A CATALOG OF SELECTED
DOVER BOOKS
IN SCIENCE AND MATHEMATICS

Astronomy

BURNHAM'S CELESTIAL HANDBOOK, Robert Burnham, Jr. Thorough guide to the stars beyond our solar system. Exhaustive treatment. Alphabetical by constellation: Andromeda to Cetus in Vol. 1; Chamaeleon to Orion in Vol. 2; and Pavo to Vulpecula in Vol. 3. Hundreds of illustrations. Index in Vol. 3. 2,000pp. 6⅛ x 9¼.

Vol. I: 0-486-23567-X
Vol. II: 0-486-23568-8
Vol. III: 0-486-23673-0

EXPLORING THE MOON THROUGH BINOCULARS AND SMALL TELE-SCOPES, Ernest H. Cherrington, Jr. Informative, profusely illustrated guide to locating and identifying craters, rills, seas, mountains, other lunar features. Newly revised and updated with special section of new photos. Over 100 photos and diagrams. 240pp. 8¼ x 11. 0-486-24491-1

THE EXTRATERRESTRIAL LIFE DEBATE, 1750–1900, Michael J. Crowe. First detailed, scholarly study in English of the many ideas that developed from 1750 to 1900 regarding the existence of intelligent extraterrestrial life. Examines ideas of Kant, Herschel, Voltaire, Percival Lowell, many other scientists and thinkers. 16 illustrations. 704pp. 5⅜ x 8½. 0-486-40675-X

THEORIES OF THE WORLD FROM ANTIQUITY TO THE COPERNICAN REVOLUTION, Michael J. Crowe. Newly revised edition of an accessible, enlightening book recreates the change from an earth-centered to a sun-centered conception of the solar system. 242pp. 5⅜ x 8½. 0-486-41444-2

A HISTORY OF ASTRONOMY, A. Pannekoek. Well-balanced, carefully reasoned study covers such topics as Ptolemaic theory, work of Copernicus, Kepler, Newton, Eddington's work on stars, much more. Illustrated. References. 521pp. 5⅜ x 8½. 0-486-65994-1

A COMPLETE MANUAL OF AMATEUR ASTRONOMY: TOOLS AND TECHNIQUES FOR ASTRONOMICAL OBSERVATIONS, P. Clay Sherrod with Thomas L. Koed. Concise, highly readable book discusses: selecting, setting up and maintaining a telescope; amateur studies of the sun; lunar topography and occultations; observations of Mars, Jupiter, Saturn, the minor planets and the stars; an introduction to photoelectric photometry; more. 1981 ed. 124 figures. 25 halftones. 37 tables. 335pp. 6½ x 9¼. 0-486-40675-X

AMATEUR ASTRONOMER'S HANDBOOK, J. B. Sidgwick. Timeless, comprehensive coverage of telescopes, mirrors, lenses, mountings, telescope drives, micrometers, spectroscopes, more. 189 illustrations. 576pp. 5⅜ x 8¼. (Available in U.S. only.) 0-486-24034-7

STARS AND RELATIVITY, Ya. B. Zel'dovich and I. D. Novikov. Vol. 1 of *Relativistic Astrophysics* by famed Russian scientists. General relativity, properties of matter under astrophysical conditions, stars, and stellar systems. Deep physical insights, clear presentation. 1971 edition. References. 544pp. 5⅜ x 8¼. 0-486-69424-0

Chemistry

THE SCEPTICAL CHYMIST: THE CLASSIC 1661 TEXT, Robert Boyle. Boyle defines the term "element," asserting that all natural phenomena can be explained by the motion and organization of primary particles. 1911 ed. viii+232pp. 5⅜ x 8½.
0-486-42825-7

RADIOACTIVE SUBSTANCES, Marie Curie. Here is the celebrated scientist's doctoral thesis, the prelude to her receipt of the 1903 Nobel Prize. Curie discusses establishing atomic character of radioactivity found in compounds of uranium and thorium; extraction from pitchblende of polonium and radium; isolation of pure radium chloride; determination of atomic weight of radium; plus electric, photographic, luminous, heat, color effects of radioactivity. ii+94pp. 5⅜ x 8½. 0-486-42550-9

CHEMICAL MAGIC, Leonard A. Ford. Second Edition, Revised by E. Winston Grundmeier. Over 100 unusual stunts demonstrating cold fire, dust explosions, much more. Text explains scientific principles and stresses safety precautions. 128pp. 5⅜ x 8½. 0-486-67628-5

THE DEVELOPMENT OF MODERN CHEMISTRY, Aaron J. Ihde. Authoritative history of chemistry from ancient Greek theory to 20th-century innovation. Covers major chemists and their discoveries. 209 illustrations. 14 tables. Bibliographies. Indices. Appendices. 851pp. 5⅜ x 8½. 0-486-64235-6

CATALYSIS IN CHEMISTRY AND ENZYMOLOGY, William P. Jencks. Exceptionally clear coverage of mechanisms for catalysis, forces in aqueous solution, carbonyl- and acyl-group reactions, practical kinetics, more. 864pp. 5⅜ x 8½.
0-486-65460-5

ELEMENTS OF CHEMISTRY, Antoine Lavoisier. Monumental classic by founder of modern chemistry in remarkable reprint of rare 1790 Kerr translation. A must for every student of chemistry or the history of science. 539pp. 5⅜ x 8½. 0-486-64624-6

THE HISTORICAL BACKGROUND OF CHEMISTRY, Henry M. Leicester. Evolution of ideas, not individual biography. Concentrates on formulation of a coherent set of chemical laws. 260pp. 5⅜ x 8½. 0-486-61053-5

A SHORT HISTORY OF CHEMISTRY, J. R. Partington. Classic exposition explores origins of chemistry, alchemy, early medical chemistry, nature of atmosphere, theory of valency, laws and structure of atomic theory, much more. 428pp. 5⅜ x 8½. (Available in U.S. only.) 0-486-65977-1

GENERAL CHEMISTRY, Linus Pauling. Revised 3rd edition of classic first-year text by Nobel laureate. Atomic and molecular structure, quantum mechanics, statistical mechanics, thermodynamics correlated with descriptive chemistry. Problems. 992pp. 5⅜ x 8½. 0-486-65622-5

FROM ALCHEMY TO CHEMISTRY, John Read. Broad, humanistic treatment focuses on great figures of chemistry and ideas that revolutionized the science. 50 illustrations. 240pp. 5⅜ x 8½. 0-486-28690-8

Engineering

DE RE METALLICA, Georgius Agricola. The famous Hoover translation of greatest treatise on technological chemistry, engineering, geology, mining of early modern times (1556). All 289 original woodcuts. 638pp. 6¾ x 11.   0-486-60006-8

FUNDAMENTALS OF ASTRODYNAMICS, Roger Bate et al. Modern approach developed by U.S. Air Force Academy. Designed as a first course. Problems, exercises. Numerous illustrations. 455pp. 5⅜ x 8½.   0-486-60061-0

DYNAMICS OF FLUIDS IN POROUS MEDIA, Jacob Bear. For advanced students of ground water hydrology, soil mechanics and physics, drainage and irrigation engineering and more. 335 illustrations. Exercises, with answers. 784pp. 6⅛ x 9¼.
0-486-65675-6

THEORY OF VISCOELASTICITY (Second Edition), Richard M. Christensen. Complete consistent description of the linear theory of the viscoelastic behavior of materials. Problem-solving techniques discussed. 1982 edition. 29 figures. xiv+364pp. 6⅛ x 9¼.   0-486-42880-X

MECHANICS, J. P. Den Hartog. A classic introductory text or refresher. Hundreds of applications and design problems illuminate fundamentals of trusses, loaded beams and cables, etc. 334 answered problems. 462pp. 5⅜ x 8½.   0-486-60754-2

MECHANICAL VIBRATIONS, J. P. Den Hartog. Classic textbook offers lucid explanations and illustrative models, applying theories of vibrations to a variety of practical industrial engineering problems. Numerous figures. 233 problems, solutions. Appendix. Index. Preface. 436pp. 5⅜ x 8½.   0-486-64785-4

STRENGTH OF MATERIALS, J. P. Den Hartog. Full, clear treatment of basic material (tension, torsion, bending, etc.) plus advanced material on engineering methods, applications. 350 answered problems. 323pp. 5⅜ x 8½.   0-486-60755-0

A HISTORY OF MECHANICS, René Dugas. Monumental study of mechanical principles from antiquity to quantum mechanics. Contributions of ancient Greeks, Galileo, Leonardo, Kepler, Lagrange, many others. 671pp. 5⅜ x 8½.   0-486-65632-2

STABILITY THEORY AND ITS APPLICATIONS TO STRUCTURAL MECHANICS, Clive L. Dym. Self-contained text focuses on Koiter postbuckling analyses, with mathematical notions of stability of motion. Basing minimum energy principles for static stability upon dynamic concepts of stability of motion, it develops asymptotic buckling and postbuckling analyses from potential energy considerations, with applications to columns, plates, and arches. 1974 ed. 208pp. 5⅜ x 8½.
0-486-42541-X

METAL FATIGUE, N. E. Frost, K. J. Marsh, and L. P. Pook. Definitive, clearly written, and well-illustrated volume addresses all aspects of the subject, from the historical development of understanding metal fatigue to vital concepts of the cyclic stress that causes a crack to grow. Includes 7 appendixes. 544pp. 5⅜ x 8½.   0-486-40927-9

Mathematics

FUNCTIONAL ANALYSIS (Second Corrected Edition), George Bachman and Lawrence Narici. Excellent treatment of subject geared toward students with background in linear algebra, advanced calculus, physics and engineering. Text covers introduction to inner-product spaces, normed, metric spaces, and topological spaces; complete orthonormal sets, the Hahn-Banach Theorem and its consequences, and many other related subjects. 1966 ed. 544pp. 6⅛ x 9¼. 0-486-40251-7

ASYMPTOTIC EXPANSIONS OF INTEGRALS, Norman Bleistein & Richard A. Handelsman. Best introduction to important field with applications in a variety of scientific disciplines. New preface. Problems. Diagrams. Tables. Bibliography. Index. 448pp. 5⅜ x 8½. 0-486-65082-0

VECTOR AND TENSOR ANALYSIS WITH APPLICATIONS, A. I. Borisenko and I. E. Tarapov. Concise introduction. Worked-out problems, solutions, exercises. 257pp. 5⅜ x 8¼. 0-486-63833-2

AN INTRODUCTION TO ORDINARY DIFFERENTIAL EQUATIONS, Earl A. Coddington. A thorough and systematic first course in elementary differential equations for undergraduates in mathematics and science, with many exercises and problems (with answers). Index. 304pp. 5⅜ x 8½. 0-486-65942-9

FOURIER SERIES AND ORTHOGONAL FUNCTIONS, Harry F. Davis. An incisive text combining theory and practical example to introduce Fourier series, orthogonal functions and applications of the Fourier method to boundary-value problems. 570 exercises. Answers and notes. 416pp. 5⅜ x 8½. 0-486-65973-9

COMPUTABILITY AND UNSOLVABILITY, Martin Davis. Classic graduate-level introduction to theory of computability, usually referred to as theory of recurrent functions. New preface and appendix. 288pp. 5⅜ x 8½. 0-486-61471-9

ASYMPTOTIC METHODS IN ANALYSIS, N. G. de Bruijn. An inexpensive, comprehensive guide to asymptotic methods—the pioneering work that teaches by explaining worked examples in detail. Index. 224pp. 5⅜ x 8½ 0-486-64221-6

APPLIED COMPLEX VARIABLES, John W. Dettman. Step-by-step coverage of fundamentals of analytic function theory—plus lucid exposition of five important applications: Potential Theory; Ordinary Differential Equations; Fourier Transforms; Laplace Transforms; Asymptotic Expansions. 66 figures. Exercises at chapter ends. 512pp. 5⅜ x 8½. 0-486-64670-X

INTRODUCTION TO LINEAR ALGEBRA AND DIFFERENTIAL EQUATIONS, John W. Dettman. Excellent text covers complex numbers, determinants, orthonormal bases, Laplace transforms, much more. Exercises with solutions. Undergraduate level. 416pp. 5⅜ x 8½. 0-486-65191-6

RIEMANN'S ZETA FUNCTION, H. M. Edwards. Superb, high-level study of landmark 1859 publication entitled "On the Number of Primes Less Than a Given Magnitude" traces developments in mathematical theory that it inspired. xiv+315pp. 5⅜ x 8½. 0-486-41740-9

CALCULUS OF VARIATIONS WITH APPLICATIONS, George M. Ewing. Applications-oriented introduction to variational theory develops insight and promotes understanding of specialized books, research papers. Suitable for advanced undergraduate/graduate students as primary, supplementary text. 352pp. 5⅜ x 8½.
0-486-64856-7

COMPLEX VARIABLES, Francis J. Flanigan. Unusual approach, delaying complex algebra till harmonic functions have been analyzed from real variable viewpoint. Includes problems with answers. 364pp. 5⅜ x 8½.
0-486-61388-7

AN INTRODUCTION TO THE CALCULUS OF VARIATIONS, Charles Fox. Graduate-level text covers variations of an integral, isoperimetrical problems, least action, special relativity, approximations, more. References. 279pp. 5⅜ x 8½.
0-486-65499-0

COUNTEREXAMPLES IN ANALYSIS, Bernard R. Gelbaum and John M. H. Olmsted. These counterexamples deal mostly with the part of analysis known as "real variables." The first half covers the real number system, and the second half encompasses higher dimensions. 1962 edition. xxiv+198pp. 5⅜ x 8½. 0-486-42875-3

CATASTROPHE THEORY FOR SCIENTISTS AND ENGINEERS, Robert Gilmore. Advanced-level treatment describes mathematics of theory grounded in the work of Poincaré, R. Thom, other mathematicians. Also important applications to problems in mathematics, physics, chemistry and engineering. 1981 edition. References. 28 tables. 397 black-and-white illustrations. xvii + 666pp. 6⅛ x 9¼.
0-486-67539-4

INTRODUCTION TO DIFFERENCE EQUATIONS, Samuel Goldberg. Exceptionally clear exposition of important discipline with applications to sociology, psychology, economics. Many illustrative examples; over 250 problems. 260pp. 5⅜ x 8½.
0-486-65084-7

NUMERICAL METHODS FOR SCIENTISTS AND ENGINEERS, Richard Hamming. Classic text stresses frequency approach in coverage of algorithms, polynomial approximation, Fourier approximation, exponential approximation, other topics. Revised and enlarged 2nd edition. 721pp. 5⅜ x 8½. 0-486-65241-6

INTRODUCTION TO NUMERICAL ANALYSIS (2nd Edition), F. B. Hildebrand. Classic, fundamental treatment covers computation, approximation, interpolation, numerical differentiation and integration, other topics. 150 new problems. 669pp. 5⅜ x 8½. 0-486-65363-3

THREE PEARLS OF NUMBER THEORY, A. Y. Khinchin. Three compelling puzzles require proof of a basic law governing the world of numbers. Challenges concern van der Waerden's theorem, the Landau-Schnirelmann hypothesis and Mann's theorem, and a solution to Waring's problem. Solutions included. 64pp. 5⅜ x 8½.
0-486-40026-3

THE PHILOSOPHY OF MATHEMATICS: AN INTRODUCTORY ESSAY, Stephan Körner. Surveys the views of Plato, Aristotle, Leibniz & Kant concerning propositions and theories of applied and pure mathematics. Introduction. Two appendices. Index. 198pp. 5⅜ x 8½. 0-486-25048-2

Math–Decision Theory, Statistics, Probability

ELEMENTARY DECISION THEORY, Herman Chernoff and Lincoln E. Moses. Clear introduction to statistics and statistical theory covers data processing, probability and random variables, testing hypotheses, much more. Exercises. 364pp. 5⅜ x 8½. 0-486-65218-1

STATISTICS MANUAL, Edwin L. Crow et al. Comprehensive, practical collection of classical and modern methods prepared by U.S. Naval Ordnance Test Station. Stress on use. Basics of statistics assumed. 288pp. 5⅜ x 8½. 0-486-60599-X

SOME THEORY OF SAMPLING, William Edwards Deming. Analysis of the problems, theory and design of sampling techniques for social scientists, industrial managers and others who find statistics important at work. 61 tables. 90 figures. xvii +602pp. 5⅜ x 8½. 0-486-64684-X

LINEAR PROGRAMMING AND ECONOMIC ANALYSIS, Robert Dorfman, Paul A. Samuelson and Robert M. Solow. First comprehensive treatment of linear programming in standard economic analysis. Game theory, modern welfare economics, Leontief input-output, more. 525pp. 5⅜ x 8½. 0-486-65491-5

PROBABILITY: AN INTRODUCTION, Samuel Goldberg. Excellent basic text covers set theory, probability theory for finite sample spaces, binomial theorem, much more. 360 problems. Bibliographies. 322pp. 5⅜ x 8½. 0-486-65252-1

GAMES AND DECISIONS: INTRODUCTION AND CRITICAL SURVEY, R. Duncan Luce and Howard Raiffa. Superb nontechnical introduction to game theory, primarily applied to social sciences. Utility theory, zero-sum games, n-person games, decision-making, much more. Bibliography. 509pp. 5⅜ x 8½. 0-486-65943-7

INTRODUCTION TO THE THEORY OF GAMES, J. C. C. McKinsey. This comprehensive overview of the mathematical theory of games illustrates applications to situations involving conflicts of interest, including economic, social, political, and military contexts. Appropriate for advanced undergraduate and graduate courses; advanced calculus a prerequisite. 1952 ed. x+372pp. 5⅜ x 8½. 0-486-42811-7

FIFTY CHALLENGING PROBLEMS IN PROBABILITY WITH SOLUTIONS, Frederick Mosteller. Remarkable puzzlers, graded in difficulty, illustrate elementary and advanced aspects of probability. Detailed solutions. 88pp. 5⅜ x 8½. 65355-2

PROBABILITY THEORY: A CONCISE COURSE, Y. A. Rozanov. Highly readable, self-contained introduction covers combination of events, dependent events, Bernoulli trials, etc. 148pp. 5⅜ x 8¼. 0-486-63544-9

STATISTICAL METHOD FROM THE VIEWPOINT OF QUALITY CONTROL, Walter A. Shewhart. Important text explains regulation of variables, uses of statistical control to achieve quality control in industry, agriculture, other areas. 192pp. 5⅜ x 8½. 0-486-65232-7

Physics

OPTICAL RESONANCE AND TWO-LEVEL ATOMS, L. Allen and J. H. Eberly. Clear, comprehensive introduction to basic principles behind all quantum optical resonance phenomena. 53 illustrations. Preface. Index. 256pp. 5⅜ x 8½.   0-486-65533-4

QUANTUM THEORY, David Bohm. This advanced undergraduate-level text presents the quantum theory in terms of qualitative and imaginative concepts, followed by specific applications worked out in mathematical detail. Preface. Index. 655pp. 5⅜ x 8½.   0-486-65969-0

ATOMIC PHYSICS (8th EDITION), Max Born. Nobel laureate's lucid treatment of kinetic theory of gases, elementary particles, nuclear atom, wave-corpuscles, atomic structure and spectral lines, much more. Over 40 appendices, bibliography. 495pp. 5⅜ x 8½.   0-486-65984-4

A SOPHISTICATE'S PRIMER OF RELATIVITY, P. W. Bridgman. Geared toward readers already acquainted with special relativity, this book transcends the view of theory as a working tool to answer natural questions: What is a frame of reference? What is a "law of nature"? What is the role of the "observer"? Extensive treatment, written in terms accessible to those without a scientific background. 1983 ed. xlviii+172pp. 5⅜ x 8½.   0-486-42549-5

AN INTRODUCTION TO HAMILTONIAN OPTICS, H. A. Buchdahl. Detailed account of the Hamiltonian treatment of aberration theory in geometrical optics. Many classes of optical systems defined in terms of the symmetries they possess. Problems with detailed solutions. 1970 edition. xv + 360pp. 5⅜ x 8½. 0-486-67597-1

PRIMER OF QUANTUM MECHANICS, Marvin Chester. Introductory text examines the classical quantum bead on a track: its state and representations; operator eigenvalues; harmonic oscillator and bound bead in a symmetric force field; and bead in a spherical shell. Other topics include spin, matrices, and the structure of quantum mechanics; the simplest atom; indistinguishable particles; and stationary-state perturbation theory. 1992 ed. xiv+314pp. 6⅛ x 9¼.   0-486-42878-8

LECTURES ON QUANTUM MECHANICS, Paul A. M. Dirac. Four concise, brilliant lectures on mathematical methods in quantum mechanics from Nobel Prize-winning quantum pioneer build on idea of visualizing quantum theory through the use of classical mechanics. 96pp. 5⅜ x 8½.   0-486-41713-1

THIRTY YEARS THAT SHOOK PHYSICS: THE STORY OF QUANTUM THEORY, George Gamow. Lucid, accessible introduction to influential theory of energy and matter. Careful explanations of Dirac's anti-particles, Bohr's model of the atom, much more. 12 plates. Numerous drawings. 240pp. 5⅜ x 8½. 0-486-24895-X

ELECTRONIC STRUCTURE AND THE PROPERTIES OF SOLIDS: THE PHYSICS OF THE CHEMICAL BOND, Walter A. Harrison. Innovative text offers basic understanding of the electronic structure of covalent and ionic solids, simple metals, transition metals and their compounds. Problems. 1980 edition. 582pp. 6⅛ x 9¼.   0-486-66021-4

TENSOR CALCULUS, J.L. Synge and A. Schild. Widely used introductory text covers spaces and tensors, basic operations in Riemannian space, non-Riemannian spaces, etc. 324pp. 5⅜ x 8¼.   0-486-63612-7

ORDINARY DIFFERENTIAL EQUATIONS, Morris Tenenbaum and Harry Pollard. Exhaustive survey of ordinary differential equations for undergraduates in mathematics, engineering, science. Thorough analysis of theorems. Diagrams. Bibliography. Index. 818pp. 5⅜ x 8½.   0-486-64940-7

INTEGRAL EQUATIONS, F. G. Tricomi. Authoritative, well-written treatment of extremely useful mathematical tool with wide applications. Volterra Equations, Fredholm Equations, much more. Advanced undergraduate to graduate level. Exercises. Bibliography. 238pp. 5⅜ x 8½.   0-486-64828-1

FOURIER SERIES, Georgi P. Tolstov. Translated by Richard A. Silverman. A valuable addition to the literature on the subject, moving clearly from subject to subject and theorem to theorem. 107 problems, answers. 336pp. 5⅜ x 8½.   0-486-63317-9

INTRODUCTION TO MATHEMATICAL THINKING, Friedrich Waismann. Examinations of arithmetic, geometry, and theory of integers; rational and natural numbers; complete induction; limit and point of accumulation; remarkable curves; complex and hypercomplex numbers, more. 1959 ed. 27 figures. xii+260pp. 5⅜ x 8½.
                                                           0-486-63317-9

POPULAR LECTURES ON MATHEMATICAL LOGIC, Hao Wang. Noted logician's lucid treatment of historical developments, set theory, model theory, recursion theory and constructivism, proof theory, more. 3 appendixes. Bibliography. 1981 edition. ix + 283pp. 5⅜ x 8½.   0-486-67632-3

CALCULUS OF VARIATIONS, Robert Weinstock. Basic introduction covering isoperimetric problems, theory of elasticity, quantum mechanics, electrostatics, etc. Exercises throughout. 326pp. 5⅜ x 8½.   0-486-63069-2

THE CONTINUUM: A CRITICAL EXAMINATION OF THE FOUNDATION OF ANALYSIS, Hermann Weyl. Classic of 20th-century foundational research deals with the conceptual problem posed by the continuum. 156pp. 5⅜ x 8½.
                                                           0-486-67982-9

CHALLENGING MATHEMATICAL PROBLEMS WITH ELEMENTARY SOLUTIONS, A. M. Yaglom and I. M. Yaglom. Over 170 challenging problems on probability theory, combinatorial analysis, points and lines, topology, convex polygons, many other topics. Solutions. Total of 445pp. 5⅜ x 8½. Two-vol. set.
                      Vol. I: 0-486-65536-9   Vol. II: 0-486-65537-7

Paperbound unless otherwise indicated. Available at your book dealer, online at **www.doverpublications.com**, or by writing to Dept. GI, Dover Publications, Inc., 31 East 2nd Street, Mineola, NY 11501. For current price information or for free catalogues (please indicate field of interest), write to Dover Publications or log on to **www.doverpublications.com** and see every Dover book in print. Dover publishes more than 500 books each year on science, elementary and advanced mathematics, biology, music, art, literary history, social sciences, and other areas.

"EMPIRE" BY INTEGRATION

The United States and
European Integration,
1945–1997

Geir Lundestad

OXFORD UNIVERSITY PRESS

OXFORD
UNIVERSITY PRESS

Great Clarendon Street, Oxford OX2 6DP

Oxford University Press is a department of the University of Oxford.
It furthers the University's objective of excellence in research, scholarship,
and education by publishing worldwide in

Oxford New York

Auckland Bangkok Buenos Aires Cape Town Chennai
Dar es Salaam Delhi Hong Kong Istanbul Karachi Kolkata
Kuala Lumpur Madrid Melbourne Mexico City Mumbai Nairobi
São Paulo Shanghai Taipei Tokyo Toronto

Oxford is a registered trade mark of Oxford University Press
in the UK and in certain other countries

Published in the United States
by Oxford University Press Inc., New York

British Library Cataloguing in Publication Data
Data available

Library of Congress Cataloging in Publication Data
Lundestad. Geir. 1945-
Empire by integration : the United States and European
Integration, 1945-1997 / Geir Lundestad.
Includes bibliographical references.
1. Europe—foreign relations—United States. 2. United States—
Foreign relations—Europe. 3. Europe—Economic integration—
History. I. Title.
D1065.U5L86 1997
327.7304—dc21 97-22509

ISBN-13: 978-0-19-878211-7

Typeset by Graphicraft Typesetters, Hong Kong Ltd.,
Printed in Great Britain

Biddles Ltd., King's Lynn
www.biddles.co.uk

Preface and Acknowledgments

THERE are many, many books that deal with aspects of American–Western European relations from 1945 till today. Although the subject is certainly touched upon in many of these books, relatively few of them analyze in any detail what is perhaps the most central aspect of these relations during this long period, namely the United States and European integration. The few books that do take up this topic tend to focus on what may be seen as, but of course are not, rather limited topics, such as for instance the Marshall Plan or the European Coal and Steel Community.

As might be expected, with ever more source material being made available in more and more capitals, historians have been able to move up in time and cover not only newer, but also larger parts of the story. Still, so far only one book exists that attempts to deal on the basis of these new sources with American policy towards European integration on a larger scale: Pascaline Winand's *Eisenhower, Kennedy, and the United States of Europe* (1993). But, as the title suggests, even this book is largely limited to the decade from 1953 to 1963.

So there seems to be a need for a larger overview, for a first effort to cover the entire period from 1945 until the present. This book tries to fill that need. It could easily have become a very long book; instead this is a rather short one.

When you want to write a short book about a vast topic, certain consequences follow. First, I have had to stick to the main lines of policy. Therefore, I frequently refer to "the United States" and "Washington," although different attitudes to European integration could of course be found in both of these places. I try to show that on the whole there was a relatively consistent American policy on European integration, a policy that underwent surprisingly few major changes in the long period here being analyzed.

Second, I have attempted to utilize the existing literature, however unsatisfactory, as fully as possible. Naturally, all historians depend on those who have gone before them. In my case this has been particularly necessary.

I, like other historians, also depend on the sources available. My most important source of historical documents has been the invaluable *Foreign Relations of the United States* (FRUS). On Western Europe and European integration this series is now available up through the Johnson administration, and although this historical record has become sketchier and sketchier it does still provide a solid base of documents for the period from 1945 until 1968. Unfortunately no similar record exists on the European side, which has meant that the European side has had to be downplayed even more than would have been natural in what is after all a study of *American* policy. For the years after 1968 I have had to rely on public statements, memoirs, contemporary analyses, interviews, and similarly inadequate materials. My findings for this later period are therefore more tentative than for the earlier years.

Third, I have tried to identify particularly important points in the historical process. Only on these points have I tried to go into the more extensive record in the form of the abundance of documents that can be found in many relevant archives in the United States, but particularly in the single most important depository, the National Archives. I have identified three such turning points, 1949–50, 1962–3, and 1969–70. The first point has to do with the very beginnings of European integration, what led to the crucial first step in the form of the proposal in 1950 for the European Coal and Steel Community (ECSC); the second deals with the strongest challenge to the American policy of European integration in an Atlantic framework, in the person of president Charles de Gaulle, his rejection of Britain's membership in the EEC, and the signing of the Franco–German treaty in January 1963. A third turning point can be identified in the Nixon–Kissinger years, when Washington modified its support for European integration a great deal, but this period has had to be dealt with largely from public sources.

The emphasis on these turning points has created what may be seen as a certain imbalance in the book, in the sense that certain parts of the analysis will be relatively detailed and close to the historical sources while other parts will be quite general and distant from the sources. I do not really see this as a major problem. Even in a work as sweeping as mine, turning points deserve more attention than other points.

Fourth, but really most important, when you want to write a short book about a vast topic you have to find the appropriate level of analysis. I have chosen to set my study of the main lines of US policy on European integration within one particular context, a comparative one in which American policy is compared with the policies of other Great Powers in the areas of the world they dominated. My main arguments in this context will be presented shortly.

The book represents a first, and hopefully useful, survey of a huge story, a survey that will undoubtedly be modified later on many points, large and small. Nevertheless, my hope is that this short book will benefit not only students who "have" to study this topic and need a short introduction to "the United States and European integration", but also researchers contributing to further analysis and debate.

No further apologies or explanations will be offered. Some thanks are due, however. First, I want to thank the members of the Norwegian Nobel Committee, the awarders of the Nobel peace prize, and the staff of the Nobel Institute for so cheerfully having tolerated my physical and mental absences from my daily duties when I was at work on this book. The library of the Institute has, as always, been most useful and the staff most helpful: for example, Bjørn Helge Feen compiled much of the Bibliography for me. I am also grateful to Peter Naess at the reference center of the American embassy in Oslo for his assistance. At Oxford University Press I am particularly obliged to senior editor Tim Barton, for his interest in my work, to T. W. Bartell who did the copyediting, and to Gary Hall who compiled the index.

Second, many scholars have assisted me in my work on this manuscript. In particular I want to thank Frode Liland for his highly appreciated research assistance. Without Frode's tall stack of photocopies from the National Archives in Washington, as well as his many other services, this book would have lacked much of whatever scholarly merit it might possess. On the American side, John Lewis Gaddis has encouraged me in my work for many years and offered detailed criticism of an early version of this manuscript. In more recent years Melvyn Leffler has taken on a similar role and he too criticized an early version. He also provided useful advice on a later version of the manuscript. I have been truly fortunate in having two such wonderful, though rather different, friends. In a way the main interpretations of my book represent an effort to keep them both moderately happy. US ambassador to NATO Robert E. Hunter has given me expert advice on American policy towards European integration, particularly in the Carter and Clinton years. On the Norwegian side, Tor Egil Førland, Rolf Tamnes, and Odd Arne Westad offered useful comments on an early draft.

For their assistance they are all to be credited; the shortcomings and mistakes are all mine.

Contents

1

INTRODUCTION AND BASIC ARGUMENTS

THIS study presents two basic arguments. First, it argues that the United States promoted the integration of Western Europe, rather strongly until the mid-1960s, less strongly after that. By promoting the unity of the most important area under its influence, the United States behaved rather differently from other leading powers in history.

Throughout history empires have been ruled from an imperial center. This imperial center has almost always tried to guard its special position and if there was one development it feared, it was the emergence of anything that looked even remotely like an alternative center. Divide-and-rule was an important imperial technique in keeping the empire's subjects in their place. Among modern empires, this description can be applied to relatively loose empires, such as the Austrian and the British ones, and to more centralized ones such as the French and particularly the Soviet empire. For Vienna, London, Paris, and Moscow it was entirely out of the question to promote an alternative center, since this might come to weaken the position of the imperial capital. Therefore, in promoting the integration of Western Europe the United States was clearly different from other Great Powers.

Second, while the American attitude was in some ways unique, the United States still wanted to exercise some form of control over Western Europe. Twice in the twentieth century it had intervened massively to prevent Europe from being dominated by a hostile power. The United States, like other Great Powers, protected its interests. After the Second World War these interests expanded dramatically. US efforts to control and dominate were, of course, based on American values, in the same way other powers exercised domination based on theirs. On the American side, these values left a wide scope for European self-organization. Thus, while the overall objective of the United States may not in principle have been very different from those of other Great Powers, the way in which the US defined its control and the methods it used to maintain this control were indeed rather different from those of other Great Powers.

Whether the American role after 1945 was so dominant that we should call the areas where the United States made its influence the most strongly felt an "empire" or simply "a sphere of influence" may be debated.[1] Unlike traditional empires, most of the countries under some sort of American influence were independent. At the same time, however, there could be little doubt about the predominant overall role of the United States. In the looser sense of the term, the American sphere of influence could well be called an "empire." This, then, is the term I shall be using for the American role. To distinguish the American "empire" from more traditional ones, I shall put the American version in inverted commas.

This American "empire," unlike the earlier empires mentioned, contained many of the key areas of the world, with Western Europe being the most important one. In Western Europe Washington was able to organize NATO, control the larger part of crucial Germany, keep the Communists out of power, include the region in the American-organized system of freer trade, and greatly enhance the influence of American culture. In a comparative perspective this was an outstanding record. The fact that many Europeans supported these same objectives does not detract from this fact. In the importance of the areas it ruled over and in some respects even the effectiveness of its control, America's "empire" compared favorably with those of more formal empires.[2]

---

[1] For my own previous analysis and use of these terms, see Geir Lundestad, *The American "Empire" and Other Studies of US Foreign Policy in a Comparative Perspective* (Oxford and Oslo: Oxford University Press, 1990), 31–115, particularly 37–9. See also Geir Lundestad (ed.), *The Fall of Great Powers: Peace, Stability, and Legitimacy* (Oslo and Oxford: Scandinavian University Press, 1994), particularly 383–402.

[2] For elaboration of this argument, see my *The American "Empire"*, particularly 39–85. Most American historians and political scientists probably perceive the imperial analogy as anti-American while many Europeans dislike the degree of

Thus, on the one hand, the United States clearly organized its "empire" differently from those of other Great Powers. Washington actually favored the creation of a supranational Europe with its own political bodies and, accordingly, at least the possible development of an alternative political center. As the "father" of European integration, Jean Monnet, put it, the American insistence on European integration "is the first time in history that a great power, instead of basing its policy on ruling by dividing, has consistently and resolutely backed the creation of a large Community uniting peoples previously apart."[3]

Yet, on the other hand, the United States protected its preeminent position. This obvious fact was clearly reflected in its attitude to European integration. Again, two points are particularly

American control the analogy implies. The term "empire" has, however, been used by others with a meaning very similar to mine. See for instance Zbigniew Brzezinski, *Game Plan: How to Conduct the U.S.–Soviet Contest* (New York: Atlantic Monthly Press, 1986), where he writes: "I use the term 'empire' as morally neutral to describe a hierarchical system of political relationships, radiating from a center. Such an empire's morality is defined by how its imperial power is wielded, with what degree of consent on the part of those within its scope, and to what ends. This is where the distinctions between the American and Soviet imperial systems are the sharpest" (16).

Charles S. Maier has argued that in the shared ideals, the cooperation of transnational elites, the important common institutions, and the elements of consensus, the American relationship with Western Europe resembled the Athenian empire and not the Roman one since the latter "forcibly incorporated other peoples in a common legal framework ruled from the center." Maier prefers the term "analog of empire" for the American role. For this, see his "Alliance and Autonomy: European Identity and U.S. Foreign Policy Objectives in the Truman Years," in Michael J. Lacey (ed.), *The Truman Presidency* (Cambridge: Cambridge University Press, 1989), 273–98, particularly 274–6. See also his "Analog of Empire: Constitutive Moments of United States Ascendancy after World War II," unpub. paper presented at the Woodrow Wilson Center, Washington, DC, 30 May 1989.

American domination on some points may well be combined with European initiative on others. One parallel could perhaps be the present international free market system. Undoubtedly this system has a strong impact on the economies of most countries within it. Still, within this common international framework the various countries pursue many different policies, with vastly different economic and political results. Or, as Maier puts it with reference to the American–European relationship, under Truman "the groundwork was laid not just for an imperial subordination to Washington but for a genuine revival of national traditions and of autonomous historical possibilities for Europeans." See his "Alliance and Autonomy," 297–8.

[3] Francois Duchêne, *Jean Monnet: The First Statesman of Interdependence* (New York: Norton, 1994), 386.

important. First, while the United States was indeed different from other Great Powers, it did not pursue its pro-integrationist policy primarily for the sake of the Western Europeans. Washington certainly thought its policy best also for them, but naturally it had its own motives for supporting an integrated Europe. These motives will be discussed shortly, but let it be stressed from the very outset that none were more important than the "double" containment of Germany and the Soviet Union. Washington's abiding concern about the role of Germany is perhaps the most striking thread of my study.

Second, while the United States supported an integrated Western Europe, this was not to be an independent Europe in the sense of the "third force" often discussed, particularly on the European left. In the American perspective, the integrated Europe was always to be fitted into a wider Atlantic framework. Through this Atlantic framework, the United States would presumably be able to protect its leading role within the Western world, although this could not be *guaranteed* once a supranational Europe had been established. Perhaps we could call this policy hegemony, or even "empire" by integration.

2

THE PUBLIC AMERICAN POSITION, 1945–1997

M OST of the historians who have written about the United
States and European integration have indeed stressed the
American support for such integration.[1] Let me, however, under-
line how relatively consistent the American position has been over

[1] Since this is not a study of integration as such, I see no need to go into the
question of exactly how the term should be defined. The focus here is simply on
the American attitude to supranational organization in Europe from the Marshall
Plan to the European Union.

Some basic accounts of European integration are Richard Vaughan, *Post-War
Integration in Europe* (London: Croom Helm, 1976) and *Twentieth-Century Europe:
Paths to Unity* (London: Croom Helm, 1979); Walter Lipgens, *A History of European
Integration, 1945–47. Vol. 1: The Formation of the European Unity Movement* (London:
Oxford University Press, 1982); Wilfried Loth, *Der Weg nach Europa: Geschichte der
europäischen Integration 1939–1957* (Göttingen: Vandenhoeck & Ruprecht, 1982);
John Gillingham, *Coal, Steel, and the Rebirth of Europe, 1945–1955: The Germans and
the French from the Ruhr Conflict to Economic Community* (Cambridge: Cambridge
University Press, 1991); Derek W. Urwin, *The Community of Europe: A History of
European Integration since 1945*, 2nd edn. (London: Longman, 1995). Two particu-
larly stimulating accounts, both by Alan S. Milward, are *The Reconstruction of
Western Europe 1945–51* (Berkeley: University of California Press, 1984) and *The
European Rescue of the Nation-State* (London: Routledge, 1992). For analyses par-
ticularly of American policy on European integration, see Max Beloff, *The United
States and the Unity of Europe* (Washington, DC: Brookings, 1963); Ernst H. van
der Beugel, *From Marshall Aid to Atlantic Partnership: European Integration as a Con-
cern of American Foreign Policy* (Amsterdam: Elsevier, 1966); Michael Hogan, *The
Marshall Plan: America, Britain, and the Reconstruction of Western Europe, 1947–1952*
(Cambridge: Cambridge University Press, 1987); Pascaline Winand, *Eisenhower,
Kennedy, and the United States of Europe* (London: Macmillan, 1993); Klaus Schwabe,
"The United States and European Integration: 1947–1957," in Clemens Wurm
(ed.), *Western Europe and Germany: The Beginnings of European Integration 1945–1960*

a fifty-year period. I shall focus first, though rather briefly, on the public position, in part because this position is of some importance in itself, in part because, as we shall later see, this public position corresponded fairly closely with the more "private" positions of the various administrations in Washington.[2]

After some hesitation in 1945–6, from 1947 onwards the United States supported European, meaning Western European, integration. In delivering his famous Marshall Plan speech at Harvard on 5 June 1947, secretary of state George C. Marshall wanted the Europeans to establish comprehensive forms of cooperation among themselves. He stated that the drawing up of a European recovery program "is the business of the Europeans." The role of the United States should consist of "friendly aid in the drafting of a European program and of later support of such a program so far as it may be practical for us to do so."[3] Washington's major disappointment with the Marshall Plan was that the Europeans did not go much further in their integration than they did.

When, in the 1950s, the Europeans finally began to work out more concrete forms of cooperation, Washington gave strong support to these initiatives from the very beginning. Soon after French foreign minister Robert Schuman launched the idea of a European Coal and Steel Community (ECSC) in May 1950, president Harry S. Truman, despite initial doubts about the cartel aspects of the idea, underlined that the United States welcomed "this act of

(Oxford: Berg, 1995); Pierre Melandri, *Les États-Unis face à l'unification de l'Europe 1945–1954* (Lille: Université de Lille III, 1979); Gérard Bossuat, *L'Europe occidentale à l'heure américaine 1945–1952* (Paris: Éditions Complexe, 1992); Francis H. Heller and John R. Gillingham (eds.), *The United States and the Integration of Europe: Legacies of the Postwar Era* (New York: St. Martin's Press, 1996).

[2] By "public position" I mean primarily the position of the United States as expressed by the president or, in cases where it was obvious that this represented Washington's joint policy, by other prominent policymakers. This position was then expressed in public speeches or, occasionally, in formal conversations with foreign leaders.

[3] Marshall's speech is found, among other places, in US Department of State, *A Decade of American Foreign Policy: Basic Documents, 1941–49* (Washington, DC: Government Printing Office, 1950), 1268–9. While Washington clearly expected the Soviet Union to exclude itself from the aid offer, it hoped that at least some of the Central and Eastern European countries would join. It was no big surprise, however, that they had to say no. For these events, see my *The American Non-Policy towards Eastern Europe 1943–1947* (Oslo: Universitetsforlaget, 1975), 397–408. After this, "European integration" referred only to integration in Western Europe.

constructive statesmanship". The proposal provided "the basis for establishing an entirely new relationship between France and Germany and opens a new outlook for Europe."[4] The members of the ECSC were France, West Germany, Italy, Belgium, the Netherlands, and Luxembourg and the organization went into effect in 1952.

The United States supported the European Defense Community (EDC)—to be made up of the same six countries—to such an extent that in December 1953 secretary of state John Foster Dulles presented his famous threat that if the EDC were not established, "That would compel an agonizing reappraisal of basic United States policy."[5] The implication was that the US might withdraw from Europe. Although this is sometimes overlooked in the literature, president Dwight D. Eisenhower quickly gave explicit support to his secretary's threat.[6] In the end, however, although the French national assembly rejected the EDC in August 1954, the American forces remained.

In the deliberations leading to the founding of the European Atomic Energy Commission (EURATOM) and the European Economic Community (EEC) in 1957, where again the same six continental countries were involved, the United States maintained a much lower profile than on the EDC question. Yet there was no doubt about the Eisenhower administration's enthusiastic support. As the president himself told a French delegation in early 1957, "he felt that the day this common market [the EEC] became a reality would be one of the finest days in the history of the free world, perhaps even more so than winning the war."[7] On another occasion Eisenhower expressed the hope that he would "live long enough to see a United States of Europe come into existence."[8] Thus, the United States definitely wanted European integration to

---

[4] US Department of State, *Bulletin*, 29 May 1950, 828. For a similar statement by Acheson, see US Department of State, *Foreign Relations of the United States* (*FRUS*), 1950: III, Secretary of State to certain diplomatic offices, 2 June 1950, 714.

[5] *FRUS*, 1952–4: V. 1, Statement by the Secretary of State to the North Atlantic Council, 14 Dec. 1953, 463.

[6] *Public Papers of the Presidents. Dwight D. Eisenhower, 1953*, 842–3.

[7] Declassified Documents Reference Service, 1992, 0440, meeting Eisenhower–French delegation, probably 26 Feb. 1957. See also *FRUS*, 1955–7: IV, Report by the Subcommittee on Regional Economic Integration of the Council on Foreign Economic Policy to the Council, 15 Nov. 1956, 483–4; *Public Papers of the Presidents. Dwight D. Eisenhower, 1956*, 1038–45.

[8] *FRUS*, 1955–7: IV, Memorandum of conversation Eisenhower–Etzel, 6 Feb. 1957, 517

go far beyond economic integration. Eisenhower and Dulles both gave the Europeans many an uplifting sermon on the importance of creating federal institutions. Their ultimate hope was that the American federal experience would be repeated on the European continent.[9]

In the negotiations between the EEC, or the Common Market, and the European Free Trade Association (EFTA, established in 1959 and consisting of Britain, Sweden, Denmark, Norway, Austria, Switzerland, and Portugal) to overcome the split between the inner six and the outer seven, as the two groups were also called, both the Eisenhower and the Kennedy administration made it clear that while they wanted the split overcome, this was not to be done at the expense of the Common Market structure. The British, not the EEC, ought to make the basic concessions. President John F. Kennedy put it very clearly: "It is best for the Atlantic Community if the United Kingdom joined the EEC on an unconditional basis."[10]

As indicated in the president's reference to "the Atlantic Community," a shift in Washington's attitude was under way. No longer was the emphasis to be simply on the need for as comprehensive a European integration as possible. This integration had to take place within an Atlantic framework as well. The American leadership role, which had earlier been more or less assumed, was now explicitly underlined in the form of the need for Atlantic cooperation. In his famous speech on Atlantic interdependence on 4 July 1962, Kennedy formally stated that "We do not regard a strong and united Europe as a rival but as a partner. To aid its progress has been the basic object of our foreign policy for 17 years." A declaration of interdependence was to be drawn up between the new union emerging in Europe and the United States.[11]

Even after president Charles de Gaulle of France had shown that the idea of European integration could be used to challenge the United States quite directly, Washington continued to support the objective of European integration. As president Lyndon B. Johnson himself stated on 3 May 1966, the US believed that "the drive for

[9] Jean Monnet, *Memoirs* (London: Collins, 1978), 379–89; *FRUS*, 1955–7: IV, Telegram from the Secretary of State to the Embassy in Germany, 1 July 1955, 308. For Dulles's early ideas on European integration, see Ronald W. Pruessen, *John Foster Dulles: The Road to Power* (New York: Free Press, 1982), particularly 307–12, 324–9, 334–57.
[10] *FRUS*, 1961–3: XIII, Memorandum of conversation Kennedy–Adenauer, 13 Apr. 1961, 6.   [11] *Public Papers of the Presidents. John F. Kennedy, 1962*, 538.

unity in Western Europe is not only desirable but we believe it is necessary." This was so because "Every lesson of the past and every prospect for the future argue that the nations of Western Europe can only fulfill their proper role in the world community if increasingly they act together."[12]

Yet in the very same speech Johnson also declared that "It remains our conviction that an integrated Atlantic defense is the first necessity and not the last result of the building of unity in Western Europe, for expanding partnership across the Atlantic, and for reconciling differences with the East."[13] European integration had to be fitted into an Atlantic framework which de Gaulle's challenge helped make ever more explicit on the American side.

Later administrations were to repeat the same themes, and were to keep searching for ever-new formulations in ever-new declarations that could create the best basis for an improved Atlantic relationship between the United States and the more integrated Europe, whether this was called the European Economic Community (EEC), the European Communities (EC), or the European Union (EU).[14]

In his speech launching the so-called Year of Europe (1973), Richard M. Nixon's national security adviser Henry A. Kissinger argued that "No element of American postwar policy has been more consistent than our support of European unity. We encouraged it at every turn." In building a new Atlantic structure, "We will continue to support European unity."[15]

Nevertheless, Nixon and Kissinger did little to hide the fact that the United States was actually re-evaluating Washington's traditional policy of strong support for European integration. For the first time the problems that European integration did indeed present to the United States were openly discussed. The two sides of the Atlantic did not have identical political interests and they competed fiercely in certain economic areas. President Nixon himself pointed to "the problems which European integration implied for

---

[12] *Public Papers of the Presidents. Lyndon B. Johnson, 1966*, 477.   [13] Ibid.

[14] "European Economic Community" was the official term until 1967, when the EEC, the ECSC, and EURATOM were merged and the term for the new unit became "the European Communities" (sometimes also in the singular form, "Community"). With the adoption of the Maastricht decisions, as of 1 Nov. 1993, this was in turn changed to "the European Union."

[15] US Department of State, *Bulletin*, 14 May 1973, 593–8. The quotations are from 595 and 598.

the United States and for our political and economic relations with our allies across the Atlantic."[16] As we shall see, in the end Washington concluded that the whole matter of European integration was best left largely to the Europeans themselves. They, not the United States, should be the ones pushing for such integration.

Jimmy Carter criticized his Republican predecessors for having neglected Western Europe. Unlike Nixon, Ford, and Kissinger, he would give "unqualified support" to the EC. As the first American president to visit the headquarters of the European Community in Brussels, he believed that "this meeting symbolizes America's abiding commitment to a strong and united Europe and to the European Community."[17]

The administration of Ronald Reagan kept up some of the integrationist rhetoric. On 24 March 1982, in the president's statement on the twenty-fifth anniversary of the signing of the Treaty of Rome and the establishment of the EEC, Reagan's first real statement on European integration since his inauguration, he repeated the traditional litany: "Let me reaffirm clearly the support of this administration for European unity. We consider a strong and united Europe not a rival, but a partner."[18]

At the same time, however, Reagan stressed that much had changed since the signing of the Rome treaties in 1957. A stronger and more united Europe had emerged; Europe should therefore shoulder a bigger share of the free world's responsibilities.[19] The Europeans ought to do much more in defense, within the NATO framework of course, and Reagan denounced "European protectionism." Unlike his predecessors, he frequently went public with American–EC economic disputes, mostly about agricultural products, but about other items as well.[20]

George Bush wanted to emphasize the overall political cooperation between the United States and the European Community and to play down the more or less inevitable economic disputes. "What a tragedy, what an absurdity it would be if future historians

---

[16] *Public Papers of the Presidents. Richard M. Nixon, 1973*, 222.

[17] *Public Papers of the Presidents. Jimmy Carter, 1978*, 34; René Schwok, *U.S.–EC Relations in the Post-Cold War Era: Conflict or Partnership?* (Boulder, Colo.: Westview, 1991), 32–3.

[18] *Public Papers of the Presidents. Ronald Reagan, 1982*, 374.

[19] Ibid.; US Department of State, *Gist*, The European Community, Apr. 1986, 2.

[20] *Public Papers of the Presidents. Ronald Reagan, 1982*, 1480; *1983*, 31; *1985*, 796–8, 809–10, 1053–4; *1986*, 417, 506, 610, 904, 1650; *1987*, 37, 1548–50.

attribute the demise of the Western alliance to disputes over beef hormones and wars over pasta."[21]

Speaking for the Bush administration, secretary of state James Baker referred to "a Europe united. This was the goal of Monnet and Schuman. This was the goal supported by the United States of Marshall and Acheson. This was the goal contained in the Treaty of Rome and more recently in the European Single Act [sic]." Baker went on to declare that "the United States supports this goal today with the same energy it did 40 years ago."[22] The Single European Act of 1986 was to turn the EC into a fully integrated market by the end of 1992. Again, while an integrated Europe was to be supported, it was to be firmly contained within the Atlantic framework. The Transatlantic Declaration on US–EC Relations of 23 November 1990, with its system for regular consultations between the two parties, was to be the formalized expression of the new relationship.

Finally, the Clinton administration has continued the rhetorical policy of its predecessors. As president William J. (Bill) Clinton himself declared on 9 January 1994, in his first major policy address on European integration, "My administration supports European Union, and Europe's development of stronger institutions of common purpose and action. We recognize that we will benefit more from a strong and equal partner than from a weak one."[23] The support was combined with the traditional emphasis on the need for a new Atlantic statement and new mechanisms, but this time the Europeans were even more interested in such a statement than were the Americans. At the US–EU Summit in Madrid on 3 December 1995, president Clinton, together with the leaders of the EU countries and the EU Commission, launched the Transatlantic Initiative with a New Transatlantic Agenda "designed to move the transatlantic relationship from consultation to joint action on a wide range of issues."[24]

Although the public statements of the presidents, or their secretaries of state, provide only a partial record of the various administrations' policies, on the whole these statements reflected America's

[21] *Public Papers of the Presidents. George Bush, 1989*, 584.

[22] USIS (United States Information Service), Address as prepared for delivery by Secretary of State James Baker, 12 Dec. 1989, 4–5.

[23] *Public Papers of the Presidents. William J. Clinton, 1994*, 9.

[24] USIS, "Joint U.S.–EU Action Plan," 3 Dec. 1995, 1; see also USIS, Speech by Secretary of State Warren Christopher, 2 June 1995, 1, 9.

overall approach fairly well. Two main reasons can be found for the correspondence of public with internal views. First, any administration's policy also has to be presented in public. In a democracy it easily leads to misunderstandings as well as to attacks on the administration if the discrepancy between the public and the internal positions is too large. Second, at least in the long run the natural tendency to please the Europeans with statements of support was held in check by the equally legitimate concern to please Congress and the American public with expressions both of American leadership and of diligence in protecting US interests, which certainly included economic interests.

Yet, as we shall see, the American position was really more complex than this simple overview might seem to indicate.

3

THE MOTIVES FOR AMERICA'S SUPPORT OF EUROPEAN INTEGRATION

W HAT, then, were the basic motives for the American policy of supporting European integration, a policy so consistently proclaimed and to a large extent even pursued by virtually every American administration from Truman's to Clinton's?

Obviously such a deep-seated attitude flowed from many different sources. Yet, without simplifying matters too much, these sources, or motives, may be arranged in five different clusters, which we may refer to respectively as the American model, a more rational and efficient Europe, a reduced American burden, the containment of the Soviet Union, and finally, the containment even of Germany.

I am prepared to argue that for virtually the entire period covered here this list puts the five elements in an ascending order of importance, with the last two being particularly important and closely linked. The "double containment" of the Soviet Union and of Germany represented the answer to immediate American security concerns while the first three clusters of motives represented longer-term interests. As almost always happens in politics, the short term is more important than the long one, but all five clusters worked strongly in favor of the United States supporting European integration.

In addition, as we shall see in later chapters, when doubts began to develop in the 1960s about the inherent compatibility of European integration and American leadership, the fact that the United States had for so long been pursuing the policy it had became in itself a source of continued support for European integration. So did the fact that the Europeans were themselves moving in the direction of closer integration.

As numerous observers have noted, Americans tend to see many features of the American model as universal, as something the rest of the world should emulate. This is certainly the case with the American federal system, political democracy, and free and open markets.[1] (The extent to which these ideals are truly American, and not European, will not be discussed here. Federalism is certainly more exclusively American than democracy and open markets. The point here is that they have been perceived as American by policymakers in Washington.)

In March 1947 senators J. William Fulbright and Elbert D. Thomas and congressman Hale Boggs introduced a very simple nineteen-word resolution in Congress: "That the Congress favors the creation of a United States of Europe, within the framework of the United Nations." The resolution was never actually voted on by Congress, but it represented an early example of American-inspired ideas being applied to the new situation in Europe.[2]

References to the importance of the American model were particularly plentiful in connection with the Marshall Plan, the first American effort to promote the integration of Western Europe. In historian Michael Hogan's slightly exaggerated words, "the Marshall Plan had aimed to remake Europe in an American mode."[3] Thus, in the Economic Cooperation Act of 1948, Congress stated in the introduction that

Mindful of the advantages which the United States has enjoyed through the existence of a large domestic market with no internal trade barriers, and believing that similar advantages can accrue to the countries of Europe, it is declared to be the policy of the United States to encourage these countries through a joint organization to exert sustained common efforts ... which will speedily achieve that economic cooperation in Europe which is essential for lasting peace and prosperity.[4]

[1] For a recent stimulating treatment of this theme, see Tony Smith, *America's Mission: The United States and the Worldwide Struggle for Democracy in the Twentieth Century* (Princeton: Princeton University Press, 1994), particularly 146–76.

[2] Robert H. Ferrell, "The Truman Era and European Integration," in Heller and Gillingham, *The United States and the Integration of Europe*, 33–7.

[3] Hogan, *The Marshall Plan*, 445.

[4] US Department of State, *A Decade of American Foreign Policy*, 299.

Many Congressmen long had rather simplistic notions about the ease with which Europe could develop on the pattern of the thirteen original American colonies and they frequently lectured Europeans on the importance of the American lesson, usually with rather ambiguous results at best. Such statements were not, however, entirely limited to Congressmen. Some prominent officials spoke in similar ways, with the 31 October 1949 speech by Economic Cooperation Administration (ECA) head Paul Hoffman perhaps offering the most striking example.[5]

Although statements about the American model were especially numerous and explicit in 1947–8, they remained a permanent part of US policy. The federalist attitude of Eisenhower and Dulles has already been mentioned. Eisenhower frequently talked about how every European country would benefit from close integration and often cited "the development of the American historical pattern as an illustration of the point he was making."[6] In his interdependence speech Kennedy proclaimed that "The nations of Western Europe, long divided by feuds far more bitter than any which existed among the 13 colonies, are today joining together, as our forefathers sought, to find freedom in diversity and in unity, strength."[7]

To pick a very recent example, after Clinton had met on 14 June 1995 with French president Jacques Chirac and president of the European Commission Jacques Santer for the semi-annual summit specified in the November 1990 US–EC declaration, the American spokesman started his summary of the reasons for Washington's support of European integration by declaring that "we believe an integrated Europe through the European Union, fosters democracy among former enemy countries in Western Europe, encourages the development of democracy in free markets and the Central European Baltic countries who wish to join it . . ."[8] So, although

[5] For Hoffman's speech, see Hogan, *The Marshall Plan*, 273–4. For Congressional attitudes, see for instance *FRUS*, 1951: IV. 1, Ambassador Bruce to the Acting Secretary of State, 10 Nov. 1951, 63–4; ibid., Consul Andrews to the Acting Secretary of State, 20 Nov., 21 Nov., 22 Nov., 24 Nov., 27 Nov., 1 Dec., 11 Dec. 1951, 64–5, 66, 67–8, 69–70, 70–2, 73–5, 75–6, 80–2. The theme of the United States shaping Europe in its own image may of course be overdone. Naturally most American observers recognized that there were significant differences between the United States and the countries of Western Europe, particularly in their social structures and their economic policies.

[6] *FRUS*, 1955–7: IV, Editorial Note (Remarks by Eisenhower), 349.

[7] *Public Papers of the Presidents. John F. Kennedy, 1962*, 538.

[8] USIS, 15 June 1995: US–European Summit Discussed, 2.

the argument was more convoluted now, for fifty years the American model of federalism, democracy, and free markets was promoted in Europe as in much of the rest of the world.

Closely related to the importance of the American model was Washington's emphasis on an integrated Europe being a more rational and efficient Europe. The economic side was obvious. As NATO commanding general Dwight D. Eisenhower stated in July 1951, Europe could not solve its problems as long as it was "divided by patchwork territorial fences": "Once united, the farms and factories of France and Belgium, the foundries of Germany, the rich farmlands of Holland and Denmark, the skilled labor of Italy, will produce miracles for the common good."[9]

On the political side, integration would not only do away with old-fashioned nationalism, but would also make it easier for the United States to deal with Western Europe. The first thought was succinctly expressed by Dulles when he said that Americans "believed firmly that the division of Europe was the cause of wars in the past. The Europeans have an obligation to tie themselves together . . ."[10] Nixon phrased the same point slightly differently: "Unity would replace the devastating nationalist rivalries of the past."[11] The second thought was most clearly expressed in Kennedy's rhetorical question: "I'm the president of the United States, but who's the president of Europe?"[12] Both for Europe and for the United States, it would be much easier to negotiate new transatlantic agreements and understandings if the constant "squabbling" of the Europeans could be avoided. One Western European center was the most efficient way of running that part of Europe.

Most administrations recognized that there was a possible danger in promoting a federated Europe: what if this more united Europe decided to oppose the United States? Naturally, the United States was opposed to a united Europe controlled by a hostile power. The point in this context, however, is that from Soviet expert George Kennan in 1946–7 to Henry Kissinger in the early

---

[9] *U.S. Department of State, Bulletin, 30 July 1951,* 164.

[10] *FRUS, 1955–7:* IV, Memorandum of conversation Dulles–Erhard, 7 June 1955, 291–2.

[11] Schwok, *U.S.–EC Relations in the Post-Cold War Era,* 220.

[12] Comment by Pierre Melandri in Robert O. Paxton and Nicholas Wahl (eds.), *De Gaulle and the United States: A Centennial Reappraisal* (Oxford: Berg, 1994), 224. For a recent expression of the same sentiment, see *The Economist,* 5 Aug. 1995, 29.

1970s—and even more recent policymakers for that matter—they all tended to argue that not only did Europeans have to solve European problems, but that at least in a long-term perspective European dependence was undesirable even for the United States.

In the discussions surrounding the Marshall Plan, Kennan thus pointed out that the US must insist "for the sake of clarity, for the sake of soundness of concept, and for the sake of the self-respect of the European peoples, that the initiative be taken in Europe and that the main burden be borne by the governments of that area." The United States could not really help those who were not willing to help themselves.[13] Indeed, as Marshall was to underline, it had to be the business of the Europeans to draw up a united recovery program.[14]

Similarly, when Harold Stassen, director of the Foreign Operations Administration, argued in October 1956 that it might be best to keep Europe weak and divided, Eisenhower replied that "weakness could not cooperate, weakness could only beg." Accordingly, the United States had to build up self-confidence and strength in the Western European nations if they were to be good allies.[15]

McGeorge Bundy, Kennedy's national security adviser, argued that partial dependency, as against equal mutual reliance, was not good for the pride or the judgment of free men, and when "one power is very much stronger than its allies there is an unhealthy tendency to seek special and unique connections at the center. It would be better if Western Europe were one great power."[16] Kennan's original "dumbbell" concept of the United States on one side of the Atlantic cooperating with a relatively unified Europe on the other side was in part resurrected by the Kennedy administration, "meaning that an economic and political alliance is stronger if it has been agreed to by partners of equal weight on both sides [of the Atlantic]."[17]

No one thought more directly in Great Power terms on these matters than Henry Kissinger. As we shall see, he was to question the realism of the underlying assumption in Washington's policy,

---

[13] FRUS, 1947: III, Kennan to Acheson, 23 May 1947, 227.
[14] US Department of State, A Decade of American Foreign Policy, 1269.
[15] Geoffrey Warner, "Eisenhower, Dulles and the Unity of Western Europe," International Affairs, 69:2 (1993), 325–6.
[16] US Department of State, Bulletin, 12 Mar. 1962, 423.
[17] Henry A. Kissinger, "What Kind of Atlantic Partnership?," The Atlantic Community Quarterly, 7 (1969), 27.

i.e. that a more united Western Europe would necessarily follow the lead of the United States. Still, he too concluded that Europe's state of dependence was also bad for the United States. Europe's shirking of responsibility led to criticism of the United States, almost regardless of what policies Washington pursued. A more responsible Europe would remedy this shortcoming; it could even temper the unfortunate mood swings Kissinger felt characterized American foreign policy. He therefore concluded that a more pluralistic world was "profoundly" in America's long-term interest. "Political multipolarity, while difficult to get used to, is the precondition for a new period of creativity."[18]

The broad agreement in Washington on this point reflected a consideration of real importance. Yet, one should not necessarily take all these statements about the undesirability of European dependence on the United States at face value. It is easy to go against dependence as such; it is more difficult to do so when independence actually leads to opposition. We also have to keep in mind that virtually all American policymakers definitely wanted even a united Europe to cooperate closely with the United States within an Atlantic framework. Most policymakers probably assumed that Europe would come to do so. Somehow Europe was to be both independent of and dependent on the United States at the same time.

In many different ways European integration could also lighten the heavy burden put upon the United States after the Second World War. Probably the main reason why the United States insisted on the Europeans working out an integrated four-year economic plan —a measure which was unthinkable in the US itself—to implement Marshall's words at Harvard was to make sure that the Europeans would not come back and ask for more money at the end of the four years.

Eisenhower kept insisting that European unity "would mean early independence from aid from America and other Atlantic countries."[19] He very much wanted to reduce US federal spending, and that certainly included a reduction in defense spending. Time and again Eisenhower returned to the need to bring "the boys home" as soon as possible. He kept hoping that this would

[18] Henry A. Kissinger, *White House Years* (Boston: Little, Brown and Company, 1979), 81–6, particularly 86. See also Kissinger, "What Kind of Atlantic Partnership?." [19] US Department of State, *Bulletin*, 30 May 1951, 164.

be possible "in a few years' time," which he generally estimated to be four to ten years. He could be "mad as hell" at "the European habit of taking our money, resenting any slight hint as to what *they* should do, and then assuming, in addition, full right to criticize us as bitterly as they may desire." After a more united Europe had developed, the United States would, in the president's words, even "be permitted to sit back and relax somewhat."[20] Dulles similarly argued that complete sovereignty for the many nations of Europe was "a luxury which European countries can no longer afford at US expense."[21]

It was another matter that this motive of reducing the US burden and, particularly, bringing "the boys home" did not go over well with most Europeans. They strongly favored American financial assistance and military guarantees in the form of American troops stationed in Europe. Eisenhower's firm support for the EDC was undoubtedly in part related to his desire to reduce the American troop presence in Europe. To communicate this motive openly, however, could easily undermine support in Europe for the EDC. This situation sometimes led to rather confusing statements in Washington about the effect EDC ratification would have on the American troop level. Dulles tried to square the circle by arguing that defeat of the EDC would give an even stronger impetus to a US withdrawal from Europe.[22]

[20] Stephen E. Ambrose, *Eisenhower: The President* (New York: Simon and Schuster, 1984), 143–5, 404–6; *FRUS*, 1955–7: IV, Editorial Note (Remarks by Eisenhower), 349; Thomas M. Sisk, "Forging the Weapon: Eisenhower as NATO's Supreme Allied Commander, 1950–1952," in Günther Bischof and Stephen E. Ambrose (eds.), *Eisenhower: A Centenary Assessment* (Baton Rouge, La.: Louisiana State University Press, 1995), 74–8, 82–3. For another interesting, recent analysis, see Saki Dockrill, "Cooperation and Suspicion: The United States' Alliance Diplomacy for the Security of Western Europe, 1953–54," *Diplomacy and Statecraft*, March 1994, 138–82. See also Hans-Jürgen Grabbe, "Konrad Adenauer, John Foster Dulles, and West German-American Relations," in Richard H. Immerman (ed.), *John Foster Dulles and the Diplomacy of the Cold War* (Princeton: Princeton University Press, 1990), 109–32; Ernest R. May, "The American Commitment to Germany, 1949–1955," in Lawrence S. Kaplan (ed.), *American Historians and the Atlantic Alliance* (Kent, Oh.: Kent State University Press, 1991), 52–80.

[21] *FRUS*, 1955–7: XXVI, Memorandum of conversation Dulles–Adenauer, 4 May 1957, 240.

[22] General Records of the Department of State, National Archives (NA), 662a.00/12-1353, Memorandum of conversation Dulles–Adenauer. See also John Charmley, *Churchill's Grand Alliance: The Anglo-American Special Relationship 1940–1957* (London: Hodder & Stoughton, 1995), 274–5.

Kennedy was not so afraid of federal expenditures as his Republican predecessor, but he was quite concerned about America's negative balance of payments and shared the view that if the United States were to do less, and even Kennedy thought it should, Europe had to do more. A united Europe would be capable of playing a greater role in the common defense, of doing more for the poorer nations, of joining with the United States and others in lowering trade barriers and resolving commercial and financial problems, and even of "developing coordinated policies in all economic, political, and diplomatic areas."[23]

For Nixon, who in many ways came to see the United States as declining and other powers, including Western Europe, as rising, the need for the United States to do less was even more obvious. This was expressed in the so-called Nixon doctrine of July 1969. Nixon's pessimism reflected many different factors: Soviet strategic equality with the US, the frustrations of Vietnam, and a deteriorating balance of payments and even of trade. Vis-à-vis Europe Nixon stressed that "a highly cohesive Western Europe would relieve the United States of many burdens."[24]

As we shall see, starting in the late 1950s American policy-makers began to worry about the balance of payments situation. Increasing concern was being expressed about the EEC/EC keeping American goods out. To the American preoccupation with what Europe could do to relieve the American burden in Europe and elsewhere was soon added the basic question of whether the European Community would benefit the United States economically. Although the answer to this question was rather complicated and involved difficult calculations, most administrations concluded that the creation of new trade between the United States and Western Europe outweighed the relative diversion of American trade away from Western Europe (and vice versa) which had to be expected from an arrangement like the EC. The Reagan administration, however, was particularly ambiguous on this point. Under Reagan the term "Fortress Europe" was frequently heard.

[23] Public Papers of the Presidents. John F. Kennedy, 1962, 538.
[24] Schwok, U.S.–EC Relations in the Post-Cold War Era, 220. The best treatment of the Nixon doctrine is found in Robert S. Litwak, Détente and the Nixon Doctrine: American Foreign Policy and the Pursuit of Stability, 1969–1976 (Cambridge: Cambridge University Press, 1984).

George Bush's secretary of state James Baker flatly stated that "Americans will profit from access to a single EC market."[25] The Clinton administration put the economic case—an integrated Europe would allow the US to do business with a single address—in the following rather rosy, though ungrammatical, terms: "That Europe, economically, the stronger it is, the better it is for us, not the weaker. The stronger it is, the more exports from the United States Europe will draw . . ."[26] Despite such optimistic overall conclusions, there were of course many aspects of EC economic policies to which the United States objected strongly.

While some policymakers, despite the tenor of the statements above, occasionally felt somewhat ambivalent about the economic benefits to the United States of a more united Europe, Washington's faith in the contribution such a Europe could make to the containment of the Soviet Union remained constant for forty-five years. Although the Marshall Plan was not formally directed against anyone, in reality the containment of the Soviet Union formed a most important part of the background for the Plan.[27] NATO was clearly directed against the Soviet Communist threat. Eisenhower and Dulles almost constantly lectured their audiences on the importance of the West standing firm and united against Soviet Communism. Eisenhower set the tone when, as commander of NATO, he argued that "It is a truism that where, among partners, strength is demanded in its fullness, unity is the first requisite." This fact had special application in Europe: "It would be difficult to overstate the benefits . . . that would accrue to NATO if the free nations of Europe were truly a unit."[28]

---

[25] Roy H. Ginsberg, "EC–US Political/Institutional Relations," in Leon Hurwitz and Christian Lequesne (eds.), *The State of the European Community: Policies, Institutions and Debates in the Transition Years* (Boulder, Colo.: Lynne Rienner, 1991), 393.

[26] USIS, US–European Summit Discussed, 15 June 1995, 2.

[27] Some of the best books and articles on the political aspects of the Marshall Plan are: Hogan, *The Marshall Plan*; John Gimbel, *The Origins of the Marshall Plan* (Stanford, Calif.: Stanford University Press, 1976); Scott Jackson, "Prologue to the Marshall Plan: The Origins of the American Commitment for a European Recovery Program," *Journal of American History*, March 1979, 1043–68. For the best short summary of the motives for the Marshall Plan, see Melvyn P. Leffler, *A Preponderance of Power: National Security, the Truman Administration, and the Cold War* (Stanford, Calif.: Stanford University Press, 1992), 159–64.

[28] US Department of State, *Bulletin*, 30 July 1951, 164.

Similarly, referring to a more united Europe, McGeorge Bundy asked rhetorically why the United States supported this objective so strongly "since great states do not usually rejoice in the emergence of other great powers." He gave the answer himself: "The immediate answer here is in the current contest with the Soviet Union." The United States and Western Europe had a common interest in resisting Communist expansion.[29]

Starting with the Truman administration, but more frequently in the Eisenhower administration, it was also argued that European integration could do more than simply contain the Soviet threat. It could even help "liberate" Eastern Europe by attracting the "satellites." Eisenhower himself thus expressed the hope that "A solid power mass in Western Europe would ultimately attract to it all the Soviet satellites, and the threat to peace would disappear."[30]

After the end of the Cold War, when the Eastern European "satellites" did indeed break away from Soviet domination, their membership in the European Union, in the words of a Clinton administration spokesman, "encourages the development of democracy in free markets and the Central European Baltic countries who wish to join it . . ."[31]

If, however, I were to stress *one* crucial motive for the American promotion of European integration, it would have to be the need to integrate Germany with Western Europe in general and with France in particular. This motive was particularly strong in the period from the late 1940s until the early 1960s, i.e. in the formative years both of European integration and of American support for it. Statements about Germany's crucial role abound in the sources and the urgency of many of these statements is quite remarkable.

In 1946–7 it became increasingly clear to policymakers in Washington that the western zones of Germany had to be rehabilitated. To rebuild western Germany without also giving economic assistance to France would have provoked a furious reaction from the

[29] Ibid., 12 Mar. 1962, 423.
[30] *FRUS*, 1955–7: IV, Editorial Note (Remarks by Eisenhower), 349; *FRUS*, 1952–4: VII, NSC document 160/1, 17 Aug. 1953, 510–20; Thomas Alan Schwartz, *America's Germany: John J. McCloy and the Federal Republic of Germany* (Cambridge, Mass.: Harvard University Press, 1991), 283. For the Truman administration, see Leffler, *A Preponderance of Power*, 284.
[31] USIS, US–European Summit Discussed, 15 June 1995, 2.

French. This German–French connection also formed an important part of the background for the Marshall Plan. The further reconstruction of Germany also strengthened the case for the American security guarantee to Western Europe (including France, of course) which formed the backbone of NATO.[32]

In Washington as in most European capitals the reconstruction of western Germany was seen as necessary, but it was still undertaken with considerable uneasiness. What policies would the new Germany pursue? In the words of Republican foreign policy expert John Foster Dulles in 1947–9: was there any guarantee that the leadership would not be seized by "militant and vengeful persons who will surely again be found in Germany?" Would some try to "play both ends against the middle" and "develop a bargaining position between East and West?" Would "economic pressure" be used to achieve "a mastery of western Europe which they could not achieve by arms?"[33]

On 23 May 1949, the German Federal Republic was formally established. If the new state was to achieve equality, and it had to if a nationalistic reaction was to be prevented, then integration was really the only alternative to full independence. Such independence, practically everybody agreed, was just not possible.

In the combination of Germany's need for equality and of Europe's need to contain Germany lay probably the deepest roots of European integration. The French had to take the lead in integrating Germany since the British had clearly demonstrated their unwillingness to do so. And in 1950 the French finally did take the lead.[34] David Bruce, certainly one of the key policymakers on European integration in the Truman, Eisenhower, and even the Kennedy administration, argued in June 1950, after Schuman had launched his Coal and Steel Initiative, that to bring "non-communized Germany into closest possible communion with its western neighbors" had been one of the great objectives in US foreign policy. For a long

[32] This is the argument presented somewhat one-sidedly in Gimbel, *The Origins of the Marshall Plan* and Timothy P. Ireland, *Creating the Entangling Alliance: The Origins of the North Atlantic Treaty Organization* (Westport, Conn.: Greenwood, 1981). In their eagerness to play up the Franco–German dimension, these authors downplay the more traditional concern with the Soviet Communist threat.

[33] The quotations are from Ronald W. Pruessen, "Mixed Messages: U.S.–E.U. Relations in the 1990s and Traditional Patterns of Transatlantic Ambivalence," unpub. paper presented at the May 1996 Brussels Conference on Decision-Making in U.S.–E.U. Relations, 8.

[34] These events are further analyzed in Ch. 4. See also Ch. 10.

time the obstacles to such an achievement seemed almost insuperable. Various expedients were discussed and found impracticable. "Then the French proposal, audacious in nature, comprehensive in conception opened up new possibility of European integration and at least offered prospect of moderating century old antagonism between French and Germans."[35]

Acheson instructed US embassies in Europe that the "US attaches greatest importance Schuman principles as contribution French–German *rapprochement*."[36] Dulles proclaimed that "the conception is brilliantly creative and could go far to solve the most dangerous problem of our time, namely the relationship of Germany's industrial power to France and the West."[37]

In the discussions on the European Defense Community, Eisenhower could become quite alarmist about Germany's future. In his talks with Churchill in July 1954, before the French vote on the EDC, he underlined that "we could not afford to lose Germany even though we were to lose France." He raised the question "as to the point at which action to preserve Germany would be required on our part."[38] When, in January 1956 in an internal document, Dulles summed up the reasons for the US support for European integration, as opposed to looser forms of cooperation, at least two of the three reasons he mentioned had to do with Germany:

a. Problem of tying Germany organically into Western Community so as to diminish danger that over time a resurgent German nationalism might trade neutrality for reunification with view seizing controlling position between East and West.

b. The weakness of France and need to provide positive alternative to neutralism and "defeatism" in that country.

[35] FRUS, 1950: III, Ambassador Bruce to the Secretary of State, 4 June 1950, 716. David Bruce played a crucial role in at least one major crisis in each of the Truman, Eisenhower, and Kennedy administrations: the adoption of the EDC on the American side in 1951, the move to the NATO solution after the EDC failure in 1954, and the response to de Gaulle's actions in January 1963. Bruce was ambassador to France 1949–52, under-secretary of state 1952–3, special observer to the EDC talks and US representative to the ECSC 1953–4, ambassador to West Germany 1957–9, and ambassador to Great Britain 1961–9. For a recent well-written biography of Bruce, see Nelson D. Lankford, *The Last American Aristocrat: The Biography of Ambassador David K.E. Bruce* (Boston: Little, Brown and Company, 1996).

[36] FRUS, 1950: III, Secretary of State to certain diplomatic offices, 8 July 1950, 740.

[37] Ibid., Acting Secretary of State to the Secretary of State, 10 May 1950, 695–6.

[38] FRUS, 1952–4: V. 1, Memorandum of conversation Eisenhower–Churchill. 27 June 1954, 985–7.

c. The solidifying of new relationship between France and Germany which has been developing since 1950 through integration movement.[39]

In May 1961 Kennedy told British prime minister Harold Macmillan that America's central interest in the EEC question was political: "We believe that only with growing political coherence in Western Europe can we look to a stable solution of the place of Germany."[40] Two weeks later he told French president Charles de Gaulle that in addition to the economic and political strengthening of Europe, there was also another reason why the US favored the European Economic Community: "It is because it contributes to tie West Germany to Europe. It is not clear what will happen in Germany after Adenauer and, therefore, every tie which links Germany to Europe should be welcome."[41] The fear of what might follow Adenauer had been even more pronounced in the Eisenhower administration than it was under Kennedy.

In the period of maximum concern with Germany, the 1940s and 1950s, the ultimate fear was that Germany would side with the Soviet Union. European integration was thus to contain both the Soviet Union and Germany. (This was "double containment." In some respects Washington felt that even France and other Western European allies of the United States had to be contained—"triple containment."[42])

Again and again, members of the Eisenhower administration returned to this worst of horror scenarios. After the French national assembly had rejected the EDC in August 1954, Dulles told the National Security Council that the heart of the matter was whether or not the US would be able to preserve NATO. "The Soviets successfully used Mendes-France to kill, or at least to maim, EDC. Will they now try to destroy NATO?" If they did that

[39] FRUS, 1955-7: IV, Telegram from the Secretary of State to the Embassy in Belgium, 26 Jan. 1956, 399. See also ibid., Letter from the Secretary of State to Macmillan, 10 Dec. 1955, 363. For similar arguments as presented in NSC 160, "United States Position with Respect to Germany" in August 1953, see FRUS, 1952-4: V, 799, n. 2.

[40] FRUS, 1961-3: XIII, Telegram from the Department of State to the Embassy in the United Kingdom, 23 May 1961, 20-1.

[41] Ibid., Memorandum of conversation Kennedy–de Gaulle, 2 June 1961, 25.

[42] Ronald W. Pruessen, "Cold War Threats and America's Commitment to the European Defense Community: One Corner of a Triangle," Journal of European Integration History, Spring 1996, 51-69. Pruessen's "triple containment" is really subsumed in my conclusion that the United States pursued European integration as a way of controlling Europe as part of the American "empire."

successfully the West would be in big trouble. In such a situation Germany might well choose not to rearm. There would be heavy pressure for Germany to accommodate the Soviet Union. Moscow "could dangle the possibility of unification of Germany, rectification of the Polish frontier, and economic advantages." Dulles's conclusion was that "there is no good alternative if the French torpedo the NATO solution, and we must not assume that we can go ahead independently to rearm Germany if the French won't agree."[43]

The Soviets held strong cards, and if they played them cleverly, Washington's consuming fear was that the Germans would be tempted by the siren songs of neutrality. Adenauer held them in place. He rejected Soviet overtures, in the form of Soviet proposals for unification, particularly the one in March 1952, but, again, what would happen after him? When in March 1960 Macmillan warned against the views of a new generation of Germans, undersecretary of state Douglas Dillon responded that "it was just this possibility" that had made Washington push European integration "in order that the new German generation would not have free hand to play East against West or various part of Europe against each other or even Europe against US."[44]

In the preparations for Kennedy's visit to Europe in June–July 1963, under-secretary of state George Ball, the person largely responsible in the Kennedy administration for European integration, pointed out that up to now the Germans had "largely been tractable" because of their fear of the Soviet Union and the fact that the US alone could provide an effective defense. Changes were under way, however, on both sides of the Iron Curtain,

and the possibility of some Soviet overture to a post-Adenauer Germany must not be overlooked. . . . In those changed circumstances a Germany not tied closely and institutionally to the West can be a source of great hazard. Embittered by a deepening sense of discrimination and bedeviled by irredentism, a Germany at large can be like a cannon on shipboard in a high sea [emphasis in original].[45]

[43] FRUS, 1952–4: V. 2, Memorandum of discussion, 215th meeting of the NSC, 24 Sept. 1954, 1266.

[44] NA, 611.41/3–2060, Herter to various embassies, 3.

[45] FRUS, 1961–3: XIII, Memorandum from Ball to President Kennedy, 20 June 1963, 209. For similar fears expressed by Ball to Kennedy in April 1961, see NA, 611.41/4–161, Memorandum for the President from Ball, 3.

While Eisenhower and especially Dulles had had a very close relationship with Adenauer, in 1960 the president was clearly becoming frustrated with the German chancellor's "increasingly confirmed . . . rigidity" and his "growing senility."[46] The Kennedy administration quickly came to feel that Adenauer was much too rigid on East–West matters, including the status of Berlin and even of East Germany.[47] Despite this, as the Ball quotation indicates, even the Kennedy administration was quite concerned about post-Adenauer Germany becoming a loose cannon. Adenauer was too rigid, but the good thing about him was that he was a guarantor against any form of Soviet–German deal. As we shall see, Washington's support for the Multilateral Nuclear Force (MLF) in NATO illustrated the American fear that if the Germans were discriminated against, even in the nuclear field, they might come to respond in dangerously nationalistic ways. Germany could not be discriminated against, but neither could it be set free. Integration was the obvious answer.

As Germany proved a loyal supporter of European integration even after Adenauer had retired and German political life stabilized on the political center, the overriding fear about Germany's position gradually abated. Yet the process was rather slow. Alarmist analyses and statements were still made. In fact, de Gaulle's independence gave them new life. His policies allegedly represented a threat not only to the United States, but also to Germany. As president Johnson told British prime minister Harold Wilson in May 1966, there was a grave danger that the Germans would come to feel that they had been cast adrift. A growing sense of insecurity on their part could lead to "a fragmentation of European and Atlantic relations which would be tragic for all of us. On our part, we cannot risk the danger of a rudderless Germany in the heart of Europe."[48]

[46] *FRUS*, 1958–60: IX, Memorandum of conference with President Eisenhower, 14 Mar. 1960, 218–20; ibid., Memorandum of conference with President Eisenhower, 17 Mar. 1960, 239–40. See also Thomas A. Schwartz, "The Berlin Crisis and the Cold War," *Diplomatic History*, Winter 1997, 139–48.

[47] Frank A. Mayer, *Adenauer and Kennedy: A Study in German-American Relations, 1961–1963* (London: Macmillan, 1996) deals with the growing differences between the two leaders. See also Thomas Alan Schwartz, "Victories and Defeats in the Long Twilight Struggle: The United States and Western Europe in the 1960s," in Diane B. Kunz (ed.), *The Diplomacy of the Crucial Decade: American Foreign Relations during the 1960s* (New York: Columbia University Press, 1994), 122–7.

[48] *FRUS*, 1964–8: XIII, Telegram from Johnson to Wilson, 21 May 1966, 396. See also ibid. 397–8.

Germany's position remained an important consideration even with later administrations. In Nixon and Kissinger's guarded response to chancellor Willy Brandt's *Ostpolitik* a lingering fear of the "specter" of "classic German nationalism" could still be found, although somewhat less dramatic now than before. "Only a federal Europe," Kissinger wrote, "could end Europe's wars, provide an effective counterweight to the USSR, bind Germany indissolubly to the West, and share with us the burdens and obligations of world leadership."[49]

With Germany's unification in 1990, the concern about the country's position came back in a different form. Thus, the Clinton administration recently pointed out that one of the reasons why it encouraged the European Union was because "it provides a home for Germany to act out its future in an integrated Europe and not independent of it . . ."[50] While hardly anyone doubted the integrationist and democratic credentials of Helmut Kohl, no one could be entirely certain what the future leaders of united Germany would come to stand for. Thus, in a way Germany could never live down the legacy of the two world wars.

[49] Henry A. Kissinger, *Years of Upheaval* (Boston: Little, Brown and Company, 1982), 143–8; Kissinger, *White House Years*, 81, 389, 409.

[50] USIS, US–European Summit Discussed, 15 June 1995, 2.

4

THE UNITED STATES AND THE BEGINNINGS OF EUROPEAN INTEGRATION, 1945–1950

D URING and immediately after the Second World War the United States was actually largely skeptical of European integration. The Roosevelt administration feared that such integration could come to mean spheres of influence politically and autarchy economically. Germany might also come to dominate an integrated Europe. When in late 1945 Washington began to modify this skepticism, the emphasis was at first on loose all-European integration in the form of the Economic Commission for Europe (ECE). The ECE included the Soviet Union and Eastern Europe and came to deal largely with minor practical matters.[1]

With the Marshall Plan the United States came out firmly in support of Western European integration, and now integration on as comprehensive a scale as possible. The Soviet Union and Communism had to be contained; the western zones of Germany had to be integrated with a revitalized Western Europe in general and with France in particular.

Washington soon became disappointed with the very limited steps the Europeans were taking in the direction of integration. When they did not set up the kind of effective organization to administer the Marshall Plan assistance that the Truman administration had hoped for, the Europeans were pressured into making a new report, although even the new report proved rather disappointing

---

[1] Beloff, *The United States and the Unity of Europe*, 1–12; Hogan, *The Marshall Plan*, 27–8; Winand, *Eisenhower, Kennedy, and the United States of Europe*, 1–11.

from an American integrationist point of view.[2] From 1947 to 1950 disappointment pretty much described the American reaction to what the Europeans were doing. No customs union was established (except the union between the Benelux countries—Belgium, the Netherlands, and Luxembourg—and this union was not really an American initiative). The Organization for European Economic Cooperation (OEEC), which was set up to administer the Marshall aid, became much too weak an organization. The so-called free lists for trade among the OEEC countries took too long to work out and there were too many reservations. Thus, although progress was made on integration, Washington thought this progress slow, much too slow.

The Truman administration clearly felt there was a lack of leadership on the European side. The natural leaders, the British, were holding back. Clement Attlee's Labour government was interested in cooperation with the Western Europeans as illustrated, on the defense side, by the Dunkirk treaty of 1947 with the French and the Brussels treaty of 1948 which also included the Benelux countries, and, on the economic side, by the British role in setting up the OEEC, however imperfect from the American point of view. In late 1947 to early 1948 foreign secretary Ernest Bevin even displayed an interest in some sort of West European customs union.

Yet for Britain, relations with Western Europe had to be carefully balanced by relations with the Commonwealth and with the United States. This was true both politically and economically. Whenever the Foreign Office took the slightest interest in a customs union, the Treasury and the Board of Trade would inevitably refer to Britain's global obligations, the special role of sterling, and the importance of the Commonwealth. With Bevin being rather half-hearted in the first place, this opposition would suffice to kill off any dramatic British initiatives. The traditional distance to the European continent was increased by the political distance between Labour ruling in Britain and more conservative forces dominating the governments on the continent. To many in Britain, not only on the left, the continent seemed to be dominated by "conservatives, capitalists, clerics, and cartels". The different war experiences

    [2] Hogan, *The Marshall Plan*, 70–82, 124–8; Geir Lundestad, *America, Scandinavia, and the Cold War, 1945–1949* (New York: Columbia University Press, 1980), 89–94, 143–4.

were certainly relevant (with nationalism having been discredited in many quarters on the continent, but not in Britain). London's firm conclusion was that it was entirely opposed to any form of European integration that smacked of supranationality.[3]

At first it was even more difficult for the French than for the British to take any effective lead in promoting European integration. The temptation to exploit European integration to enhance France's international role was there, but it was more than counterbalanced by other factors. French governments were many and weak, and the centrist forces that dominated these governments after 1947 in practice expected London to lead on European matters. On the crucial issue of Germany, Paris had difficulties in abandoning the course defined in 1945–6, which represented an evident continuation of the French policy after the First World War: the elimination of as much centralized power in Germany as possible, the separation of the Rhineland from the German state(s), the internationalization of the Ruhr, and the economic fusion of the Saar with France. The French five-year plan for the modernization of France from 1947 (the Monnet plan) was based on German weakness in the form of inexpensive deliveries of coal from Germany to France and on France taking over traditional German markets.

In 1947–8, once reviving Germany became an essential part of the integration problem, the French at first became even more paralyzed. If the traditional French course had to be abandoned and Germany treated more leniently, most Frenchmen felt it much too risky to balance Germany more or less on their own. Britain had to be brought in to help in the containment of Germany.

[3] For good accounts of British policies, see John Young, *Britain, France and the Unity of Europe 1945–1951* (Leicester: Leicester University Press, 1984) and, by the same author, *Britain and European Unity, 1945–1992* (London: Macmillan, 1993); Geoffrey Warner, "The Labour Governments and the Unity of Western Europe, 1945–51," in Ritchie Ovendale (ed.), *The Foreign Policy of the British Labour Governments, 1945–1951* (Leicester: Leicester University Press, 1984), 61–82; Roger Woodhouse, *British Policy towards France 1945–51* (London: Macmillan, 1995); Edmund Dell, *The Schuman Plan and the British Abdication of Leadership in Europe* (Oxford: Oxford University Press, 1995). For an interesting account by a British insider, see Edwin Plowden, *An Industrialist in the Treasury: The Post-War Years* (London: André Deutsch, 1989), particularly 86–96. Plowden quotes a "forthright colleague of mine" who argued that "We are being asked to join the Germans, who had started two world wars, the French, who had in 1940 collapsed in the face of German aggression, the Italians, who had changed sides, and the Low Countries, of whom not much was known but who seemed to have put up little resistance to Germany" (93).

Economically, France was still rather protectionist. That protectionism helped kill both the customs union with Italy, which the two had informally agreed in March 1949, and the loose schemes of cooperation with Italy and the Benelux countries (Fritalux) which were being discussed.[4]

There matters remained for a long time. France would not launch a major initiative on European integration without Britain being included, and Britain simply refused to take part in any form of supranational integration. Still, the French were gradually moving. In June 1948 the French national assembly accepted the London agreements which pointed the way to an independent West Germany. Foreign minister Georges Bidault persuaded the assembly that it had to choose between cooperation, including cooperation with the western zones of Germany, and isolation. Robert Schuman became French foreign minister in July 1948 and, as a native of Alsace-Lorraine, he had an obvious interest in Franco–German reconciliation. Schuman had strong backing from Jean Monnet who, starting in 1948, became a most ardent spokesman for European integration. Monnet was soon to become Washington's favorite European.[5]

Partly as a result of the political reconstruction of Western Germany, the French took the lead on the creation of a potentially supranational Council of Europe. The State Department issued a statement declaring that "We favor the taking by the Europeans

[4] Young, *Britain, France and the Unity of Europe* offers a good account of French policies. For a more comprehensive account of the early years, see his *France, the Cold War and the Western Alliance. 1944–1949: French Foreign Policy and Post War Europe* (Leicester: Leicester University Press, 1990). F. Roy Willis, *France, Germany and the New Europe 1945–1967* (Oxford: Oxford University Press, 1968), is still useful. For the economic side, see Frances Lynch, "Resolving the Paradox of the Monnet Plan: National and International Planning in French Reconstruction," *Economic History Review*, 37:2 (1984), 229–43. Italy was basically sympathetic to anything that could make it a valuable partner for the West, enhance its international status, and strengthen cooperation with the United States and France in particular. For a good, short account of Italy's position on European integration, see Antonio Varsori, "Italy's Position towards European Integration (1947–58)," in Christopher Duggan and Christopher Wagstaff (eds.), *Italy in the Cold War: Politics, Culture and Society 1948–58* (Oxford: Berg, 1995), 47–66.

[5] For a good analysis of these developments, see Young, *Britain, France and the Unity of Europe*, 108–43 and his *France, the Cold War and the Western Alliance*, 194–7, 211–13. See also Carolyn Woods Eisenberg, *Drawing the Line: The American Decision to Divide Germany, 1944–1949* (Cambridge: Cambridge University Press, 1996), 398–403.

themselves of any steps which promote the idea of European unity or which promote the study of practical measures and the taking of such measures."[6]

But again, Britain, despite her strong opposition to supranationalism, was to be included in the European Council ("this talking shop in Strasbourg," as Bevin called it[7]). This seemed like a vicious circle. Really significant European integration could not be achieved with Britain and it could not be achieved without Britain. Washington was becoming increasingly frustrated by the lack of progress.

Yet signs of change could also be detected on the American side. In 1949 the Truman administration was finally realizing that Britain simply would not take any lead on European integration. In fact, London was becoming more and more Atlantic in its approach and Washington was at least in part accepting this, as illustrated most clearly by the close Anglo–American cooperation in NATO and in connection with the devaluation of the pound in September 1949. In its work to set up the European Payments Union (EPU) in 1949–50, Washington again cooperated closely with London. Obviously a payments union without Britain would be much less valuable than one where it was included.[8]

If, with the very partial exception of the EPU, Britain was absolutely refusing to take a constructive lead on European integration, then the United States was now preparing to proceed without it. The reason for Washington's rapidly growing impatience was evident: developments in West Germany could not be put on hold. Germany had to be integrated into a European framework and if Britain would not take the lead in establishing such a framework, others had to do it. In May 1949 the West German state was formally established. The Truman administration was insisting that the controls on Germany had to be modified and eventually lifted. On this point the British largely supported the Americans. European integration was the obvious solution for Washington, and to a lesser extent even for London. Britain understood that French–German reconciliation was necessary, but was held back by the

[6] *FRUS*, 1948: III, Secretary of State Marshall to the embassy in France, 27 Aug. 1948, 222–3.

[7] Peter Hennesy, *Never Again: Britain 1945–51* (London: Jonathan Cape, 1992), 340.

[8] NA, 762.00/3–2250, Secretary of State Acheson to the embassy in the United Kingdom.

fact that it could not itself join any supranational organization. From the American point of view something now *had* to be accomplished. The alternatives of, on the one hand, continuing to hold Germany down and, on the other, giving it full freedom to act were simply not acceptable.

On 19 October 1949, secretary of state Dean Acheson warned that there were signs in West Germany of events taking "a familiar and dangerous nationalist turn." This trend would continue unless German energies were integrated into those of Western Europe as a whole. "The danger is that the time to arrest and reverse this trend is already very short." The French had to take the lead and they had to do this "promptly and decisively." No longer could Paris keep waiting for London to act. "The key to progress towards integration is in French hands," Acheson stated and he continued, "even with the closest possible relationship of the US and the UK to the continent, France and France alone can take the decisive leadership in integrating Western Germany into Western Europe." This was "the last chance for France to take the lead" if "Russian or German, or perhaps Russian–German domination, is to be avoided."[9]

At a joint meeting on 21–2 October, the most important US ambassadors in Europe were skeptical about the practicality of Acheson's conclusions. They argued that no European integration which was to include Germany was possible without the participation of Great Britain. The French just would not chance it more or less alone with the Germans.[10]

The skepticism of the ambassadors made Acheson soften his position somewhat: "We agree with you . . . that France alone cannot lead . . . and that British influence and assistance is also essential." However, he did not wish "to see progress retarded by British reluctance" and he therefore reaffirmed his basic point that the French had to take some sort of lead.[11] On 30 October Acheson accordingly told Schuman that "Now is the time for French initiative to integrate the German Federal Republic promptly and

[9] *FRUS*, 1949: IV, Secretary of State to the embassy in France, 19 Oct. 1949, 469–70.

[10] *FRUS*, 1949: IV, 472–96, particularly Meeting of US ambassadors at Paris, 21–2 Oct. 1949, 493.

[11] *FRUS*, 1949: IV, Secretary of State to the embassy in the United Kingdom, 24 Oct. 1949, 345; see also Schwabe, "The United States and European Integration: 1947–1957," 119–30.

decisively into Europe." France should agree to give the West Germans more independence in their political affairs and also take the lead in bringing Germany into all relevant international organizations. To do otherwise would be to weaken the democratic forces in Germany and strengthen extremism and the Soviet position there.[12]

The next months were to show, however, that the Truman administration had not really drawn the kind of clear conclusions which the October debate would appear to indicate. Washington was still confused as to how to proceed. Thus, at a meeting on 7 March 1950 with several of the key policymakers on the American side, Acheson again concluded that "What was needed was some new approach which would recapture the initiative." The EPU was certainly useful, but the successful working-out of a payments union "would have no popular appeal, there would be no holidays or torch-light parades in celebration of a payments union." What more could actually be done? The suggestions varied from Acheson's idea simply to ask UK ambassador Oliver Franks "what he thought we could do to get started" to US high commissioner to Germany John McCloy's contribution that "what was needed was a drastic step toward political unity such as the establishing of articles of confederation for Europe."[13]

Washington continued to work closely with London, particularly on the EPU.[14] True, even in financial and monetary matters, where the British influence was particularly strong, Washington was prepared to proceed without London if this was absolutely necessary. As secretary of state Acheson instructed ambassador Douglas in London on 22 March 1950, on the matter of the EPU: if agreement on a plan in which the United Kingdom would be able to participate was not going to be possible, "I should feel that we must go ahead with the development of a trade and liberalization scheme among the continental countries." In May–June, however,

[12] FRUS, 1949: III, Secretary of State to the embassy in France, 30 Oct. 1949, 622–5. See also Young, France, the Cold War and the Western Alliance, 228–31, particularly 230; Dean Acheson, Present at the Creation: My Years in the State Department (New York: Norton, 1969), 338–40.

[13] FRUS, 1950: III, Memorandum of conversation Acheson, McCloy, Douglas et al., 7 Mar. 1950, 1628–32.

[14] FRUS, 1950: III, Memorandum by Boochever to Reynolds, 29 June 1950, 663. For a general account of the establishment of the EPU, see Milward, The European Rescue of the Nation-State, 348–66.

the British modified their position sufficiently to secure an agreement to establish the EPU.[15]

Washington's sympathy for London remained strong. In April a State Department position paper once again concluded that "No other country has the same qualifications for being our principal ally and partner as the UK." The US could find "its most important collaborators and allies in the UK and the Commonwealth, just as the UK and the Commonwealth are, in turn, dependent upon us." In part because of these very sympathies, American policymakers just could not bring themselves to give up entirely on Britain taking some sort of lead on European integration. The State Department continued to express the hope that closer ties could be established between Britain and the continental states: "we would be glad to support British leadership (in conjunction with the French)." The problem of course was that no British leadership was emerging. This did not prevent the State Department from showing increasing sympathy for Britain's ties with the Commonwealth and with the United States.[16]

No significant initiative was actually taken vis-à-vis the French to follow up on Acheson's request for French leadership on 30 October. It was as if Washington would not believe that the French could undertake any major action to address the German situation.

In its search for a way out, the Truman administration looked rather desperately for new ideas. The US high commission in Germany was behind some of the most dramatic ones. On the very same day, 25 April, McCloy first recommended that the West must decisively establish a trend away from the present concept of a "Ruhr authority as an agency imposed on Germany (perhaps towards an international authority for control of all Western European coal and steel), away from MSB [the Military Security Board] (and towards full membership in NATO)." In this way Germany could begin to resume her place in Europe; and the "Germans will begin to see promise in a future by the side of Western democracies—as against East."[17]

[15] NA, 762.00/3-2250, Secretary of State Acheson to the embassy in the United Kingdom; Sally Dore, "Britain and the European Payments Union: British Policy and American Influence," in Heller and Gillingham, The United States and the Integration of Europe, 167–97, particularly 177–84.

[16] FRUS, 1950: III, Paper prepared in the State Department: Essential elements in US-UK relations, 19 Apr. 1950, 869–81, particularly 870, 874–5, 878, 880.

[17] FRUS, 1950: IV, McCloy to the Secretary of State, 25 Apr. 1950, 633–5; quotation from 635.

Here McCloy was actually suggesting what was to become Western policy: first a coal and steel community and then German membership in NATO. At the time he sent his report, however, there was little reason to believe that this would be the outcome.

Then, one hour later, McCloy reported having examined even the idea of the United States urging West Germany to take the lead on European integration. The high commission's conclusion was obvious, however: "After careful consideration" this alternative was rejected, although it appeared "very attractive at first glance."[18]

One additional idea also cropped up in Washington in March–April 1950. This was for the United States itself to take the initiative to establish what was called an International Organization in the North American–Western European Area. Again West Germany was the focal point. Germany had to be "tied" to the West. It was still deemed impossible to bring it into NATO, and the OEEC and the Council of Europe were just too weak to really tie Germany down. France would not move without Britain. Britain would not move without the United States. It therefore appeared unlikely that much progress could be made towards "that political and economic integration of Western Europe, which seems necessary to contain Western Germany unless the United States deepens its commitments to Western Europe."

The new organization was to become "the senior body" over all existing organizations, including NATO, but since this Atlantic Council, as it was also called, "must not involve anything more than cooperative action among sovereign governments," it was difficult to see exactly how its integrationist objective could be achieved.[19] In the end very little came out of this rather vague idea. Opinions in Washington were mixed. Neither the British nor the French expressed any strong interest. The French feared that under such a scheme West Germany would be given at least indirect membership in NATO. The relationship between existing organizations and the suggested one was indeed a major problem.[20]

---

[18] Ibid. 682–4; quotation from 683.

[19] NA, 396.1-LO/4-2650, May Foreign Ministers Meetings, International Organization in the North American–Western European Area, particularly 3–7, 10–12. See also NA, 396.1-LO/4-2750 SF, Minutes of US–French Bipartite Meeting; NA, 396.1-LO/4-1250, Memorandum from Bancroft to Hickerson; NA, 396.1-LO/3-3150, Telegram from Acheson to McCloy.

[20] FRUS, 1950: III, Secretary of State to the Acting Secretary of State, 16 May 1950, 659–61; ibid., Acting Secretary of State to the embassy in France, 25 May 1950, 661–2; ibid., Harriman to the Secretary of State, 15 June 1950, 662–3.

Thus, the American eagerness to build up Germany economically and politically was rapidly increasing. Even Germany's military reconstruction could be seen on the horizon. Washington made it perfectly clear that Germany *had* to be reconstructed and eventually be treated as an equal partner. If the French did not come up with ideas on how this was to be done, the United States would have to involve itself more directly. Although Washington had presented no definite idea on how to proceed, it had repeatedly indicated that some form of Western European integration was the best, and probably the only, way out.

On the French side, as early as September 1949 Schuman had referred to a "mandate" from the United States to lead on the German question.[21] Paris had long hesitated. It hoped that somehow the United States could solve the German problem for it. One way would indeed be to transform the Atlantic alliance into an economic as well as a military organization. But since Paris was strongly opposed to anything that would mean letting Germany indirectly into NATO, there was not much that could be done in a meaningful way. And Washington did not want to become too intimately involved in Europe's affairs. In the end, all that could be agreed on was a certain strengthening of the American role in the OEEC. This then became part of the framework for the dramatic initiative Paris was about to take.[22]

Paris had to act, if it were not to lose control entirely over developments in Germany. On 15 May the NATO Council was to open its meeting in London, to be preceded by a meeting of the foreign ministers of the US, the UK, and France. Although the question of Germany's contribution to the strength of the West was difficult to handle in the formal NATO context, it was obvious that the Americans would again be concerned about "speeding up the integration of Western Germany with the West, and, if possible, to relax our controls in Western Germany."[23]

[21] For the mandate, see Klaus Schwabe, " 'Ein Akt konstruktiver Staatskunst'— die USA und die Anfänge des Schumans-Plans," in Klaus Schwabe (ed.), *Die Anfänge des Schuman-Plans 1950/51/The Beginnings of the Schuman Plan* (Baden-Baden: Nomos, 1988), 219.

[22] Frances Lynch, "The Role of Jean Monnet in Setting Up the European Coal and Steel Community," in Schwabe, *Die Anfänge des Schuman-Plans*, 120–1. See also the references in n. 19.

[23] Both the tripartite meeting of the foreign ministers and of the NATO Council are extensively documented in *FRUS, 1950: III*. The quotation is from ibid., Paper prepared in the State Department, 28 Apr. 1950, 1002. For good brief

The crucial French initiative, the Schuman plan for a European Coal and Steel Community, was taken on 9 May 1950, against this rather complex background. The Americans had also been considering the idea of a coal and steel community, as we have seen from McCloy's statement, and ambassador David Bruce in Paris had discussed the concept in advance with Jean Monnet. The more specific forms were worked out in Paris. The technical work was done by Monnet and his group, and they received the political support of Robert Schuman and the French Foreign Office and, later, premier Bidault and the cabinet.[24]

After Washington's initial doubts about the cartel aspects of the Schuman plan had been resolved at least in part, the Truman administration was to give the plan full backing. This was, finally, the initiative which Washington had been searching for at least since the formation of the West German state, or even earlier. As Dulles said after Schuman had launched his plan, this was what he and Marshall had talked about in connection with the Council of Foreign Ministers meeting in Moscow in March–April 1947, "but we did not believe the French would ever accept."[25]

studies of the background for the Schuman plan, see Schwabe, "'Ein Akt konstruktiver Staatskunst,'" particularly 213–25; Pierre Gerber, "European Integration as an Instrument of French Foreign Policy," in Heller and Gillingham, *The United States and the Integration of Europe*, 57–77, particularly 66–70.

    [24] *FRUS*, 1950: III, Secretary of State to the Acting Secretary of State, 12 May 1950, 697–701. See also Duchêne, *Jean Monnet*, 190, 218, 224; Eric Roussel, *Jean Monnet* (Paris: Fayard, 1996), 519–29. For Bruce's role, see Lankford, *The Last American Aristocrat*, 221–3.

    [25] *FRUS*, 1950: III, Acting Secretary to the Secretary of State, 10 May 1950, 695–6; Schwabe, "'Ein Akt konstruktiver Staatskunst,'" 223–8.

5

THE ATLANTIC FRAMEWORK FOR EUROPEAN INTEGRATION, 1950–1960

THE fear of Germany dominating Europe was the primary reason why the United States had intervened in two world wars. In the Cold War the United States intervened again in Europe, to contain the Soviet Union. And the US was still quite concerned about Germany's role. The United States was obviously opposed to the integration of Europe if this took place under the leadership of a hostile power. Therefore, American support for European integration was clearly premised on certain conditions being fulfilled. By far the most important of these was that the more united Europe remain friendly to the United States. To make certain that this happened, the new Europe had to be fitted into a wider Atlantic framework. This framework was established first through the Marshall Plan and the OEEC and then, much more importantly, through NATO. Gradually the General Agreement on Tariffs and Trade (GATT) also came to constitute an important part of this framework. To a large extent this "Atlantic framework" was a code phrase for overall American leadership. There was never any real doubt that Western Europe belonged to the American "empire."

In early 1948 the United States had still been reluctant to join Western Europe in a common Atlantic security organization. Instead the Truman administration had emphasized the contribution the Western Europeans should make to their own defense. Only in March 1948 did Washington agree to start confidential talks with Britain and Canada about an Atlantic defense system. This was done in response to urgent British messages after Soviet moves towards Czechoslovakia and Finland, and the rumors about a Soviet-pact proposal to Norway.[1]

Once the talks on an Atlantic system started, it is remarkable how quickly the Truman administration abandoned the emphasis on the Western Union formed through the Brussels treaty of March 1948. Washington still insisted on the Europeans contributing to their own defense, but this was now to be done through the Atlantic organization being formed, i.e. through what in April 1949 became NATO.

There were several reasons for this change of emphasis. On the American side the Western Union of Britain, France, Belgium, the Netherlands, and Luxembourg included only some of the right members. Washington saw Portugal with the Azores, Denmark with Greenland, and Norway as essential in a strategic context. On the European side there was little desire to underline the role of the Western Union. For London in particular it had been formed at least in part to make it easier to bring the Americans in. The Europeans considered the American security guarantee crucial and they struggled hard to make it as automatic as possible. Britain preferred cooperating with the Americans to working with the continentals. On the French side too many wanted to speak directly with Washington, and not through some sort of British command, which could easily have become the case under a strong Western Union.

Most important of all, however, the Americans insisted on a leadership role if they were to join an Atlantic defense organization. This could more easily be done through NATO than through Kennan's dumbbell concept of cooperation between two (equal) sides of the Atlantic. The result was that the American policy went almost full circle: from stressing the importance of a European defense organization, the Truman administration in fact became concerned that the Western Union not interfere in NATO matters.[2]

---

[1] The change in US policy in March 1948 is discussed in my *America, Scandinavia, and the Cold War, 1945-1949*, 171-93. See also Escott Reid, *Time of Fear and Hope: The Making of the North Atlantic Treaty 1947-1949* (Toronto: McClelland and Stewart, 1977).

[2] Lawrence S. Kaplan, *The United States and NATO: The Formative Years* (Lexington, Ky.: University of Kentucky Press, 1984), 82-3, 88-92; NA, 396.1-LO/5-850, Telegram from the Secretary of State to the embassy in the United Kingdom; Klaus Schwabe, "The Origins of the United States' Engagement in Europe, 1946-1952," in Francis H. Heller and John R. Gillingham (eds.), *NATO: The Founding of the Atlantic Alliance and the Integration of Europe* (London: Macmillan, 1992), 169-80; Gerber, "European Integration as an Instrument of French Foreign Policy," 64-5.

In the early years the Atlantic framework for European integration was rarely explicitly formulated. Under the Marshall Plan Washington emphasized the aspect of European self-help. With NATO American leadership became obvious, but too much insistence on this could easily undermine an effective European defense contribution. In the 1950s it was more or less taken for granted that the United States and Europe had the most basic interests in common. These interests definitely included the Atlantic framework and American leadership.

In the 1950s the emphasis on the Atlantic framework could easily be carried too far. In historical perspective, the Eisenhower administration in particular was remarkable not for its largely implicit emphasis on this framework, but rather for the strong and direct support it gave to European integration. The British kept pushing for unambiguously Atlantic solutions, whether in the form of German rearmament in NATO, an OEEC approach to cooperation in atomic energy, an Atlantic free trade area to "dilute" the EEC, or even putting all the European institutions—the ECSC, EURATOM, and the Common Market—into some sort of Atlantic setting. All these efforts were, however, *opposed* in Washington. While the US agreed that there should definitely be a wider Atlantic framework for European integration, with this framework already in place the United States, unlike Britain, insisted that the "six should increasingly act as a unit within Atlantic organization, and that integrity of developing institutions of six-country Community should be safeguarded."[3]

As we have already seen, Washington pursued European integration with considerably more fervor than the six ECSC/EEC countries themselves. From 1949 to 1960 the United States apparently channeled a total of 3–4 million dollars into supporting various federalist activities in Europe, much of this through intelligence contacts. In 1950 Washington helped bring about a change of leadership in the European Movement, away from Churchill's cautious British attitude to Belgian foreign minister Paul-Henri Spaak's continental approach.[4] European federalists had excellent connections

[3] *FRUS*, 1955–7: IV, Circular telegram from the Secretary of State, 7 Mar. 1957, 535–6. See also Miriam Camps, *European Unification in the Sixties: From the Veto to the Crisis* (London: Oxford University Press, 1967), particularly 236–57.

[4] Richard J. Aldrich, "European Integration: An American Intelligence Connection," in Anne Deighton (ed.), *Building Postwar Europe: National Decision-Makers and European Institutions, 1948–63* (London: Macmillan, 1995), 159–79; Beloff, *The*

on the American side, and none more so than Jean Monnet, who had easy access to the highest officials through most of the 1950s and 1960s.[5]

In the negotiations leading to the European Coal and Steel Community, the United States did not stress the Atlantic framework at all. In fact, no such framework was even foreseen, except the ECSC's loose connections with the OEEC and even GATT. Washington made little or no effort to bring Britain in. The Labour government clearly did not want to join, and any further talk of British membership might therefore have obstructed the whole effort.[6]

In this case the lack of insistence on the Atlantic framework is explained largely by the nature of the Schuman initiative. It was revolutionary in its integrationist concept, but dealt only with the organization of coal and steel, products where an Atlantic framework was not natural, at least not in a short-term perspective. An explicit Atlantic emphasis would have run directly counter to the objective of getting the French–German integration process started. As under the Marshall Plan, the Truman administration stressed greater European self-sufficiency, in part to reduce American costs. Finally, the ECSC would not represent any challenge to the crucial part of the Atlantic framework in the form of NATO.

The defense area was at the core of the Atlantic framework. After the outbreak of the Korean War, the Truman administration soon concluded that German resources were needed also on the military side. This conclusion was presented to the NATO foreign ministers' meeting in New York in September 1950. Again the Americans underlined what had to be done, in this case that West Germany had to be rearmed, but exactly how this was to be done was to be decided later. Clearly rearmament within NATO was the solution initially favored by Washington. In the negotiations

United States and the Unity of Europe, 72–5. See also *FRUS*, 1955–7: IX, NSC 5720: Status of United States programs for national security as of June 30, 1957, 11 Sept. 1957, 605.

[5] Monnet, *Memoirs*, particularly 465, 472; Duchêne, *Jean Monnet*, particularly 231, 244, 326–8; George W. Ball, *The Past has Another Pattern: Memoirs* (New York: Norton, 1982), 69–99; Clifford Hackett, *Monnet and the Americans: The Father of a United Europe and his U.S. Supporters* (Washington, DC: Jean Monnet Council, 1995); Walt W. Rostow, "Jean Monnet: The Innovator as Diplomat," in Gordon A. Craig and Francis L. Loewenheim (eds.), *The Diplomats 1939–1979* (Princeton: Princeton University Press, 1994), 257–88.

[6] Hogan, *The Marshall Plan*, 367–74.

on West Germany's rearmament flowing from the NATO meeting in September, Washington openly stressed the Atlantic or NATO framework, because at first it seemed unlikely that German rearmament could be undertaken in any other context. In a circular to US embassies in Europe, Acheson pointed out that the "North Atlantic framework, which finds increasingly concrete expression in NATO, is accordingly framework within which we seek maximum development of common action in pursuit of basic objectives common to North America and Western Europe." Within this framework the US could also support purely European actions, but only "insofar as they promote our common interests and strengthen North Atlantic community."[7]

After French defense minister René Pleven (prime minister August 1951–January 1952) came to insist in October 1950 on a European context in the form of the European Defense Community, the Truman administration at first disliked this approach. It was seen as militarily unsound, as discriminating strongly against Germany, and as excessively reducing the role of NATO. The French were allegedly trying to have it both ways, promoting the integration of and maintaining discrimination against Germany at one and the same time. At worst, the French proposal could be a way of postponing, even preventing West German rearmament. All the other countries also preferred the NATO over the EDC approach. Still, the French view could not simply be overlooked. And after all, it was Washington's policy even in the defense area "to encourage further moves towards greater unity on Continent and particularly Franco–Ger *rapprochement*." Some sort of compromise between the American and the French proposals had to be found.[8]

[7] *FRUS*, 1951: III. 1, Secretary of State to certain diplomatic offices, 29 Jan. 1951, 761. See also *FRUS*, 1950: III, Secretary of State to the embassy in the United Kingdom, 14 Nov. 1950, 450–2.

[8] *FRUS*, 1950: III, Secretary of State to the embassy in the United Kingdom, 14 Nov. 1950, 450. For an analysis of West German rearmament written long ago, but still illuminating, see Laurence W. Martin, "The American Decision to Rearm Germany," in Harold Stein (ed.), *American Civil-Military Decisions: A Book of Case Studies* (Birmingham, Ala: University of Alabama Press, 1963), 643–65. The best study of the EDC question is probably Edward Fursdon, *The European Defence Community: A History* (London: Macmillan, 1980). See also Saki Dockrill, *Britain's Policy for West German Rearmament 1950–55* (Cambridge: Cambridge University Press, 1991); Daniel Lerner and Raymond Aron (eds.), *France Defeats EDC* (New York: Praeger, 1957); Robert McGeehan, *The German Rearmament Question: American*

This was accomplished by December 1950. The so-called Spofford compromise, named after Charles M. Spofford, US deputy representative on the NATO Council, stressed the complementary rather than the competitive nature of the American and French plans. It clearly suggested that NATO was the immediate answer and a European army a longer-term one. In commenting upon this compromise, Acheson reiterated that "We favor this solution as long as it is clearly a part of and under NATO umbrella."[9] The details would have to be worked out later, but in any European army within NATO the most obvious forms of discrimination against Germany had to be ended.

In July 1951 high commissioner John McCloy, ambassador David Bruce, and NATO commander Dwight Eisenhower, at least indirectly assisted by Jean Monnet, persuaded the Truman administration that the United States should basically accept the French EDC plan. In their opinion, it was really the only way to get the French to rearm. They also saw it as "a major, and probably decisive, step toward European political federation." In his diary Eisenhower wrote that a satisfactory solution to the European security problem could be found only in "a U.S. of Europe—to include all countries now in NATO" as well as West Germany, and some neutrals which he later left out. "If *necessary*, U.K. could be omitted" (emphasis in original).[10]

The Truman administration, at first somewhat grudgingly, and the Eisenhower administration, quite wholeheartedly, supported the EDC approach. So complete was the conversion that the two administrations in fact did so despite the French soon beginning to display a curious lack of faith in their own plan. In Washington's new analysis, not only did France have to be brought along—and

Diplomacy and European Defense after World War II (Urbana, Ill.: University of Illinois Press, 1971). For the most recent study of this question, see David Clay Large, *Germans to the Front: West German Rearmament in the Adenauer Era* (Chapel Hill, NC: University of North Carolina Press, 1996).

[9] *FRUS*, 1951: III. 1, Secretary of State to the embassy in France, 28 June 1951, 802; Fursdon, *The European Defence Community*, 92–9.

[10] *FRUS*, 1951: III. 1, Memorandum by McCloy, 1 Sept. 1951, 875; Martin F. Herz, *David Bruce's "Long Telegram" of July 3, 1951* (Lanham, Mass.: University Press of America, 1978); Lankford, *The Last American Aristocrat*, 228–9, 232–4, 237–41. Bruce called Monnet "the foremost political philosopher of the Twentieth Century." For this, see ibid. 209. See also Winand, *Eisenhower, Kennedy, and the United States of Europe*, 28–30, 36–9; Louis Galambos (ed.), *The Papers of Dwight David Eisenhower. XII: NATO and the Campaign of 1952* (Baltimore: Johns Hopkins

the best way to do so would appear to be by supporting its plan—
but the more West Germany was bound up with France the better, and the more difficult it would be for Moscow to tempt the
Germans with neutrality.

For the Republicans in particular it certainly mattered that an
effective European unit would reduce expenditures for the United
States both in terms of money and military forces. Congress continued to be strongly pro-integrationist and in 1953 passed the
Richards amendment, which aimed to channel 50 per cent of relevant US military assistance through the EDC. The amendment
was at first opposed by the Eisenhower administration, which argued
that the United States "can and must encourage unity in Europe,
but we cannot compel unity." The final decisions on the EDC "must
be taken by the nations directly concerned." In 1954 the administration and Congress worked out compromise language to step up
pressure on the French and the Italians, who still had not ratified
the EDC treaty.[11]

The Eisenhower administration invested so much prestige in the
EDC that Dulles, supported by the president, threatened "an agonizing reappraisal" if the French assembly did not pass the proposal.
It is indeed remarkable that the Eisenhower administration went
as far as it did in trying to promote European defense cooperation
through the EDC.

Yet even the EDC was to be subordinated to NATO. With the
exception of West Germany, where most of the US troops in Europe were stationed anyway, the members of the EDC would all
be members also of NATO. American troops would remain in Europe, although both the Truman and the Eisenhower administration refused to give any guarantees of permanence on this point.
The American nuclear umbrella would apply. Especially in time
of war the EDC governing bodies would fall under the NATO
Supreme Commander, who was an American. NATO would control strategic planning for the EDC, including troop withdrawals

University Press, 1989), 801. Dean Acheson actually argues that he changed "independently" of Bruce, McCloy, and Eisenhower. For this, see his *Present at the
Creation*, 557. Acheson's statement seems somewhat suspect, however, in view
of his earlier position.

[11] *FRUS*, 1952–4: V. 1, Memorandum by Merchant to the Secretary of State,
16 June 1953, 792–4; ibid., Editorial Note, 973–4; ibid., Dulles to the embassy in
France, 10 July 1954, 995–6; *FRUS*, 1952–4: V. 2, Memorandum of conversation
by Merchant, 30 Aug. 1954, 1117.

for overseas duties. As Dulles pointed out to the NATO Council in December 1953, an integrated European Community and the wider Atlantic Community would depend on each other. "These two structures will differ but they must be built together. Each is vital to the success of the other and each today, happily, is in fact being built."[12]

In a paradoxical twist, Washington was soon being pressured by Paris to modify an EDC project which only the French had initially favored. The truth was that support for the EDC was never that strong in France. The Communists and the Gaullists opposed the EDC all along. Many Socialists in particular were disappointed that Britain would not join and that ties with NATO were not even stronger than they actually were. Others in the political center used the EDC to attract American support for the French position in Indochina. The implication was that if Washington supported Paris in Indochina, Paris would return the favor by approving the EDC. After France's position had collapsed at Dien Bien Phu, the French assembly turned the EDC down on 30 August 1954.[13]

The Eisenhower administration was at first somewhat unwilling to give up the project and considered "punishing" the French for their behavior. London had actually favored a NATO solution all along. Prime minister Winston Churchill described the EDC as a "sludgy amalgam" and now he told Eisenhower that "I do not blame the French for rejecting EDC but only for inventing it."[14] Even after Washington came to support the NATO course which London was finally pushing openly, Dulles was still unhappy to see European supranationality go: "This was always to me the most important aspect of EDC."[15]

---

[12] FRUS, 1952–4: V. 1, Statement by the Secretary of State to the North Atlantic Council, 14 Dec. 1953, 462; Fursdon, The European Defence Community, 179–80, 186, 207–9. See also Rolf Steininger, "John Foster Dulles, the European Defense Community, and the German Question," in Richard H. Immerman (ed.), John Foster Dulles and the Diplomacy of the Cold War (Princeton: Princeton University Press, 1990), 79–108.

[13] Fursdon, The European Defence Community, 266–99. For a recent study which argues strongly—probably too strongly—that the French used the EDC primarily to extract US support in Indochina, see Jasmine Aimaq, For Europe or Empire? French Colonial Ambitions and the European Army Plan (Lund, Sweden: Lund University Press, 1996), particularly 182–92, 231–7.

[14] FRUS, 1952–4: V. 2, Churchill to Eisenhower, 17 Sept. 1954, 1225–6.

[15] FRUS, 1952–4: VI, Memorandum of conversation Eisenhower–Chaban-Delmas, 20 Mar. 1952, 1192–4.

The major reason why the EDC road had initially been chosen was that the French had refused to let West Germany directly into NATO. But after first having rejected the EDC and then on Christmas Eve rejecting even the entry of Germany into NATO, the French national assembly finally approved the new agreements in their entirety on 30 December 1954. West Germany was to be admitted into NATO, as well as into a strengthened Brussels-pact Western Union, now renamed the Western European Union (WEU). In the end Paris felt it had little choice after having created such a crisis in the alliance. If it rejected even NATO membership, a separate treaty between the United States, Britain, and West Germany seemed most likely, hardly an enticing idea for the French. French public opinion seems all along to have disliked the NATO option the least.[16]

Dulles kept feeling that there was just too little supranationality in the NATO solution, but he had had no specific alternative proposal prepared in case the EDC failed.[17] Therefore, in the end he had no choice but to praise British foreign secretary Anthony Eden's conception as "brilliant and statesmanlike."[18] The British initiative "at least avoided the disaster of a neutralized Germany, an isolated France, and Soviet domination of Europe." Militarily Dulles saw it as an advantage to have Britain tied more closely to the European continent—and this was part of the new solution— but politically it involved a country, the United Kingdom, "which is not as ready to develop supra-national agencies. This was something of a disadvantage."[19]

After the dramatic failure of the EDC, European integration quickly came to focus on two new projects. The first was EURATOM, which was an extension of the so-called functionalist

[16] *FRUS*, 1952–4, V. 2, Acting Secretary Smith to Eisenhower, 10 Sept. 1954, 1160–1; Fursdon, *The European Defence Community*, 303–37; Georges-Henri Soutou, "France," in David Reynolds (ed.), *The Origins of the Cold War in Europe* (New Haven: Yale University Press, 1994), 114–17.

[17] For Washington's more general approach to alternatives to the EDC, see *FRUS*, 1952–4, V. 1, Editorial Note, 859–60.

[18] *FRUS*, 1952–4, V. 2, Report on the Secretary of State's conversations with Adenauer and Eden, 16–17 Sept. 1954, 1216–17. The most recent study of Eden's role after the French defeat of the EDC is found in David Dutton, *Anthony Eden: A Life and Reputation* (London: Arnold, 1997), 302–6.

[19] *FRUS*, 1952–4: V. 2, Memorandum of discussion, 216th meeting of the NSC, 6 Oct. 1954, 1379–80.

or sectoral approach supported by Monnet in particular. Monnet argued that it was logical to move from one energy field, coal and steel, to another, atomic energy, especially when this new field appeared to be highly promising technologically and without too many vested interests. The other project was the more comprehensive common market approach supported by the Benelux countries in general, and by Dutch foreign minister Johan Willem Beyen in particular. This was a more ambitious project, so ambitious in fact that it had been discussed earlier without much success. The two projects were soon fused, in the sense that Monnet and Beyen supported each other's ideas.[20]

The United States adopted a lower profile after the failure of the EDC. The heavy American pressure during the EDC debate was thought to have backfired. As we have already seen, however, there could be no doubt about Washington's continued support for the most comprehensive forms of European integration.

Thus, concerning the EURATOM plans, Dulles instructed the embassy in Bonn that the United States particularly welcomed the recognition of the need for Europe to continue to advance "beyond cooperative arrangements to Federal institutions, with necessary transfer of sovereign power." Without giving the impression of any American pressure, the State Department wished to "encourage and support Germans and other Europeans advocating such views."[21]

The United States clearly had it in its power to make or break EURATOM. In the nuclear field Western Europe was quite dependent on the United States both for technical expertise and uranium. Washington could cooperate with Europe either through EURATOM or bilaterally. It generally preferred the first course, although bilateral agreements were also concluded with the member countries. To have concluded only bilateral agreements would, in the words of Monnet, have made the European countries the "atomic satellite" of the United States. The US Atomic Energy Commission and the American atomic energy industry, the former being especially concerned about lax security, the latter being eager to obtain quick bilateral deals with the various European countries,

---

[20] The best analysis of this new phase of European integration is found in Milward, *The European Rescue of the Nation-State*, 173–223.

[21] *FRUS*, 1955–7: IV, Telegram from the Secretary of State to the embassy in Germany, 1 July 1955, 308.

and both worrying about the "socialist" nature of EURATOM, favored the bilateral route. Eisenhower supported the State Department in its preference for the supranationality of EURATOM.[22]

The most ambitious American ideas of 1947-9 for a customs union under the OEEC were rather similar to the European common market project of the 1950s. So in principle Washington was a strong supporter of the common market concept. Tactically, however, it was now afraid that the concept was simply too ambitious, and thus could easily lead to failure again. The project was seen as rather general and unlikely to meet with a speedy response, particularly from protectionist France. The British, who agreed to send an observer to the Spaak committee set up after the Messina meeting of the continental Six in June 1955, quickly excused themselves from further efforts. In the memorable words of its observer: "The future treaty which you are discussing has no chance of being agreed; if it was agreed, it would have no chance of being ratified; and if it were ratified, it would have no chance of being applied. And if it was applied, it would be totally unacceptable to Britain."[23]

Before the meeting of the six ECSC countries in Venice in May 1956, Dulles therefore cabled the US embassies that he certainly hoped that the approval of the EURATOM treaty, which was of such immediate importance, "would not be held up until complex and doubtless lengthy Common Market negotiations concluded."[24]

Paris was, however, showing a more favorable attitude to the common market than had been expected. The French wanted to counteract the negative impression they had created of themselves as a result of the EDC failure. They also had a strong interest in EURATOM since the French nuclear industry was the most advanced on the continent.

[22] Insa Schwarz, "The United States and the Creation of the European Atomic Energy Community 1955-58," *Historians of Contemporary Europe Newsletter*, Dec. 1992, 209-24; Jonathan E. Helmreich, "The United States and the Formation of EURATOM," *Diplomatic History*, Summer 1991, 387-410; Winand, *Eisenhower, Kennedy, and the United States of Europe*, 83-108. For the "atomic satellite" comment and Monnet's views in more detail, see Pascaline Winand, "European Insiders Working Inside Washington: Monnet's Network, Euratom and the Eisenhower administration," unpub. paper presented at the Commonwealth Fund conference, London University, 16-17 Feb. 1996, especially 12-13.

[23] Roy Denman, *Missed Chances: Britain and Europe in the Twentieth Century* (London: Cassell, 1996), 196-200; quotation from 198-9.

[24] *FRUS*, 1955-7: IV, Telegram from the Secretary of State to the embassy in Belgium, 24 May 1956, 444.

The Venice meeting therefore gave a bigger push to the common market discussions than Washington had foreseen. In drawing up a more definite US position on the market, and British (counter)plans for a wider OEEC free trade area within which the common market could be fitted, Eisenhower simply joined the two together and publicly stated that nothing had been more heartening than the recent announcement of two new proposals that would further advance the economic integration of Europe. "We watch these exciting new developments with the keenest interest. Because, my friends, as Europe grows stronger economically we gain in every way."[25] Despite the openness of this statement, in early 1957, as further progress was made on the common market, Eisenhower, as we have already seen, praised the project in the highest terms.

On 25 March 1957, Belgium, France, Italy, Luxembourg, the Netherlands, and the Federal Republic of Germany signed the treaties of Rome, which established the EEC and EURATOM. New members would in principle be required to adhere to the terms of these treaties. The treaties were rather quickly ratified by the six countries. Dulles sent his warm congratulations to the key politicians in France and Germany.[26]

The United States gave priority to the plans of the Six over the British Atlantic schemes. The common market had to be established *before* the six countries entered into negotiations with the British. Otherwise, London might dilute the new unit too much.[27] In the 1950s few Americans believed more strongly in the good cause of European integration than did Eisenhower and Dulles. As Dulles explained to British foreign secretary Harold Macmillan in December 1955, a six-nation community might well evolve protectionist tendencies and show a trend toward greater independence. "In the long-run, however, I cannot but feel that the resultant increased unity would bring in its wake greater responsibility and

---

[25] *FRUS*, 1955-7: IV, Report by the Subcommittee on Regional Economic Integration of the Council on Foreign Economic Policy to the Council, 15 Nov. 1956, 483–4.

[26] *FRUS*, 1955-7: IV, Dulles to the embassy in France, 25 July 1957, 561.

[27] See for instance *FRUS*, 1958–60: VII. 1, Circular instruction from the Department of State, 13 Feb. 1958, 14–16. For a good short analysis of early British reactions to the EEC, see Sabine Lee, "Staying in the Game? Coming into the Game? Macmillan and European Integration," in Richard Aldous and Sabine Lee (eds.), *Harold Macmillan and Britain's World Role* (London: Macmillan, 1996), 123–36.

devotion to the common welfare of Western Europe."[28] In fact, Britain should be encouraged to join the Six *only* if it was prepared to accept supranationality and the ultimate goal of some sort of European federation. Otherwise it might end up ruining this historic development.

Despite its opposition to Britain's explicit Atlanticism, the Eisenhower administration continued to take the wider Atlantic framework for granted. The Six would operate within the NATO structure. Until de Gaulle came to power, no one in NATO really disputed American pre-eminence. However, the founding of the EEC created a need to fit the new organization into a reformed Atlantic economic framework. As we shall see, America's balance of payments problems and then the evolution of de Gaulle's policies also considerably strengthened Washington's emphasis on the Atlantic framework. While this framework had been largely implicit until 1958–9, thereafter it became a constant and explicit part of US policy. The fact that John Foster Dulles—who combined strong support for both European and Atlantic integration—became ill and had to leave office in April 1959, and was replaced by the more Atlantic-oriented Christian Herter, helped smooth this transition.

In 1958–9 Washington took two important initiatives which aimed to strengthen the economic part of this Atlantic framework. The first was the proposal of October 1958 to launch a new GATT round. This fifth such round—which became known as the Dillon round (1958–62) after under-secretary of state for economic affairs Douglas Dillon—aimed, like the previous four rounds, at establishing lower tariffs among the industrialized countries. This was a general objective which the Truman and Eisenhower administrations had both been pursuing, with rather lukewarm support from Congress. There was no doubt that the creation of the EEC added a special dimension to this effort. Thus, in September 1959 the interdepartmental Council of Foreign Economic Policy (CFEP) stated that the new round was motivated by the need to bring about a lowering of the common external tariff of the EEC "in order to assure that United States exports have continuing access to this increasingly vital market and to help ease adjustments between the Community and other countries in the GATT."[29]

---

[28] *FRUS*, 1955–7: IV, Letter from the Secretary of State to Macmillan, 10 Dec. 1955, 363.

[29] *FRUS*, 1958–60: IV, Policy statement by the Council on Foreign Economic Policy, 24 Sept. 1959, 232.

The bargaining strength of the Eisenhower and later the Kennedy administration in the Dillon round was considerably reduced by the Congressional skepticism to freer trade. When the EEC proposed a 20 per cent cut in most of its common external tariff, something which both the Eisenhower and the Kennedy administration strongly favored, the US could respond to this offer only after strong presidential leadership had been exerted vis-à-vis both Congress and a Department of Agriculture which was disappointed that reductions could not also be secured in the Community's rather protectionist Common Agricultural Policy (CAP).[30] The frustrating experience with the Dillon round was to lead the Kennedy administration to fight hard for much greater US flexibility in a new round of GATT negotiations, the Kennedy round.

The second initiative the Eisenhower administration took led to the transformation of the OEEC into the Organization for Economic Cooperation and Development (OECD). Again this was an initiative that gradually emerged. The OEEC might well have been reformed anyway, but the formation of the EEC probably speeded up the process. In the new organization the United States and Canada would become direct members and the US would then presumably be playing the leading role; the OECD could also provide a most useful setting for upcoming negotiations between the EEC and EFTA, a setting which could help Washington avert the danger of the two organizations reaching a free trade area agreement at the economic expense of the United States; finally, the new organization also aimed at increasing the role of the Europeans in development assistance. The OECD convention went into effect on 30 September 1961, but it came to represent no dramatic change compared to its predecessor. In the end neither the US nor most Europeans really wanted a very strong organization.[31] Yet both the OECD and, particularly, the GATT rounds meant a

---

[30] For accounts of the Dillon round, see Alfred E. Eckes, Jr., *Opening America's Market: U.S. Foreign Trade Policy since 1776* (Chapel Hill, NC: University of North Carolina Press, 1995), 180–3; Heidi Storeheier, *US Policy towards the European Free Trade Association 1959–1963* (Norwegian University of Technology and Science Cand. philol. thesis, 1996), 59–64, 91–100, 141–3.

[31] FRUS, 1958–60: IV, Memorandum from Herter to Eisenhower, 24 Nov. 1959, 58–9; FRUS, 1961–3: XIII, Circular telegram from the Department of State, 27 Oct. 1961, 43–5; John F. Kennedy Library, *Report to the Honorable John F. Kennedy by the Task Force on Foreign Economic Policy*, 31 Dec. 1960, 15, 112–17. See also Winand, *Eisenhower, Kennedy, and the United States of Europe*, 128–36, 150–2; Storeheier, *US Policy towards the European Free Trade Association*, 77–9, 140–1, 150–1.

considerable strengthening of the Atlantic framework for European integration.

In August 1960 the State Department instructed the embassy in Paris that US policy rested on the view that "NATO should be principal forum for cooperation and consultation among member nations, with this forum complemented in economic field by the OECD when it comes into being." Compared to earlier instructions, this represented a definite strengthening of the Atlantic framework, although the cable went on to state that the US continued to feel that European integration "is of vital importance both for the member countries and as measure to increase overall strength of the Alliance."[32]

With this kind of Atlantic framework, rather implicit at first, then more explicit, it was evident that Washington did not really see Western Europe as an independent actor. Europe might occasionally come to have positions different from those of the United States, but the assumption was nearly always that the two sides of the Atlantic would continue to share the most basic interests.

True, before the founding of NATO, Washington, in the words of John D. Hickerson, head of the State Department's Office of European Affairs, had envisaged "the creation of a third force which was not merely the extension of US influence but a real European organization strong enough to say "no" both to the Soviet Union and the United States," if America's actions should require this. As we have seen, with the creation of the Atlantic defense organization, a development to which Hickerson himself contributed so mightily, the "third force" quickly became aligned with the United States.[33]

In September 1952, when asked about the possibility of the Community of Six emerging as a "third force," David Bruce, now under-secretary of state, replied that "little consideration has been given in the US to this possibility." He pointed to "the overwhelming and uncritical Congressional and public support of European integration."[34]

---

[32] FRUS, 1958–60: VII, Telegram from the Department of State to the embassy in France, 22 Aug. 1960, 296.

[33] FRUS, 1948: III, Memorandum of conversation by Hickerson, 21 Jan. 1948, 11; Lundestad, America, Scandinavia, and the Cold War, 167–98.

[34] FRUS, 1952–4: VI. 1, Summary minutes of the Chiefs of Mission meeting, London, 24–6 Sept. 1952, 655. See also Declassified Documents Reference Service, 1995, Memorandum of conversation Williamson–Hirsch, 20 Oct. 1952, 1731.

Under Eisenhower and even under Kennedy, references can still be found to an integrated Europe representing such a "third force". Most of these references, however, simply meant that a united Europe would be a third important actor in international politics, after the United States and the Soviet Union. The implication was almost never that it would be an independent unit standing in the middle between the two existing superpowers; it was just an additional one. The expectation was almost always that it would be standing rather close to the United States.

Eisenhower repeatedly talked about Western Europe as a "third force," but always in this context of the united Europe cooperating with the United States. Thus, in November 1954 he told French premier Pierre Mendès-France that Western Europe "should be the third great force in the world," but went on to add that the US "was related by culture and blood to countries of Western Europe and in this sense was a product of Western Europe. For this reason we favor a strong Western Europe."[35] In February 1956 the president referred to the industrial capacity of a united Europe and then expressed his belief that "such a 'third force' *working with the rest of the free world* would change the whole complexion of present circumstances and insure peace" (emphasis mine).[36] Earlier he had even talked about "developing in Western Europe a third great power bloc, after which development the United States would be permitted to sit back and relax somewhat."[37]

There were those who felt there was a risk in promoting a united Western Europe. It could after all come to represent an *independent* "third force." Inside the State Department, in 1948-9, Theodore Achilles had played an important role in drawing up US policy towards Western Europe. In November 1952, as minister to France, he argued, first, that a united Europe *outside* the framework of the Atlantic community would not be in the American interest since it could become neutralist or unable to withstand Soviet pressure. This was a rather conventional conclusion, but he then went on to argue that even "A Europe united within a developing Atlantic unity may or may not be in our national interest."

[35] *FRUS*, 1952-4: V. 2, Minutes of meeting Eisenhower-Mendès-France, 22 Nov. 1954, 1482.
[36] *FRUS*, 1955-7: IV, Memorandum of conversation Eisenhower-Mayer, 8 Feb. 1956, 409. See also ibid., Memorandum of conference with the president, 6 Feb. 1957, 517.
[37] Ibid., Editorial note (Remarks by President Eisenhower), 349.

It could be helpful, as the Brussels treaty had originally been, but as Atlantic unity developed, "we may find a six-nation knot within it an unnecessary and possibly harmful complication." The basic task for America was to develop Atlantic unity.[38] Stassen's comment from October 1956 in the same vein has already been mentioned. More vaguely, a National Intelligence Estimate of 29 July 1958 predicted that over the next ten years a more independent Western Europe might emerge. This would alter relations within NATO. While increased European unity would strengthen the overall position of the West, it would also "encourage the development of a political 'third force' which would seek more energetically than either of the great powers to establish the means and modes of coexistence."[39]

In their agnosticism or even skepticism toward European unity, such voices were either in a small minority, such as Achilles and Stassen, or rather vague, as in the National Intelligence Estimate. The conclusion even of the Estimate was after all that "we believe that the essential concept of an Atlantic Community based on close ties between the US and Western Europe will probably remain unimpaired."[40] The great majority of the Eisenhower administration was both supportive of European integration and optimistic about the extent to which Western Europe and the United States would continue to cooperate.

The Kennedy and later administrations rarely used the expression "third force." This was probably because general de Gaulle was now the spokesman of a more truly independent Europe. Washington certainly did not want to express support for this kind of "third force." Instead, the Atlantic framework was to be stressed more explicitly than ever. Thus, secretary of state Dean Rusk told French ambassador Hervé Alphand that the "third force" issue touched a very sensitive nerve. "The concept that Europe could be the arbiter between the US and the Soviets was basically fallacious. Europe was the key issue outstanding between the US and USSR." Rusk even vaguely threatened that if ever Europe decided to play an independent role, "issues between the US and the USSR would be greatly reduced." The US rather than Europe would be the

[38] FRUS, 1952–4, VI. 1, Memorandum by the minister in France (Achilles), 28 Nov. 1952, 242.
[39] FRUS, 1958–60, VII. 1, National Intelligence Estimate, 29 July 1958, 63–4.
[40] Ibid. 64.

"third force" in any such combination.[41] George Ball, in referring to a united Europe, stated that while in de Gaulle's view such a Europe should be independent from the United States, the US, on the other hand, wanted "to insure that a united Europe works with us ever more closely in the framework of an Atlantic alliance."[42]

As we shall see, the Atlantic theme was to remain a constant one with all later administrations from Johnson's to Clinton's.

[41] *FRUS*, 1961–3: XIII, US–French Exploratory Talks Rusk–Alphand, 28 May 1962, 709. See also ibid., Memorandum of conversation Rusk–Strauss, 9 June 1962, 406.

[42] Ibid., Scope paper prepared in the Department of State, 11 June 1962, 106. See also ibid., Memorandum of conversation Ball–de Murville, 21 May 1962, 94.

6

DE GAULLE'S CHALLENGE TO THE ATLANTIC FRAMEWORK, 1960–1969

Two main challenges were to arise to the American policy of support for a more united Western Europe inside an Atlantic framework, or inside the American "empire." One was political, and came in the form of president de Gaulle and his vision of a Europe relatively independent of the United States. The other was economic and was expressed in Washington's concern about the effects a more united Europe would have on American economic interests.

A revolt of right-wing elements in Algiers led to Charles de Gaulle coming to power in France on 1 June 1958, and the fall of the Fourth Republic. Within a few months de Gaulle created a constitution for the new Fifth Republic based on the strong presidential powers he had sought as early as 1945–6. De Gaulle's main objective was to strengthen the position and "gloire" of France as much as possible. To accomplish this, in September 1958 he insisted that "a world-wide organization" of the United States, the United Kingdom, and France be created. This organization should, on the one hand, "take common decisions in political questions affecting world security" and, on the other hand, "draw up and, if necessary, implement plans of strategic action, particularly where the use of nuclear weapons is concerned." In other words, a directorate of the three was to run the Western world. The French nuclear program already in existence was greatly speeded up.

In opposition the general had been quite skeptical to the European Economic Community, but only a few days after he became prime minister he signalled that he would respect the agreements which France had already signed. This included the treaties of Rome. In fact de Gaulle soon came to promote the development of a common foreign and defense policy for the EEC. However, this, like his policy towards the EEC in general, was to be based on a curious combination of French leadership and respect for national, particularly French, sovereignty.[1]

Early American reactions to de Gaulle were rather favorable. influenced as they were by the analysis that he had saved France from a deep political crisis. A National Intelligence Estimate of 29 July 1958 concluded that if de Gaulle should fail, his most probable successor would come from the authoritarian right, and "there would be a prolonged period of serious unrest and possible civil strife with far-reaching consequences for France's position in Europe and NATO."[2] Even in late 1959 the National Security Council concluded that

There is little question as to France's importance to the Western Alliance. or that the Gaullist experiment offers the best hope in decades of rejuvenating France as a strong ally. Nor is there any argument that a strong if nationalistic France is so important to long-run US interests that, to the extent compatible with US interests, we should do all we reasonably can to accommodate De Gaulle.[3]

De Gaulle was a conservative politician and his anti-Communism was evident, particularly in his early years as president. He saw himself as the staunch protector of West Germany against the Soviet Union and resisted Soviet ideas on Berlin so firmly that he came to feel that Washington was just too willing to negotiate with Moscow. Later, in October 1962, he was to back the Kennedy administration in its response to the Soviet installation of missiles in Cuba. After that, however, he was to confront Washington directly over Vietnam and China, to approach the Soviet Union, and to take his ideas about a Europe stretching "from the Atlantic

---

[1] The best biography of de Gaulle is probably Jean Lacouture, *De Gaulle*. The French edition of this biography is in three volumes, the abridged English edition is in two. Vol. 2 of the English edition, *De Gaulle. The Ruler: 1945–1970* (London: Harvill, 1991) is the most relevant here. The quotation about the directorate is from 217.

[2] *FRUS*, 1958–60: VII. 1, National Intelligence Estimate, 29 July 1958, 62.

[3] *FRUS*, 1958–60: VII. 2, National Security Council Report, Statement of US Policy on France, 4 Nov. 1959, 306. See also Frank Costigliola, *France and the United States* (New York: Twayne, 1992), especially 124–32.

to the Urals" in a direction that really worried policymakers in Washington.[4]

So the full challenge from de Gaulle developed only gradually. Yet even by 1960 it had become obvious that the general would represent a challenge to traditional American leadership in NATO. In 1959 France withdrew its Mediterranean fleet from NATO's command. Washington was opposed to de Gaulle's proposal of a triumvirate running NATO or even the (Western) world. No such formal arrangement could be permitted to develop. It gave the wrong impression of Washington's policies; the British did not like the idea, nor did the smaller NATO countries; and Washington resented the implication in de Gaulle's idea that France would be speaking on Germany's part.

Eisenhower still wondered if there were not some way the US could get outside the so-called Standing Group of the Military Committee already existing in NATO, made up of the US, the UK, and France, "into a real tripartite discussion of strategic and military questions *in return for which de Gaulle would get on with NATO*" emphasis in original).[5] This search for a compromise which could give de Gaulle some of the substance of tripartite leadership in less direct ways than he had proposed actually continued well into the Kennedy administration. Kennedy was prepared to offer France the position of SACEUR (Supreme Allied Commander, Europe), but in the end these efforts led to nothing.[6]

In the Kennedy administration under-secretary George Ball largely handled questions having to do with European integration. Ball was perhaps Monnet's closest friend in Washington, the competition on this point being rather tough, but Ball, even more than Monnet, combined the European with the Atlantic approach.[7]

In a March 1961 circular to the relevant embassies in Europe, the incoming Kennedy administration repeated the emphasis on an

---

[4] A collection of fine analyses of French–American relations under de Gaulle is found in Robert O. Paxton and Nicholas Wahl (eds.), *De Gaulle and the United States: A Centennial Reappraisal* (Oxford: Berg, 1994).

[5] *FRUS*, 1958–60: VII. 2, Memorandum of telephone conversation Eisenhower–Herter, 1 July 1960, 397.

[6] Ibid., Letter from Eisenhower to de Gaulle, 30 Aug. 1960, 413–17; *FRUS*, 1961–63: XIII, Telegram from Rusk to the State Department, 7 Aug. 1961, 673; Wolfram Kaiser, *Using Europe, Abusing the Europeans: Britain and European Integration, 1945–63* (London: Macmillan, 1996), 160–2.

[7] Ball's own story is told in his *The Past has Another Pattern*, particularly pt. 3, "Monnet, Europe, and Law Practice," and pt. 5, "The Kennedy Years."

explicit Atlantic framework: the State Department "supports in principle any further cooperation among Six in political or other fields which will strengthen and bolster NATO."[8] The Acheson report of the same month, which Kennedy had commissioned, strongly underlined the need for an Atlantic framework.[9] In Kennedy's own conversations with German foreign minister Heinrich von Brentano in April 1961, the president again stressed the Atlantic side. Despite the economic problems the EEC presented for the United States, "In the interest of a stronger Atlantic Community ... we are prepared to meet these problems." Again, however, there was to be no dilution of the unity of the Six: it was best for the Atlantic Community "if the United Kingdom joined the EEC on an unconditional basis."[10]

The meeting between presidents Kennedy and de Gaulle in June 1961, their first and their last, went relatively well, although the disagreement on NATO, particularly on nuclear strategy, was obvious. The United States was strongly opposed to France developing its own nuclear weapons, as it had been after the first French test detonation had taken place in 1960. On the EEC the two agreed that the tying down of Germany was perhaps the most profound reason for the EEC.[11]

The split between France and the United States kept growing, however. On the EEC de Gaulle favored a French-led, slightly protectionist Community based on the nation state while Kennedy advocated a supranational group with open borders to the outside world, particularly to the Atlantic community. To accomplish this he wanted Britain to join the EEC.

The Eisenhower administration had been afraid that British membership in the EEC could not be accomplished without diluting

[8] FRUS, 1961-3: XIII, Circular telegram from the Department of State, 24 Mar. 1961, 4.

[9] John F. Kennedy Library, A Review of North Atlantic Problems for the Future, Mar. 1961, particularly 24-6; Winand, Eisenhower, Kennedy, and the United States of Europe, 171-2, 179-80.

[10] FRUS, 1961-3: XIII, Memorandum of conversation Kennedy–Adenauer, 13 Apr. 1961, 6-7. See also David Nunnerly, President Kennedy and Britain (London: Bodley Head, 1972), 163-92; Rolf Steininger, "Grossbritannien und de Gaulle: Das Scheitern des britischen EWG-Beitritts im Januar 1963," Vierteljahrshefte für Zeitgeschichte, Jan. 1996, 111-15.

[11] FRUS, 1961-3: XIII, Memorandum of conversation Kennedy–de Gaulle, 2 June 1961, 23-5; ibid., Memorandum of conversation Kennedy–de Gaulle, 1 June 1961, 309-16.

the EEC. Therefore, the administration had really done little to encourage the British to apply. Always optimistic and believing that all good things could be achieved at the same time, the Kennedy administration decided to work more actively to bring Britain in, but without this having the effect of diluting the EEC significantly. A presidential directive of 20 April 1961 put it this way: "The Six should be encouraged to welcome U.K. association with the Community and not set the price too high for such association, providing that there is to be no weakening of essential ties among the Six."[12]

The hope was that the integration process in the EEC had reached the "point of no return" and that the community might therefore be somewhat more flexible now than earlier.[13] British membership was necessary to strengthen the EEC's Atlantic orientation. It could also serve to neutralize the growing feud with de Gaulle. Washington clearly played down the significance of the so-called "special relationship" between the United States and Britain, always more special to the latter than to the former.[14] The UK should not be encouraged to oppose or stay aloof from European integration "by doubts as to the US attitude or by hopes of a 'special' relation with the US."[15] Instead, as a senior member of the administration formulated it, "We hoped that if England went into Europe, it would take a sense of 'special relationship' with it, and that we would then have a 'special relationship' with Europe."[16]

On 31 July 1961, Britain applied for membership in the EEC. The decision reflected the growing importance of Western Europe in Britain's economic and foreign policy and the declining role of

[12] Ibid., Policy directive: NATO and the Atlantic Nations, 20 Apr. 1961, 287; Winand, *Eisenhower, Kennedy, and the United States of Europe*, 283–4.

[13] NA, 611.41/1–661, Barbour to Burdett, 7–8.

[14] *FRUS*, 1961–3: XIII, Policy directive: NATO and the Atlantic Nations, 20 Apr. 1961, 286–7; ibid., Memorandum of conversation Rusk–Strauss, 9 June 1962, 402. For relatively recent accounts of British–American relations, see D. Cameron Watt, *Succeeding John Bull: America in Britain's Place, 1900–1975—A Study of the Anglo-American Relationship and World Politics in the Context of British and American Foreign-Policy-Making in the Twentieth Century* (Cambridge: Cambridge University Press, 1984); David Dimbleby and David Reynolds, *An Ocean Apart: The Relationship between Britain and America in the Twentieth Century* (New York: Random House, 1988); Alan P. Dobson, *Anglo-American Relations in the Twentieth Century* (London: Routledge, 1995).

[15] *FRUS*, 1961–3: XIII, Policy directive, NATO and the Atlantic Nations, 20 Apr. 1961, 286–7.   [16] Nunnerley, *President Kennedy and Britain*, 11.

the Commonwealth—in 1961, for the first time, Britain exported more goods to Europe than to the Commonwealth. It appears that the American preference for the EEC and the pressure on Britain to join played an important role in the British decision to apply. The "special relationship" with the United States now had to be maintained inside the EEC, if there were to be any such relationship at all.[17]

Most of Washington's sympathy was still with the EEC. As Ball recommended to the president, it should be made clear to Macmillan that the British should enter the Community "only if they are prepared to accept the full implications of European unification —with the possible ultimate goal of some form of Federation."[18]

The desire to get Britain in did not, therefore, prevent the administration from supporting further integration of the Six. This could be noticed in Washington's initial response to the ideas worked out by a study commission of officials from the six countries under the leadership of Frenchman Christian Fouchet. The group deliberated from February 1961 to April 1962 and aimed to develop a "Union of States." The most striking proposal was for a common foreign and security policy based on regular consultations on the highest political levels among the member countries.[19]

A November 1961 circular from the State Department to the US embassies concerned noted that "what we know of French draft appears to be useful to this end," i.e. to "maintain momentum toward integration." Additional steps towards genuine supranational integration might follow later. The administration saw "no more inherent inconsistency between Six role in defense field and NATO than there is between Six role in economic field and OECD."[20]

Defense cooperation among the Six was thus largely acceptable as long as the wider role of NATO was recognized. The comparison with the OECD seemed to imply a surprisingly relaxed

---

[17] For a fine recent study of the British decision to apply for membership, see Wolfram Kaiser, *Grossbritannien und die Europäische Wirtschaftsgemeinschaft 1955–1961: Von Messina nach Canossa* (Berlin: Akademie Verlag, 1996), particularly 146–7, 186–92. See also Young, *Britain and European Unity, 1945–1992*, 76–9.

[18] NA, 611.41/4–161, Memorandum from Ball to the president: Relationship of United Kingdom to the European Common Market, 4.

[19] Lacouture, *De Gaulle. The Ruler: 1945–1970*, 346–50.

[20] *FRUS*, 1961–3: XIII, Circular telegram from the Department of State, 3 Nov. 1961, 48–9.

American attitude. Washington's positive response was at least in part based on an early reading of the situation inside the EEC. In January 1962 a revised French draft was presented, a draft which virtually overlooked the objections that had been presented to the first draft. Instead of only Holland being opposed to the Fouchet plan, as it first appeared, the other four members also became opposed in varying degrees to the French scheme. The Benelux countries in particular wanted to use the institutions of the Treaty of Rome instead of the more state-centered French approach and they preferred not to go into defense matters before the British had been admitted and the role of NATO clarified. These views were fully in line with Washington's real desires. In May 1962 Rusk declared that the Fouchet plan ran "counter to concept of true integration which US has long supported." In the end the EEC shelved the plan.[21]

In June 1962 the general American position on European integration was formulated, with strong emphasis on the Atlantic framework. The development of a political entity which could act as "an increasingly responsible partner in NATO and the OECD can make an important contribution to the development of an Atlantic Partnership."[22] This Atlantic approach was also very much the cornerstone of Kennedy's Grand Design as presented in Philadelphia on 4 July 1962. The United States was prepared "to discuss with a united Europe the ways and means of forming a concrete Atlantic partnership, a mutually beneficial partnership between the new union now emerging in Europe and the old American Union founded here 175 years ago."[23] Or, as the president put it more succinctly half a year later, the United States wanted "an outward-looking Europe with a strong American connection."[24]

De Gaulle's vision was clearly different from Kennedy's. The trend was therefore that US relations with France kept getting more strained. President Kennedy still tried to calm down his

[21] Ibid.; *FRUS*, 1961–3: XIII, Telegram from the embassy in Belgium to the State Department, 29 Nov. 1961, 52–3; ibid., Telegram from Rusk to the State Department, 4 May 1962, 690; Winand, *Eisenhower, Kennedy, and the United States of Europe*, 247–63; Urwin, *The Community of Europe*, 104–7; William C. Cromwell, *The United States and the European Pillar: The Strained Alliance* (London: Macmillan, 1992), 31–5.

[22] NA, The Papers of Charles S. Bohlen, Secretary's European Trip, 18–28 June 1962, 2.   [23] *Public Papers of the Presidents. John F. Kennedy, 1962*, 538–9.

[24] Schwartz, "Victories and Defeats in the Long Twilight Struggle," 131.

secretary of state, who in early May 1962 drew up a long list of grievances against the French, stressing their differences on NATO and nuclear weapons. At the same time, however, Kennedy himself strongly disliked de Gaulle's "notion that we should stay out of all of Europe's affairs while remaining ready to defend her if war should come."[25]

Well into 1962 the administration nevertheless remained reasonably optimistic about the possibilities of coming to some sort of understanding with Paris. When de Gaulle recognized how isolated he really was, he would presumably adjust his course. In June 1962 a State Department analysis thus concluded that the US objective should not be publicly to attack or isolate de Gaulle, but to let him draw for himself the conclusion that he could not bring the Germans along with him on his European conception. "Experience indicates that if he recognizes that his present tactic will not work, De Gaulle will adjust to the situation by moving in the direction of policies more nearly consistent with our own."[26]

After the State Department received reports that Adenauer was actually moving closer to de Gaulle instead of the other way around, Kennedy tried to warn Adenauer that if the British were not admitted to the EEC, this could bring Labour to power in Britain and "the Labor party did not have any position on Berlin ..." Adenauer was told that an enlarged EEC would create economic difficulties for the United States, but political considerations had to prevail. There were three massive power blocs in the Atlantic area: the US, the Six, and finally Britain and the Commonwealth. "It was absolutely necessary to join these three blocs more closely together into one Atlantic Community."[27]

In Washington evaluations about the likelihood of Britain actually being able to join the EEC fluctuated somewhat. In May–June 1962 the president seemed to be less optimistic than his secretary of state, despite the latter's pronounced disappointment with

[25] *FRUS*, 1961–3: XIII, Rusk to the State Department, 4 May 1962, 690–1; ibid., Ball to Rusk, 5 May 1962, 691–2; ibid., Rusk to the State Department, 6 May 1962, 692–3; ibid., Ball to Rusk, 9 May 1962, 694; ibid., Telegram from Kennedy to ambassador Gavin, 18 May 1962, 704. See also ibid., Telegram from the embassy in France to the State Department, 16 May 1962, 702–3; ibid., Gavin to the Secretary of State, 28 May 1962, 705–7.

[26] Ibid., Scope paper prepared in the Department of State, 11 June 1962, 107.

[27] Ibid., Memorandum of conversation Kennedy–Adenauer, 15 Nov. 1962, 125–6. Adenauer was clearly very skeptical of the British Labour Party. For this, see NA, 611.62a/10-159, Telegram from Bruce to the Secretary of State.

French policy in general.[28] On the whole, however, the atmosphere was optimistic. In early December 1962 the State Department concluded that despite serious difficulties with de Gaulle, "His ultimate aims are not irreconcilable with the interests of the West." Agriculture was seen as the main obstacle in Britain's negotiations with the Six. France's renewed energies should be "channeled in a direction which is compatible with the unity of the Alliance," and the United States should "by all means avoid giving deGaulle the feeling that we are trying to isolate him or work against him."[29] As Ball was to state after the negotiations had failed, the administration "recognized the possibility—although not the probability—that these negotiations [UK–EEC] would break down."[30]

One important tactic in working with de Gaulle was to avoid any image of an Anglo-Saxon bloc. In Washington's analysis, de Gaulle's doubts as to British membership appeared to be based on his fear that Britain would challenge French hegemony and become a permanent spokesman for American interests within the EEC. Therefore, the United States should not be seen as the sponsor of Britain in the EEC. Washington repeatedly stressed that it was not a party to the negotiations. Undue attention should be avoided on the special US–UK relationship in the nuclear field.[31]

This strategy failed. The United States *was* seen as the sponsor of Britain in the negotiations with the EEC. Washington recognized that a relationship existed between nuclear weapons and European integration. This was reflected in the October instructions to incoming ambassador to France Charles E. Bohlen. His posture on nuclear weapons "should reflect US confidence that movement toward greater unity in Europe and toward a closer US-European partnership will eventually make itself felt in the nuclear field, as elsewhere." The US had to be willing to cooperate with Europe

---

[28] *FRUS*, 1961–3: XIII, Meeting Kennedy–Malraux *et al.*, 11 May 1962, 696; ibid., Rusk to the State Department, 21 June 1962, 726–7. For an indication that Kennedy continued to be rather less optimistic about the outcome of Britain's negotiations with the Six, see NA, 375.800, Memorandum of conversation Kennedy–Haekkerup.

[29] NA, 611.41/12–762, Rusk to ambassador Bruce, particularly 5–6. See also *FRUS*, 1961–3: XIII, Circular telegram from the State Department to certain missions, 3 July 1962, 112. For US concern about the pace of the negotiations, see NA, 375.42/11–1462, Memorandum of conversation Ball–Schröder, particularly 2.

[30] NA, EC/NG EEC, Letter from Ball to senator Douglas, 15 Feb. 1963, 5.

[31] *FRUS*, 1961–3: XIII, Scope paper prepared in the Department of State, 11 June 1962, 106.

even in the nuclear field. The MLF was the recommended route, however.[32] A different form of partnership already existed in relations with Britain, and Macmillan, who understood the importance of this issue in the EEC negotiations, encouraged even de Gaulle to approach the Americans. At Nassau in December 1962, after Washington had simply cancelled the US–UK Skybolt missile project, Kennedy offered Macmillan the American Polaris missile instead. Thus, Britain was becoming more dependent than ever on the United States. De Gaulle became furious and denounced Britain for "betraying Europe."[33]

It is difficult to know whether de Gaulle would have vetoed British membership in the EEC even without the Nassau agreement. The president's famous press conference on 14 January 1963, where he shut the door on Britain, clearly suggested that the differences were fundamental. He likened British participation to the entry of an American Trojan horse. The EEC "would seem like a colossal Atlantic community under American dependence and direction, and that is not at all what France wanted to do and is doing, which is a strictly European construction."[34]

De Gaulle's veto on Britain led to a feeling of "distress" in Washington. Still, the State Department did not want to enter into a public discussion with the general. Encouraged by Italian prime minister Amintore Fanfani, Rusk at first even seemed to hope that the crisis might be temporary. The State Department tried to cheer itself up by arguing that there might well be diversions which "challenge both our patience and ingenuity. We are, however, firmly convinced of the inevitability of a more closely knit Atlantic partnership."[35]

To Adenauer the State Department expressed the strong hope that the chancellor could make his leadership felt in order to

---

[32] Ibid., Instruction for Bohlen, undated, 738. For Macmillan's ideas, see Kaiser, *Grossbritannien und die Europäische Wirtschaftsgemeinschaft*, 141–7, 186–92, and also his "The Bomb and Europe: Britain, France, and the EEC Entry Negotiations 1961–1963," *Journal of European Integration History*, 1:1 (1995), 65–85.

[33] For two good articles on these events by Frank Costigliola, though somewhat harsh on Kennedy, see "Kennedy, the European Allies, and the Failure to Consult," *Political Science Quarterly*, Winter 1995, 105–23, and "The Failed Design: Kennedy, de Gaulle, and the Struggle for Europe," *Diplomatic History*, Summer 1984, 227–51.   [34] Lacouture, *De Gaulle. The Ruler: 1945–1970*, 357–60.

[35] *FRUS*, 1961–3: XIII, Memorandum of conversation Rusk-Fanfani, 16 Jan. 1963, 144–6; ibid., Circular telegram from the Department of State, 19 Jan. 1963, 146–8.

prevent a downward turn of events which "could have most serious consequences for all of us."[36] If the other five countries held firm in opposing de Gaulle and the Germans made it absolutely clear that they would accept nothing else, then "de Gaulle may be induced to yield." German firmness was the key in this situation.[37]

When, however, de Gaulle's veto was followed on 22 January with a Franco–German treaty, Washington went into a state of "shock."[38] The treaty had been in preparation for some time and the United States had in fact supported it early on. As long as the treaty did not develop into "a Bonn–Paris axis" at the expense of NATO and the Atlantic community, French–German reconciliation was highly beneficial. French–German conflict had brought the United States into two world wars and, as Rusk told Alphand, an understanding between France and Germany for the drawing together of those two countries was therefore very much to be desired.[39]

In the new context of what seemed like a direct contest between the American concept of an Atlantic Europe and de Gaulle's European Europe, Washington's positive position was immediately reversed. George Ball made it clear that West Germany might soon have "to make a difficult choice between its relationship with France and its ties with the rest of Europe and the U.S."[40] President Kennedy called the treaty "an unfriendly act" and lectured German ambassador in Washington Heinrich Knappstein on the evils of concluding "a directorate with France" after the United States had

---

[36] NA, 611.62A/1–1963, Rusk to the embassy in Bonn.

[37] *FRUS*, 1961–3: XIII, Telegram from the State Department to the embassy in Germany, 24 Jan. 1963, 151–3.

[38] In his *The Past has Another Pattern* George Ball writes about the Franco–German treaty that "I can hardly overestimate the shock produced in Washington by this action or the speculation that followed, particularly in the intelligence community" (271).

[39] NA, 375: NATO/9–762, Memorandum of conversation Rusk–Alphand. See also NA, 651.62A/11–1462, Memorandum of conversation Ball–Schröder; NA, 651.62A/11–1662, Telegram from Bohlen to the State Department. For a more negative formulation, see *FRUS*, 1961–3: XIII, Kennedy to ambassador Gavin, 18 May 1962, 704.

[40] NA, 911.62A/1–2263, Ball to the embassy in Bonn. For the developments leading to the Franco–German agreement, see Adrian W. Schertz, *Die Deutschlandpolitik Kennedys und Johnsons: Unterschiedliche Ansätze innerhalb der amerikanischen Regierung* (Cologne: Böhlau, 1992), 190–201; Stephen A. Kocs, *Autonomy or Power? The Franco–German Relationship and Europe's Strategic Choices, 1955–1995* (Westport, Conn.: Praeger, 1995), 37–50.

tried to protect Germany by refusing to agree to the French idea of a tripartite directorate.[41] Old-time luminaries Acheson, McCloy, and general Lucius Clay used very strong language in their communications with German officials. Clay was the most dramatic, telling Knappstein that if the treaty was ratified "bedeutet dies das Ende Berlins" (this means the end of Berlin).[42] Ambassador Bohlen in Paris tried to calm Washington by pointing out that the Franco–German treaty really created no new institutions and introduced no significant new measures.[43] He did not succeed, at least not at first.

Kennedy's strongest fear was that the French would attempt to strike a deal with the Soviets which would also include the Germans. He directed that "we should concentrate our intelligence resources on finding out everything we can about discussions and negotiations between the French and the Russians." The president's language became almost warlike: the United States might not get into "an across-the-board battle with de Gaulle," but Kennedy wanted to be certain that "if de Gaulle continued to harass us, we would be in a position to defend ourselves. The U.S. military position is good but our financial position is vulnerable." Rusk commented that the United States was in Europe not because the Europeans wanted "us there but because we believe our presence there is essential to the defense of the U.S." Washington just could not permit de Gaulle "to force us out of Europe without the greatest effort to resist such a move."[44] There was disagreement about

[41] *FRUS*, 1961–3: XIII, Telegram from the Department of State to the embassy in Germany, 23 Jan. 1963, 148–50. In his report on the conversation ambassador Knappstein wrote that president Kennedy was "in spürbar schlechter Stimmung" (an obviously bad mood). For this, see *Akten zur Auswärtigen Politik der Bundesrepublik Deutschland, 1963*, 163.

[42] *Akten zur Auswärtigen Politik der Bundesrepublik Deutschland, 1963*, 200–1, 201–3, 228–9; Mayer, *Adenauer and Kennedy*, 90–2. For Acheson's very strong and very lengthy reaction against the Franco–German treaty, see NA, POL FR-UK, Reflections on the January debacle, 31 Jan. 1963.

[43] NA, 651.62A/1–2563, Bohlen to the Secretary of State, sects. 1 and 2. NA, 651.62A/1–3063, Information airgram from the State Department, gives a somewhat slanted summary of what Bohlen had actually reported from Paris.

[44] *FRUS*, 1961–3: XIII, Summary record of NSC Executive Committee meeting, no. 39, 31 Jan. 1963, 158, 161. Kennedy's fears about de Gaulle's actions were stimulated by intelligence reports. George Ball thus writes in *The Past has Another Pattern* that "There were wild rumors of a plan to pave the way for France, with Bonn's assistance, to negotiate with Moscow for a whole new European arrangement. We compared and supplemented our intelligence reports with bits and

exactly how vulnerable the United States was to French financial pressure. Treasury secretary Douglas Dillon and head of the State Department's policy planning staff Walt Rostow argued that the American position was stronger than many of the financial experts believed.[45]

The focus was on Germany. While de Gaulle had in a way done no more than could realistically have been feared, Washington was bitterly disappointed by Germany and Adenauer. Kennedy stressed that he wanted a strong letter sent to Adenauer, since the United States must not give the chancellor the impression that he could "have it both ways," i.e. close cooperation with Paris as well as with Washington. The letter of 1 February appealed for a common front against the Soviet challenge "in Berlin, in the Caribbean, and elsewhere around the world." Germany had to confirm that it belonged to the West, while "Those who feel that 45 billion dollars and 16 years of continuous economic and military assistance have earned us nothing but the hostility of certain European leaders and newspapers" were likely to press for "concepts that would end Western unity."[46] Adenauer simply responded that de Gaulle was a staunch friend of the United States. The chancellor was clearly at a loss to understand why the US had responded so negatively to a treaty it had earlier favored.[47]

---

pieces gathered by the British. We looked at all possibilities of a Paris–Bonn deal with Moscow, leading toward a Soviet withdrawal from East Germany to be followed by some form of confederation between the two parts of that severed country. That would, of course, mean the end of NATO and the neutralization of Germany" (271).

On equally alarming lines Theodore C. Sorensen writes in his *Kennedy* (New York: Bantam Books, 1966): "Thus Kennedy was briefly startled early in 1963 by a foreign intelligence report of doubtful authenticity. 'Rumors from regular and reliable sources' maintained that De Gaulle and the Soviet Union had made or were about to make a secret deal, calling for a demilitarized Central Europe, including all Germany, Greece and Turkey, the progressive withdrawal of American troops from Europe as well as Germany, and a recognition of the Oder-Neisse line. . . . Fortunately it [the report] proved groundless; but this possibility motivated many of Kennedy's inquiries in the round of meetings that followed" (643–4).

[45] *FRUS*, 1961–3: IX, Rostow to Kennedy, 4 Feb. 1963, 161–2; ibid., Dillon to Kennedy, 11 Feb. 1963, 162–4.

[46] *FRUS*, 1961–3: XIII, Summary record of NSC Executive Committee meeting, 31 Jan. 1963, 163; ibid., Letter from Kennedy to Adenauer, 1 Feb. 1963, 164–5.

[47] Ibid. 165 n. 1; NA, 375.42/1–3063, Memorandum of conversation Acheson–Knappstein, with attached letter from Adenauer to Acheson.

On 5 February Kennedy asked David Bruce, now ambassador to Britain, to undertake a study of US policies towards Europe and make recommendations for action. Bruce completed his assignment in four days. He recommended that the US continue to support British membership in the EEC, but that it make no effort to stop ratification of the Franco–German treaty. Instead of giving de Gaulle "a discreet touch of the whip" by harassing him on various issues, as Bruce himself had suggested on 30 January, he now saw the issue more constructively: "Our tactic with France must be to provide a counter attraction, not aimed at France, but at the legitimate ambitions of Europe. The opportunity for France to join in these efforts must always remain open." In the meantime, the US should work out contingency plans against "a de Gaulle assault on NATO, our trade negotiations, or our balance of payments."

The response to de Gaulle should not be imperial divide-and-rule, but for the US to continue to encourage a united Europe, a Europe which was then to be treated as an equal partner. An integrated Europe would pose dangers if it struck off on its own, seeking to play a really independent role. To minimize the chances of such a development, and to ensure that the resources of a unifying Europe were used to best effect, Washington should seek "to strengthen the instruments of partnership between Europe and the US, e.g. NATO and the OECD, at the same time as we promoted and encouraged the process of European integration." At the same time, however, Bruce still expected Europe to follow the American lead. Somehow there was to be both equality between Europe and the United States and an American lead.[48] Bruce's advice was to form the basis of US policy, in 1963 as on several earlier occasions.

Washington's various efforts to keep alive the issue of British entry into the EEC quickly proved futile. Britain simply could not be brought in against France's will. Half-baked American ideas about British "association" with the Six and activation of the

---

[48] FRUS, 1961–3: XIII, Instructions from Kennedy to Bruce, 5 Feb. 1963, 180–1; ibid., Editorial Note (Content of Bruce's report), 188. The "discreet touch of the whip" is found in NA, 375.42/1–3063, Bruce to the Secretary of State. See also Costigliola, "Kennedy, the European Allies, and the Failure to Consult," 108–9. The Bruce report is found in John F. Kennedy Library, National Security Files, Box 319, Memorandum from Bruce to president Kennedy, 9 Feb. 1963. For a presentation of the report, see Schertz, Die Deutschlandpolitik Kennedys und Johnsons, 201–5.

Western European Union were quickly dropped.[49] Most important, however, American fears of a French–Soviet deal also subsided quickly. A long letter from Moscow to Paris did not in fact represent a Soviet overture, as at least some in Washington appear to have feared. The letter was instead an attack on the Franco–German treaty.[50]

Washington's short-term objective now became to have the Franco–German treaty modified by expressions of German loyalty to the United States and to NATO. With a partial exception for Adenauer, whose fall from power had already started and who wanted to be remembered for his reconciliation with France, the German government quickly agreed to make amends. Most of its key members alleged they had indeed been shocked, first by the circumstances leading to the treaty and then by the strong American reaction to it. Faced with a choice between Washington and Paris, Bonn was quite explicit: it would choose the former. Spurred on by Monnet, who persuaded Bruce, the State Department initially preferred that the declaration of loyalty be incorporated into the ratification law instead of into a resolution by the Bundestag, as preferred by the Adenauer government. At the same time, however, any renegotiation with the French had to be avoided. The outcome of all this was that the declaration was included in a preamble to the treaty.[51]

The German government also agreed to stop the planned delivery of pipes to a Soviet project to export gas to Western Europe, deliveries which German industry had been strongly pushing

[49] NA, 375.42/1–2363, To the Secretary of State from Tyler: Outstanding issues in the UK–EEC negotiations; NA, EC/NG EEC, Memorandum from Ball to president Kennedy, 9 Feb. 1963; ibid., Memorandum of conversation Ball–Godber, 6 Feb. 1963; NA, 375.42/1–3063, Telegram from MacArthur to the State Department; NA, 375.42/1–2363, Telegram from Tuthill to the State Department.

[50] NA, POL FR-US, Memorandum of conversation Tyler–de Leusse, 1 Feb. 1963. See also NA, POL 15–1 FR XR POL/FR, Personal from Bohlen to Rusk enclosing memorandum of conversation Bohlen–Joxe.

[51] *FRUS*, 1961–3: XIII, Memorandum of conversation Rusk–Carstens, 5 Feb. 1963, 182–7; NA POL FR-WGER, Rusk to various embassies, 13 Feb. 1963; ibid., Bruce to the Secretary of State, 5 Mar. 1963; ibid., Rusk to Bruce, 7 Mar. 1963; ibid., Memorandum of conversation Ball–von Brentano, 21 Mar. 1963; *FRUS*, 1961–3: XIII, Memorandum of conversation Rusk–von Brentano, 22 Mar. 1963, 190–3; *Akten zur Auswärtigen Politik der Bundesrepublik Deutschland*, 1963, 332–4, 443–6, 467–72. See also Hans-Peter Schwarz, *Adenauer. Der Staatsmann: 1952–1967* (Stuttgart: Deutsche Verlags-Anstalt, 1991), 810–39; Schertz, *Die Deutschlandpolitik Kennedys und Johnsons*, 205–10.

for.[52] After Bonn had bowed to Washington in these ways, the State Department could again point out that it really agreed with the idea of French–German reconciliation even in the form of a separate treaty.[53]

In a logical, if not in a political, sense the preamble tended to make the treaty meaningless. Despite strong annoyance, especially on the part of Adenauer, over the Kennedy administration's signals of a more flexible policy on Berlin, the Oder–Neisse border, and even on the existence of East Germany, Bonn had to side with the United States.[54] The US was the primary guarantor of Germany's security. On a fundamental security issue the United States was clearly more important than France. Kennedy also decided to go on a trip to Europe, including Berlin and Germany, in great part to counter an earlier visit by de Gaulle. Again, the Germans were to choose, this time between Kennedy and de Gaulle. Kennedy's visit proved a big success, even bigger than de Gaulle's, not only in Germany but in most of Western Europe. The popularity of the United States at the public level had probably never been higher than during and immediately after Kennedy's journey.[55]

De Gaulle's rapidly growing independence and the sympathies he had aroused in Germany did not lead the United States to abandon the goal of European integration. The case for European integration was still seen as sound and the traditional reasons for US support still existed. In fact, although integration had been intended to prevent Germany from going its own separate way, the same argument applied even to France. Now the other European countries could perhaps prevent France from going too far off on its own. In addition, any reversal now of America's support for European integration would play directly into de Gaulle's hands, since it would strengthen charges that the US was simply following the imperial course of divide-and-rule. On the other hand, Washington

[52] *Akten zur Auswärtigen Politik der Bundesrepublik Deutschland, 1963*, 407–14; Angela Stent, *From Embargo to Ostpolitik: The Political Economy of West German–Soviet Relations, 1955–1980* (Cambridge: Cambridge University Press, 1981), 93–126.

[53] NA, POL FR-WGER, Memorandum of conversation Ball–von Brentano, 21 Mar. 1963; *FRUS*, 1961–3, XIII, Memorandum of conversation McGhee–Adenauer, 20 May 1963, 199–201.

[54] This is basically the story told in Mayer, *Adenauer and Kennedy*.

[55] Arthur M. Schlesinger, Jr., *A Thousand Days: John F. Kennedy in the White House* (Boston: Houghton Mifflin Company, 1965), 881–8; *Akten zur Auswärtigen Politik der Bundesrepublik Deutshland, 1963*, 422; Lacouture, *De Gaulle. The Ruler: 1945–1970*, 343–4.

had to lower its pro-integration profile somewhat to avoid Gaullist charges of American "domination" over Western Europe.

At the same time, the alarm over the Franco–German treaty was to have important consequences for the American policy. The Truman and particularly the Eisenhower administration had been strong supporters of Adenauer, in part because of his staunch democratic and anti-Soviet attitude, in part because he favored a high degree of European integration. Although this support had clearly waned under Kennedy, Adenauer seemed to be a fixture on the German scene. Vice-chancellor and minister of economic affairs Ludwig Erhard, on the other hand, had been seen as rather weak, especially on integration—as excessively oriented towards a free trade area at the expense of the cohesion of the Six. After the Franco–German treaty, however, the Kennedy administration became more favorable to Erhard. The minister himself made it clear to the Americans that he had at best been lukewarm to the treaty. His emphasis on the Atlantic framework was now seen as more necessary than before. Erhard thus became Washington's choice. American and, more important, widespread German dissatisfaction with *der Alte's* stubbornness in general and his growing friendship with de Gaulle in particular constituted important factors in Adenauer's resignation and Erhard's taking over as chancellor in October 1963. And Adenauer had after all reached the advanced age of 87.[56]

Britain's membership in the EEC had been seen as the single most important element in strengthening the Atlantic framework. With that membership now precluded, at least for the foreseeable future, Washington concentrated on a series of other initiatives, most of which had been developed earlier, but which were now invigorated to contain de Gaulle and to buttress the American position in general.

[56] Eckart Conze, "Hegemonie durch Integration? Die amerikanische Europapolitik und de Gaulle," *Vierteljahrshefte für Zeitgeschichte*, Apr. 1995, 337–9; Schwarz, *Adenauer*, 627–868, particularly 810–39; Volker Hentschel, *Ludwig Erhard: Ein Politikerleben* (Munich: Olzog, 1996) writes about Erhard and the Americans in this period that "Er war ihr Mann. Das wusste man in Washington" (He was their man. They knew this in Washington) (410). See also ibid. 410–25, 431–3; Hans-Jürgen Schröder, "Deutsche Aussenpolitik 1963/64", *Vierteljahrshefte für Zeitgeschichte*, July 1995, 524–8. For American contacts with Erhard and foreign minister Schröder during the January crisis, see NA, 375.42/1-2663, Ambassador Dowling to the Secretary of State; NA, 375.42/1-2863, Rusk to the embassy in Brussels; NA, 375.42/1-2963, Ambassador Tuthill to the Secretary of State.

The Kennedy administration had long been pushing the Trade Expansion Act, in part for overall trade purposes, but also to soften the impact on the United States of the EEC outer trade wall and to strengthen basic relations between the two sides of the Atlantic. The act was clearly framed with the purpose in mind of encouraging British membership in the EEC. In his message to Congress, the president had told the lawmakers that "The two great Atlantic markets will either grow together or they will grow apart." That decision would "either mark the beginning of a new chapter in the alliance of free nations—or a threat to Western unity." The act passed the House in June and the Senate in September 1962. It lay the foundation for the Kennedy round in GATT.

De Gaulle's veto added urgency to the GATT discussions. Thus, on 30 January 1963, Rusk instructed the key embassies in Europe that the US should be moving ahead as rapidly as possible with negotiations under the Trade Expansion Act. "Progress along this line will tend to minimize the damage that the French veto will cause for all of us."[57]

Also on the economic side, Washington gave thought to the further strengthening of already existing institutions, especially the OECD. Again, the important thing was to do anything that could bind the Europeans, which obviously included France, into the wider Atlantic framework. Despite even the president expressing an interest in this, no major changes were in the end undertaken in the OECD. The organization's rather cumbersome structure was based on consensus and therefore most difficult to change, especially so soon after its creation as the already reformed version of the OEEC. And the US wanted even less than most countries to limit its freedom of action in economic matters.[58]

In trying to strengthen the Atlantic framework, Washington now also put renewed emphasis on the MLF. The idea for this force had originated in the Eisenhower administration in 1960 and was expressed in the form of a fleet of surface ships, or alternatively submarines, manned by mixed crews from NATO countries under NATO command. The project was developed in part

---

[57] *FRUS*, 1961–3: XIII, Telegram from the Department of State to the embassy in Italy, 30 Jan. 1963, 155–6; Schlesinger, *A Thousand Days*, 847.

[58] NA, EC/NG EEC, Letter from Ball to senator Douglas, 15 Feb. 1963, appendix, 6–8; ibid., Memorandum of conversation Kennedy–Lange, 22 Mar. 1963. See also NA, POL FR-UK, Memorandum from Dean Acheson: Reflections on the January debacle, 31 Jan. 1963, 13–15.

to counter the growing deployment of Soviet intermediate-range missiles directed at Western Europe. Initially the idea had been to use land-based missiles, but this had proved politically difficult in most European countries and the sea-based MLF was therefore put together.

The MLF was developed even more to provide Germany with a sense of equality with atomic powers Britain and France, but without giving the Germans direct access to nuclear arms. The underlying analysis was that while France might be the most troublesome ally at the moment, the Federal Republic was in the longer run more threatening. The Germans "will reach point of despair as to their hopes of ever getting their hands on nuclear weapons by multilateral route and will therefore move, surreptitiously at first and then openly, to create their own nuclear force."[59]

In his 30 January cable Rusk even argued that the MLF represented "a specific and important way for UK to seek closer ties with Germans and Italians among alliance members seeking interdependence." The MLF was now to link Britain to the continent and contain the Gaullist challenge. In his report, Bruce too argued strongly for the MLF. If Washington were to treat the Europeans with a sense of equality, the two critical areas were the MLF and extensive political consultations with the Europeans. In the preparations for Kennedy's trip to Europe, Ball similarly warned that history indicated what the consequences of discriminating against Germany would be. In his analysis, this lesson of history applied even to discrimination in atomic weapons. The under-secretary concluded that no one had offered an effective means of tying Germany to the West except through a unified Europe within

[59] NA, 375: NATO/7-562, Ambassador Finletter to the Secretary of State. The best short account of the MLF issue is Frank Costigliola, "Lyndon B. Johnson, Germany, and 'the End of the Cold War'," in Warren I. Cohen and Nancy Bernkopf Tucker (eds.), *Lyndon Johnson Confronts the World: American Foreign Policy, 1963–1968* (Cambridge: Cambridge University Press, 1994), 173–210. See also Philip Geyelin, *Lyndon B. Johnson and the World* (New York: Praeger, 1966), 159–80; Winand, *Eisenhower, Kennedy, and the United States of Europe*, 203–43. For longer analyses, see Helga Haftendorn, *NATO and the Nuclear Revolution: A Crisis of Credibility, 1966–1967* (Oxford: Clarendon Press, 1996); John D. Steinbruner, *The Cybernetic Theory of Decision* (Princeton: Princeton University Press, 1974); Cathrine McArdle Kelleher, *Germany and the Politics of Nuclear Weapons* (New York: Columbia University Press, 1975); Jane Stromseth, *The Origins of Flexible Response* (New York: St. Martins, 1988); Schertz, *Die Deutschlandpolitik Kennedys und Johnsons*, 45–6, 94–7, 182–9, 201–15, 265–92, 333–43.

an Atlantic partnership. The MLF was a crucial element in this Atlantic framework.[60]

Kennedy himself seems to have held a more realistic view of the MLF's potential than the many State Department "theologians" on this issue. On 31 January the president did remark, however, that the US had narrowly averted the disaster which would have occurred if the British had decided to join with de Gaulle in a separate European nuclear arrangement. The even bigger fear, that Germany would join with France in some sort of nuclear cooperation, seemed to be only partially relieved by the French insistence that they had absolutely no desire to see a German finger on the French nuclear trigger.[61]

After Kennedy cooled on the MLF from the summer of 1963, Johnson began to push the idea again in the spring of 1964. In November 1964 Bundy told the president that all his top advisers still believed that the MLF, although not an end in itself, was the least unsatisfactory means of keeping the Germans firmly tied into NATO. The Central Intelligence Agency (CIA) apparently feared that Bonn would turn to Paris for nuclear assistance if Washington did not continue to push the MLF.[62] But with Britain and France not really interested; with Germany in part supporting the idea simply because the United States pushed it; with Bundy, secretary of defense Robert McNamara, the Pentagon, and the Senate increasingly lukewarm at best; and the Soviet Union opposed, the scheme was shelved soon afterwards.[63] Since the Germans were

---

[60] FRUS, 1961–3: XIII, Telegram from the Department of State to the embassy in Italy, 30 June 1963, 155; ibid., Editorial Note (Bruce report), 188; ibid., Memorandum from Ball to Kennedy, 20 June 1963, 208–9; NA, POL FR-UK, Acheson: Reflections on the January debacle, 11. See also Frank Costigliola, "Kennedy, de Gaulle, and the Challenge of Consultation," in Paxton and Wahl, De Gaulle and the United States, 190–2.

[61] FRUS, 1961–3: XIII, National Security Council meeting, 31 Jan. 1963, 161; NA, POL FR-US, Memorandum of conversation Kennedy–de Murville, 25 May 1963, 4–6.

[62] FRUS, 1964–8: XIII, Memorandum from Bundy to president Johnson, 8 Nov. 1964, 104; H. W. Brands, The Wages of Globalism: Lyndon Johnson and the Limits of American Power (New York: Oxford University Press, 1995), 99–100.

[63] FRUS, 1964–8: XIII, Memorandum from Bundy to president Johnson, 24 Nov. 1964, 121; Walt W. Rostow, The Diffusion of Power: An Essay in Recent History (New York: Macmillan, 1972), 77, 237–42, 247–9, 391–2; Costigliola, "Lyndon B. Johnson, Germany, and 'the End of the Cold War'," 181–7; Haftendorn, NATO and the Nuclear Revolution, 160–3; Schwartz, "Victories and Defeats in the Long Twilight Struggle," 128–136; Winand, Eisenhower, Kennedy, and the United States of Europe, 346–56.

clearly preferring Washington to Paris, the sense of crisis which de Gaulle had created subsided. There was less of a need to satisfy the Germans through measures such as the MLF.

It is important to remember about the MLF that, despite the complexities of the project, there was never any question of the United States actually giving up its veto power as far as the actual use of these weapons was concerned. One interesting side aspect of the debate involved the American attitude to a joint European nuclear force. This was a somewhat theoretical issue since Britain and France were not interested in a joint project. The Kennedy administration tentatively concluded that if in the long run the Europeans were to establish such a joint force, Washington should favor it on the condition that it was "thoroughly coordinated with other NATO nuclear resources with regard to control and targeting."[64] Washington's close nuclear cooperation with London gave the Americans considerable leverage in case such a force were to be created. Again, an integrated Europe had to be fitted into the wider Atlantic framework.

The United States managed to contain the Gaullist challenge. France received very little support from the other NATO allies. Washington was therefore able to insist that the dispute with de Gaulle was not between the United States and France, but between the French leader and all the other NATO countries. The Johnson administration generally refrained from public polemics with de Gaulle.

Yet there could be little doubt about the American position as such. With reference to the discussions among the Six about the future of the EEC, the State Department's European bureau concluded that it would be concerned if any such negotiations weakened rather than strengthened NATO, if they were to lead to an inward-oriented "small Europe" excluding the British for all time, if they did not promote European integration by strengthening the existing European Communities, and, on top of all this, if the negotiations "ignored the crucial collateral policy of Atlantic partnership."[65] The Atlantic framework was as important as ever.

[64] NA, 375.72/9–1362, Memorandum for McGeorge Bundy: Talking points for the president's statement to the NATO parliamentarians, Appendix: Questions and answers for NATO parliamentary delegation. See also NA, 375.42/1–2263, Tuthill to the Secretary of State.

[65] FRUS, 1964–8: XIII, Memorandum from assistant secretary of state Tyler to Rusk, 3 Feb. 1965, 185.

As was evident from the European bureau's memorandum, this did not mean that Washington had given up on further integration. On the actual form of European political union, "we have quietly supported generally "federalist" concepts and the democratization of Europe via increased Parliamentary powers, although we have made it clear that the decisions were for Europeans to take."[66]

The US continued to support the idea of British membership. Again, however, the British should be prepared to make concessions to the supranational nature of the EEC. Washington was against the EFTA neutrals joining the EEC as full members or even as associate members, since this could easily come to mean a "lowest common denominator" approach to integration and thereby slow the desired process toward supranationalism. Thus, membership for the neutrals was politically negative for the US. It would also harm American economic interests.[67]

Ever since the defeat of the EDC the various administrations in Washington had underlined that the forms European integration were to take had to be decided primarily by the Europeans themselves. As we have seen, this formal position never stopped Washington from making its views clear, but under Johnson the United States was actually becoming a less central actor than before. Yet, this had at least as much to do with the growing preoccupation with the war in Vietnam as with any change of position on European integration as such.

The relatively calm attitude to de Gaulle continued even after he took France out of NATO's military structure in March 1966 and brought about the evacuation of 26,000 US military personnel from France. Although there were many, particularly Rusk and the NATO old-timers, who wanted to give a firm, public response to de Gaulle's move—and Ball and Acheson actually did—president Johnson instructed Rusk and McNamara that

I would be grateful if you would make it known that I wish the articulation of our position with respect to NATO to be in constructive terms. I see no benefit to ourselves or our allies in debating the position of the French government. . . . we shall develop . . . proposals which would bind

[66] Ibid.

[67] Ibid.; FRUS, 1964–8: XIII, Circular telegram to certain posts in Europe, 26 Mar. 1964, 30–1; ibid., Memorandum of conversation Stoessel–Ferri, 6 Dec. 1967, 644–5. For a good account of Washington's attitude to the neutrals, see Storeheier, US Policy towards the European Free Trade Association, 137–46.

the Atlantic nations closer together; support, as best we can, the long term movement towards unity in Western Europe; and exploit the possibilities of easing East–West tensions."[68]

Johnson also quashed a proposal to transfer the latest in American science and engineering provided, as in the Marshall Plan, Europe developed an integrated framework to put this knowledge to good use. There was to be no ganging up against de Gaulle. The president's focus was now definitely on Vietnam and de Gaulle's move had not exactly come as a shock, since he had already withdrawn the French Mediterranean and Atlantic fleets from NATO control,[69] the former in 1959, the latter in 1963.

Again, much of the concern was with what Germany would do. As acting national security adviser Robert Komer told the president, "The real problem, as always, is not France but Germany."[70] Once again, various ideas for nuclear sharing with Germany were trotted out.[71] In December 1966 NATO finally established the Nuclear Defense Affairs Committee and the Nuclear Planning Group. Seven years of trying to contain something which hardly existed—a German nuclear ambition—was over. Yet the whole affair did illustrate the crucial role of Germany in American policy.

The war in Vietnam, America's balance of payments problems, the improved East–West climate, and de Gaulle's policies all helped increase pressure in Congress to reduce the number of US troops in Europe. The Johnson administration, like Kennedy's, was opposed to any weakening of the American role. They instead negotiated with the ever more affluent Germans to have them make

---

[68] FRUS, 1964–8: XIII, Memorandum from Johnson to Rusk and McNamara, 4 May 1966, 376–7. For the open attacks on de Gaulle, see Douglas Brinkley, *Dean Acheson: The Cold War Years, 1953–71* (New Haven: Yale University Press, 1992), 228–35.

[69] FRUS, 1961–3: XIII, Circular telegram from the State Department to certain European missions, 15 June 1963, 775–6; ibid., Telegram from Bohlen to the State Department, 20 Aug. 1963, 777–9; Brands, *The Wages of Globalism*, 104–8; Elizabeth D. Sherwood, *Allies in Crisis: Meeting Global Challenges to Western Security* (New Haven: Yale University Press, 1990), 130–1.

[70] FRUS, 1964–8: XIII, Acting special assistant for national security affairs, Komer, to president Johnson, 16 Mar. 1966, 337. Komer was the acting adviser after Bundy stepped down and before Rostow took over in April 1966.

[71] See, for instance, ibid., 336; FRUS, 1964–8: XIII, Memorandum of conversation Rusk–Sir Patrick Dean, 17 Mar. 1966, 340; ibid., president Johnson to Rusk, 11 Apr. 1966, 364–5; ibid., National Security Action memorandum, 22 Apr. 1966, 374–5.

payments to offset the extra American costs involved in deploying troops in Europe. In 1967, after complicated negotiations in the middle of which Erhard was replaced as chancellor by Kurt Georg Kiesinger, an agreement was signed. The American troop level was reduced only marginally, while the German payments increased significantly.[72]

In July 1967 the Wilson government renewed Britain's application for membership in the EEC. Johnson had told Wilson that he was "immensely heartened by your courageous announcement." Britain's entry would "certainly help to strengthen and unify the West." The United States would maintain a low profile in this matter, but the president told the prime minister that "if you find on the way that there is anything we might do to smooth the path, I hope you will let me know." Low profile or not, de Gaulle had not changed his mind. On 27 November he informed the world that before he could agree to Britain's entry, it would have to make "very vast and deep changes." "What France cannot do is to enter at present into a negotiation with the British and their associates which could lead to the destruction of the European structure of which she is a part."[73]

Washington frequently expressed the hope that after de Gaulle had left the scene, France would resume a more friendly course. The United States would as it were wait the general out. The US should operate on the assumption that de Gaulle's leadership of France was temporary, and that he would be succeeded by a government "more responsive to public opinion, hence more favorable to NATO, to a United Europe and to the United States."[74]

[72] Erhard's fall was in part related to the American pressure for greater German offset payments in a difficult budget situation for the Erhard government. For this, see Hentschel, *Ludwig Erhard*, 635–6. See also Gregory F. Treverton, *The Dollar Drain and American Forces in Germany: Managing the Political Economies of Alliance* (Athens, Oh.: Ohio University Press, 1978), 32–4, 114–33; Brands, *The Wages of Globalism*, 108–19; Rostow, *The Diffusion of Power*, 395–7.

[73] *FRUS*, 1964–8: XIII, Message from Johnson to Wilson, 15 Nov. 1966, 491; Denman, *Missed Chances*, 228–30. See also *FRUS*, 1964–8: XIII, Memorandum from Solomon and Stoessel to Ball, 19 July 1966, 437–8; ibid., Telegram from Rusk to certain posts in Europe, 2 May 1967, 570; ibid., Telegram from Bruce to the State Department, 25 Oct. 1967, 630–1.

[74] Ibid., Circular telegram from Rusk to the US posts in the NATO capitals, 2 Mar. 1966, 320. See also Declassified Documents Reference Service, 1994, Draft NSAM, Subject: France and NATO, 8 Oct. 1965, 2859–60; The Lyndon B. Johnson National Security Files (Frederick, Md.: University Publications of America), Microfilm, Western Europe, Reel 5, Visit of Foreign Minister Schröder, 23–4 Nov.

In a memorandum for president Johnson in December 1968, in connection with a visit by Jean Monnet to Washington, prointegrationist national security adviser Walt Rostow wrote that one of the disappointments of Johnson's presidency was that the Europeans had not come closer to unity. "It is essential to have an effective European partner if the U.S. role in the world is to be stabilised in the long term." Rostow recommended that Johnson encourage Monnet in his work: "You may wish to express the hope that he and his European Action group should maintain momentum and keep the faith." Johnson presumably did.[75] Thus, even the Johnson administration continued the old policy of pursuing a more supranational Europe, and it, like earlier administrations, did this in close cooperation with Jean Monnet.

1964; Memos of the special assistant for national security affairs: McGeorge Bundy to president Johnson, 1963–1966 (Frederick, Md.: University Publications of America), Microfilm, Memorandum from Bundy to the President, 3 Jan. 1966, with enclosure from Dillon; Costigliola, *France and the United States*, 136–48; Schwartz, "Victories and Defeats in the Long Twilight Struggle," 134–6; Lloyd Gardner, "Lyndon Johnson and De Gaulle," in Paxton and Wahl, *De Gaulle and the United States*, 257–78.

[75] Lyndon B. Johnson National Security Files, Microfilm, Reel 4, 809. See also Winand, *Eisenhower, Kennedy, and the United States of Europe*, 357–62. Rostow was another one of Monnet's strong admirers in Washington. For this, see Rostow, "Jean Monnet: The Innovator as Diplomat," in Craig and Loewenheim, *The Diplomats 1939–1979*, 257–88. No memorandum of conversation has been found for the meeting between Johnson and Monnet on December 9. This was confirmed in a letter to me of April 18, 1997 from senior archivist Regina Greenwell of the Johnson library.

7

THE EUROPEAN ECONOMIC CHALLENGE TO THE ATLANTIC FRAMEWORK, 1945–1972

D E Gaulle represented the major political challenge to the primacy of the Atlantic framework, or, more directly expressed, the American-dominated framework. The second challenge was economic, in the sense that European integration could discriminate against certain American economic interests. The European economic challenge was, however, long tempered by two considerations. The first and most important was the fact that political objectives clearly took precedence over economic ones. The second was economic. Most key policymakers concluded that however harmful European integration might be to some American interests, on the whole such integration was beneficial to the US even economically.

This pattern was displayed as early as the Marshall Plan. Here political considerations, in the form of the containment of the Soviet Union and of Communism, the integration of Western Germany, etc. were seen as justifying a certain overall discrimination against US economic interests. If Europe's acute dollar problem was to be solved, the remedy appeared simple: the Western European countries had to import relatively less from the dollar area and more from each other. Yet, this general conclusion did not prevent the Truman administration and Congress from instituting privileges for specific American business interests. Shipping and certain agricultural products provided perhaps the most striking examples.[1]

[1] The best study of these ambiguities is still Hadley Arkes, *Bureaucracy, the Marshall Plan, and the National Interest* (Princeton: Princeton University Press, 1972), particularly 153–72.

When the Truman administration supported the creation of the European Coal and Steel Community, this was again done primarily for political reasons and, more particularly, to bring about French–German reconciliation and integrate West Germany firmly with the West. The American coal and steel industries certainly did not push for the creation of the ECSC. On the whole they feared the consequences of strengthening their European competitors. On the economic side Washington was primarily concerned about the cartel aspects of the ECSC, even after Monnet and others had tried hard to calm American fears on this point.

The business interests were represented both in the Truman and in the Eisenhower administration, more strongly in the latter than in the former. Thus, in December 1953 secretary of the Treasury George Humphrey argued that Congress and business were "going to strenuously object to our using their tax money to finance additional steel competition from abroad." However, these objections could not stop either of the two administrations from supporting Monnet or from pushing the Germans in particular to negotiate and then implement the ECSC. Neither did they stop Washington from giving a 100 million dollar loan to the ECSC, but the objections were probably instrumental in making the loan considerably smaller than it would otherwise have been: 400 to 500 million dollars had actually been considered.[2]

The strong American support for the European Payments Union was also based in part on political considerations. The State Department and the Economic Cooperation Administration (later the Mutual Security Agency) saw even the EPU in the light of contain-

Arthur H. Vandenberg, chairman of the Senate Foreign Relations Committee 1947–9, provided dramatic evidence of how quickly the perspective could change. Already in June 1949 he had written in his diary that "the economic stabilization of Western Europe (in particular of Western Germany) pours a flood of new competitive commodities into the world's market . . . We are winning the Cold War, we are losing the long-range economic war." See Arthur H. Vandenberg, Jr. (ed.), *The Private Papers of Senator Vandenberg* (Boston: Houghton Mifflin, 1952), 488–91.

[2] *FRUS*, 1952–4, VI. 1, Humphrey to the Secretary of State, 8 Dec. 1953, 333–4; ibid., Draft memorandum of conversation, 15 Dec. 1953, 337–42; Gillingham, *Coal, Steel, and the Rebirth of Europe*, particularly 228–351. For earlier attempts to integrate the European coal and steel industry, see ibid. 1–44; Carl Strikwerda, "The Troubled Origins of European Economic Integration: International Iron and Steel and Labor Migration in the Era of World War I," *American Historical Review*, Oct. 1993, 1106–42.

ment, but also as a step on the long road towards multilateralism. The more negative Treasury saw the EPU as another postponement of convertibility and multilateralism. Various lobbies objected to the EPU's discrimination against American goods. Again, the State Department prevailed.[3]

From an American economic point of view European plans for a common market in agriculture, a so-called "green pool," were much more sensitive than either the ECSC or the EPU. In principle both the Truman and the Eisenhower administration supported even these plans. European integration should not exclude agriculture, but Washington was clearly uneasy about the heavy protectionist elements in these early projects.[4] In any case, the "green pool" was much too controversial for the Europeans themselves, so it came to nothing.

On EURATOM the United States again went with integration. The alternative would have been to emphasize the bilateral agreements with the different European countries. Although the US atomic industry generally favored the bilateral route, it had few problems in accepting EURATOM once the supranational approach had been adopted.[5]

With the proposals for a general common market gaining ground in 1955–6, Washington had to go beyond general political statements and analyze the whole spectrum of economic interests. The report of September 1956 by the interdepartmental Council on Foreign Economic Policy (CFEP) optimistically concluded, after meetings with US officials in Europe, that economic integration would lead to the development of strong, modern economies with higher productivity and consumption levels, and that this "in turn would result in Europe's becoming a better market for United States exports." Even the Commerce and the Treasury Departments seemed to share the upbeat mood about the economic effects of the common market.[6] In more modern terms, the creation of

[3] Dore, "Britain and the European Payments Union," 192–3.

[4] *FRUS*, 1952–4: VI. 1, 418–45, particularly Secretary of State to the embassy in France, 25 May 1952, 418–19; ibid., Kenney to the Office of the US Special Representative in Europe, 18 Mar. 1952, 428–9; ibid., Acting Secretary Smith to certain diplomatic offices, 27 May 1953, 444–5.

[5] Winand, "European Insiders Working Inside Washington," especially 26–8.

[6] *FRUS*, 1955–7: IX, Report by the chairman of the Council on Foreign Economic Policy (Randall), Sept. 1956, 24–5; Romero, "U.S. Attitudes to Integration and Interdependence: The 1950s," in Heller and Gillingham, *The United States and the Integration of Europe*, 110–14.

additional trade was seen as likely to outweigh the relative diversion of trade away from the United States.

Yet European economic integration certainly presented challenges for the United States. In the Eisenhower administration, the European proposals were seen at the working level as having to be harmonized with the general promotion of multilateral trade, the ultimate attainment of general currency convertibility, and the avoidance of large-scale discrimination against US goods or even those of certain other countries. Agriculture was quickly identified as particularly problematic, because here heavy European protectionist elements would be most likely to injure a major and growing American export interest.[7] Despite the overall positive emphasis, concrete American economic interests were not to be neglected.

American industry as such was divided over the pros and cons of the common market. The conclusion from a meeting of some forty of the major companies was that a common market would discourage US exports since the whole arrangement was based on preferences for the member countries. On the other hand, the vast integrated new market would clearly have a positive effect on US investments in Europe. One big market was much better than many small ones. For the big American oil and car companies already present in Western Europe the latter point was rather important.[8]

The CFEP consensus on the treaties of Rome was clear: the common market "is on balance in accord with United States policy objectives in Western Europe and merits United States support." The economic problems posed by the market, "including those with respect to agriculture, should be the subject of negotiations within the framework of the GATT."[9] The State Department decided that while the economic concerns were to be mentioned to the countries involved, more concrete negotiations should take place only *after* the Six had ratified the treaties of Rome. Earlier

[7] *FRUS*, 1955–7: IV, Report by the Subcommittee on Regional Economic Integration of the Council on Foreign Economic Policy to the Council, 15 Nov. 1956, 484–6; ibid., Memorandum from Dillon to Randall, 11 Apr. 1957, 552.

[8] Ibid., Memorandum from Frank to Dillon, 24 May 1957, 555–6 (French economic adviser Robert Marjolin asked that the latter point not be made public since French business interests would react negatively to such a conclusion); Mira Wilkins, "U.S. Multinationals and the Unification of Europe, 1945–1960," in Heller and Gillingham, *The United States and the Integration of Europe*, 342–55.

[9] *FRUS*, 1955–7: IV, Memorandum from Dillon to Randall, 11 Apr. 1957, 553 n. 2.

action "could seriously interfere with favorable parliamentary action" in the six member countries.[10] Nothing should be done which could slow down the establishment of the EEC.

After the treaties of Rome had been negotiated and, to Washington's surprise, quickly ratified by the Six, the administration kept up the general political encouragement. While the free trade area promoted by Britain could alleviate some of the economic problems for the United States involved in the creation of the EEC, these negotations should not delay the implementation of the common market. The State Department instructed the relevant embassies that the political importance of European integration "looking to permanent solution of age-old Franco-German problems" had committed the US to "the success of the European Common Market."[11]

Alan Milward and Federico Romero have argued that starting in 1958 the American policy towards European integration became much more negative. In this respect Romero points out that it was very fortunate that the EEC came about in 1955–7, because "if it had come about just two years later the common market would have certainly received very different treatment in Washington."[12]

The United States had run its first post-war balance of payments deficit in 1950, and this was actually repeated in most years in the 1950s, but the deficit was still relatively small and not really seen as representing a major problem. The US was after all running a substantial surplus in its balance of trade. The payments deficit also meant that Europe was receiving much-needed dollars. In 1958–9 the payments deficit increased considerably. (The trade surplus lasted until 1971.) Military expenditures and private investment abroad were seen as the main culprits.[13]

[10] US Department of State, *Bulletin*, 4 Feb. 1957, 182; FRUS, 1955–7: IV, Memorandum from Dillon to Randall, 11 Apr. 1957, 549–53.

[11] *FRUS*, 1955–7: IV, Acting Secretary Herter to the Embassy in France, 10 Oct. 1957, 564–5.

[12] Federico Romero, "Interdependence and Integration in American Eyes: From the Marshall Plan to Currency Convertibility," in Alan S. Milward *et al.*, *The Frontier of National Sovereignty: History and Theory 1945–1992* (London: Routledge, 1993), 155–81; quotation from 179. See also Milward's contribution, "Conclusions: The Value of History," particularly 198–200 and Romero, "U.S. Attitudes to Integration and Interdependence: The 1950s" 103–21, particularly 116.

[13] *FRUS*, 1958–60: IV, Memorandum prepared in the Treasury Department, 30 Oct. 1958, 91–3; ibid., Paper prepared in the State Department: International payments position of the United States, 24 July 1959, 115–20. See also Treverton,

It does indeed appear that economic considerations became more important in 1958-9. The negative balance of payments was undoubtedly one important factor behind the United States now pushing for results in the Dillon round in GATT and for the reorganization of the OEEC into the OECD. With the US experiencing economic problems, the Europeans had to carry a larger share of the burden. Washington also became more insistent that "discrimination against third countries," primarily the US, not be part of any wider free trade area between the EEC and other European countries. As under-secretary of state Douglas Dillon pointed out, US public opinion was "now very sensitive to trade discrimination against US" and would be further disturbed by new acts of discrimination. These problems ought therefore to be handled through the OEEC/OECD and GATT, where the United States was directly represented.[14]

Still, the Milward-Romero interpretation seems considerably overstated. In fact, while there were also changes in US policy towards the EEC, these were smaller than in Washington's policies towards other areas. The explanation was obvious. Political considerations, as interpreted by the State Department, continued to dominate American policy towards the EEC well after 1958. In addition, for the US the economic side included more than simply the balance of payments problems, however serious these were.

Even after the EEC came into operation in 1958, Washington hesitated to press its economic grievances. At first it was hoped that a combination of the long-awaited introduction of currency convertibility, a lowering of the EEC tariffs to the outside world, and increased European military and development spending would improve the US payments situation.[15] It also took a while to change

The Dollar Drain and American Forces in Germany, 10–12, 32–3; Thomas W. Zeiler, *American Trade and Power in the 1960s* (New York: Columbia University Press, 1992), particularly 32–3. The balance of payments referred to here is the "basic balance," i.e. current account plus long-term capital flows. On current accounts alone the US, with only a few exceptions, ran a surplus from 1945 to the early 1970s. For this, see David P. Calleo, *Beyond American Hegemony: The Future of the Western Alliance* (New York: Basic Books, 1987), 83–4, 241–2; *Economic Report of the President 1996* (Washington, DC: Government Printing Office, 1996), 392–3.

[14] *FRUS*, 1958–60: VII, Circular telegram from the State Department to certain diplomatic posts, 13 Oct. 1959; ibid., Dillon to the State Department, 13 Dec. 1959, 202–3; Storeheier, *US Policy towards the European Free Trade Association*, 65–85.

[15] *FRUS*, 1958–60: IV, Memorandum from Southard to Anderson and Dillon, 18 May 1959, 108–10; ibid., Paper prepared in the State Department: International payments position of the United States, 24 July 1959, 115–20.

established policies. In December 1959 Dillon, who had excellent connections in the business and financial community, went on a trip to Western Europe for the purpose of "promoting US exports and removing discrimination," probably the first such trip since the war by a top official. Even he, however, only argued that while the US might not have pressed adequately for liberal policies on the part of the EEC in the early stages, "we felt that as the Community became more firmly established it would be possible to apply more pressure to get them to adopt 'outward-looking' policies." Illustrating the new concern, Dillon particularly mentioned the "changed balance-of-payments situation."[16]

Largely in response to the formation of the EEC, Britain, Denmark, Sweden, Norway, Switzerland, Austria, and Portugal established the European Free Trade Association (EFTA) in 1959–60. Washington was rather negative about EFTA. While at first it primarily underlined that the new organization had to be compatible with GATT rules, the Eisenhower administration became increasingly skeptical. In October 1959 secretary Herter nevertheless told the relevant embassies that since the EFTA convention would be signed soon, "it would be counter-productive for US even to imply that it is attempting to bring influence to bear against signature."[17]

No such negative feelings were expressed towards the EEC as such. In November 1959 Herter wrote the president that the United States had "strongly supported" the EEC "for political as well as economic reasons."[18] Although even economic reasons were seen to exist for the United States to support the EEC, most of the American support flowed from political sources. In August 1960 the State Department underlined that the basic point was still that the United States continued to feel that European integration was of vital importance both for the member countries and for the overall strength of the Atlantic alliance. While a more open and liberal Community was definitely to be encouraged, primarily through new GATT negotiations, such measures should not

[16] Romero, "U.S. Attitudes towards Integration and Interdependence: The 1950s," 116; FRUS, 1958–60: VII, Memorandum of conversation Dillon–Lloyd, 8 Dec. 1959, 175–85, particularly 179, 181. See also ibid., Memorandum of discussion at the 409th meeting of the National Security Council, 4 June 1959, Attachment: Report by Beale, 219.

[17] FRUS, 1958–60: VII, Herter to certain diplomatic posts, 13 Oct. 1959, 162; Storeheier, US Policy towards the European Free Trade Association, 37–64.

[18] FRUS, 1958–60: IV, Memorandum from Herter to Eisenhower, 24 Nov. 1959, 58.

have the effect of weakening the EEC. The balance of payments situation thus made Washington increasingly skeptical toward the British plan for a free trade area and later toward EFTA, not toward the EEC. Unlike the EEC, the other two represented economic discrimination against the United States with no overall political advantage.[19]

In December 1960 Eisenhower blurted out that "We are spending too many billions all around the world without the Europeans taking a commensurate load." The Europeans had to do more "and a failure on their part to do so would bring into question our basic relationship and attitude toward these problems."[20] These were indeed strong statements on the president's part, but they were not directed at the EEC as such. Neither were they really new. Eisenhower had complained about the Europeans in terms almost as dramatic as early as November 1953.[21]

With the coming of the Kennedy administration, the concern about the balance of payments situation was to increase significantly. In 1960 the first run on the dollar took place in November during the elections and foreign dollar holdings for the first time exceeded US gold reserves.[22] Even before he took office, Kennedy appointed a task force, headed by George Ball, to look into the foreign economic policy of the United States, with emphasis on the balance of payments situation. The task force recommended a growth strategy, combining an opening of foreign markets with expansive policies in general. The US was to export its way out of the payments problem.[23]

In the Kennedy administration each department was required to calculate the foreign exchange implications of *its* activities (its "gold" budget). In April 1961 Kennedy told secretary of the Treasury Douglas Dillon that the two things that worried him the most

[19] FRUS, 1958–60: VII. 1, Telegram from Department of State to the embassy in France, 22 Aug. 1960, 294–6; ibid., Circular telegram from the Department of State, 27 June 1959, 138–9; Winand, *Eisenhower, Kennedy, and the United States of Europe*, 114–21.

[20] FRUS, 1958–60: IV, Memorandum from Eisenhower to Herter, 7 Dec. 1960, 284; Costigliola, *France and the United States*, 119–20.

[21] Ambrose, *Eisenhower: The President*, 143–4.

[22] Zeiler, *American Trade and Power in the 1960s*, 32–3; Robert M. Collins, "The Economic Crisis of 1968 and the Waning of 'the American Century'," *American Historical Review*, Apr. 1996, 399–401.

[23] John F. Kennedy Library, Report to the Honorable John F. Kennedy by the Task Force on Foreign Economic Policy, 27 Dec. and 30 Dec. 1960.

were "nuclear war and the payments deficit."[24] The new president was to return to the problems of the payments deficit again and again. Ball thought JFK's concern was related to his closeness to his businessman father. "Every weekend he went up to Hyannis Port," Ball recalled; "he came back absolutely obsessed with the balance of payments." Ball, emphasizing the political side, tried to get Kennedy to decide on these issues in settings more favorable to Ball.[25]

Washington began pushing West Germany to support the American troops there in the form of so-called offset payments.[26] Kennedy adviser John Kenneth Galbraith argued that it was foolish for the United States to increase its own balance of payments problems by promoting a strong high-tariff bloc like the EEC. Matters would allegedly become even worse with British membership. Galbraith received some support in his rather dramatic opposition to a well-established policy and he was to repeat his views later.[27] Kennedy then sent Ball a memorandum on 21 August 1961 stating that he was concerned about the economic effect upon the United States if Britain joined the EEC. "I have been informed that the effect will be extremely serious."[28]

Despite such pressure, there was to be no basic change in Washington's encouragement of European integration. Even in the August memorandum the president confirmed with regard to past US policy that "We have been in the position, of course, of encouraging the expansion of the common market for political reasons."[29] The political reasons for the American attitude had repeatedly been underlined, and they were strongly expressed even under Kennedy.

[24] Schwartz, "Victories and Defeats in the Long Twilight Struggle," 138–9; Treverton, *The Dollar Drain and American Forces in Germany*, 10. For a good account of the Kennedy administration and foreign economic policy, see William Borden, "Defending Hegemony: American Foreign Economic Policy," in Thomas G. Paterson (ed.), *Kennedy's Quest for Victory: American Foreign Policy, 1961–1963* (London: Oxford University Press, 1989), 57–85.

[25] Brands, *The Wages of Globalism*, 108–9; Treverton, *The Dollar Drain and American Forces in Europe*, 32–4; Rostow, *The Diffusion of Power*, 234–7.

[26] Treverton, *The Dollar Drain and American Forces in Germany*, 32–3; Diane B. Kunz, "Cold War Dollar Diplomacy: The Other Side of Containment," in Kunz, *The Diplomacy of the Crucial Decade*, 81–4.

[27] Schlesinger, *A Thousand Days*, 845–6. For an expression of Galbraith's attitude in 1963, see *FRUS*, 1961–3: IX, Letter and memorandum from Galbraith to Kennedy, 28 Aug. 1963, 78–86.

[28] *FRUS*, 1961–3: XIII, National Security Action Memorandum no. 76, 21 Aug. 1961, 32. [29] Ibid.

For these same political reasons the Kennedy administration was in fact pushing more directly than its predecessor for British membership in the EEC, but as we have seen, Washington was clearly against a simply commercial arrangement between the Six and Britain. As Kennedy told Macmillan in May 1961, it was because of this political conviction that the US had been willing "to face the prospect of significant—although we hope temporary—economic disadvantage to the United States in the spread of the Common Market." A customs union for the EEC, Britain, and possibly other EFTA countries would be an economic challenge to the US, without compensating political advantages, and "we should be most reluctant to see such a result." Similarly, as we have also seen, Washington did not want the neutral EFTA countries as members of the EEC because that too would mean economic discrimination against the US without any political compensation.[30]

Kennedy had expressed to Macmillan the hope that the disadvantage to the United States in a European common market would be temporary. But Ball's quick response to Kennedy's memorandum of 21 August was again to present even the economic side in an optimistic light. The under-secretary of state argued that it was inherent in a European common market that it would discriminate, at least relatively, against American goods, but, in his analysis, the common market would also lead to higher overall growth. This growth would in turn stimulate higher imports from the United States. With only 1/4 of 1 per cent higher growth than would otherwise be the case, this trade creation would compensate for the trade diversion.[31] Thus, the United States would benefit both politically *and* economically from a highly integrated common market.

Yet the best of all worlds was of course to have as much political integration as possible with as little economic discrimination

[30] *FRUS*, 1961–3: XIII, Telegram from the Department of State to the embassy in the United Kingdom, 23 May 1961, 20–1. See also ibid., Circular telegram from the Department of State, 12 Apr. 1961, 5–6; ibid., Memorandum of conversation Ball–Caccia, 2 May 1961, 10–11. For the same point expressed a few years later, see *FRUS*, 1964–8: XIII, Memorandum of conversation Hinton–Lemberger, 12 Nov. 1965, 265–6.

[31] Ibid., Memorandum from Ball to Kennedy, 23 Aug. 1961, 32–8. For a similar conclusion on Ball's part as presented in February 1963, see NA, EC/NG EEC, Letter from Ball to senator Douglas, 15 Feb. 1963, 1–2. For a less optimistic way of calculating US gains and losses in its trade with the EEC, see Lawrence B. Krause, *European Economic Integration and the United States* (Washington, DC: Brookings, 1968), 222–8.

against the US as possible, and all this with British membership in the EEC and a strong NATO–GATT framework. Two related economic areas were regarded as particularly difficult for the United States. As was to be expected, the first one was agriculture. In 1958 agriculture constituted one-third of total US exports.[32] Although agricultural exports to the EEC were going up in absolute numbers, they were declining relatively. Thus, they helped less than had been hoped in stemming the growing balance of payments deficit. Agricultural interests were also extremely well organized and well represented in Congress. Washington was therefore quite concerned about the signs that the EEC was working out a rather protectionist agricultural policy.

It was still symptomatic of the situation, however, that after a long debate the Kennedy administration decided not to present an *aide-mémoire* to the EEC countries and Britain spelling out its concerns about US agricultural interests being discriminated against in a Common Market–United Kingdom deal. This did not prevent American concerns from being presented in less formal ways.[33] As Rusk told Belgian foreign minister Paul-Henri Spaak, the United States was not willing "to accept deep economic injury, such as might result from a loss of several hundred millions of dollars a year of agricultural sales to Europe."[34]

The preferences extended by the EEC to the member countries' former colonies represented the second main area of controversy. This point had particular relevance in connection with British membership. If commercial privileges were extended to the entire Commonwealth, not only to the colonies producing tropical products,

---

[32] US Department of State, *U.S. Trade with the European Community 1958–1980*, Special Report no. 84, 28 June 1981, 3.

[33] *FRUS*, 1961–3: XIII, Memorandum of conversation Freeman–Hallstein, 17 May 1961, 15–17; ibid., Memorandum from Ball to Kennedy, 23 Aug. 1961, 34–5; ibid., Circular telegram from the Department of State, 5 Sept. 1961, 38–9; ibid., Letter from Kennedy to Mills, 23 May 1962, 97–100; ibid., Telegram from the Department of State to the embassy in Germany, 8 June 1962, 104–5; ibid., Telegram from the State Department to the mission to the European Communities, 31 July 1962, 113–16; ibid., Memorandum from Freeman to Kennedy, 26 Nov. 1962, 128–34. For the debate on whether to send the *aide-mémoire*, see also NA, 375.800/7–2762, Memorandum from Ball to McGeorge Bundy; NA, 375.800/7–3062, Memorandum from Ball to McGeorge Bundy; NA, 375.800/8–362, Under-Secretary Murphy to Ball; NA 375.800/9–1362, Ball to Murphy, 24 Sept. 1962.

[34] *FRUS*, 1961–3: XIII, Memorandum of conversation Rusk–Spaak, 27 Nov. 1962, 136.

this would mean a very substantial relative discrimination not only against the United States, but also against Latin America. Considering the products involved, the latter would be even more directly affected than the former.[35] Washington's most promising approach for minimizing direct discrimination seemed to be to work for a general reduction of protectionism through the upcoming Kennedy round in GATT.

When de Gaulle turned down British membership in the Community, this was regarded as an unmitigated disaster politically. Economically, however, it was seen differently: in an otherwise gloomy National Security Council meeting on 31 January 1963, George Ball noted that the Common Agricultural Policy would probably not go into effect now. The colonial problems would also be reduced, in part because Britain remained outside, in part because the other five EEC countries might now reject a deal even for the French colonies.[36] This analysis soon proved wrong. The EEC did work out a common agricultural policy and preferential agreements were established for the former colonies.

In March 1962 president Kennedy, with reference to the balance of payments problems, raised American duties on carpets and glass. This in turn led the EEC to suspend concessions it had already made to the US on imports of polystyrene, polyethylene, synthetic and artificial clothing, and varnishes and paint. Protectionist sentiment in Congress then led Washington to new measures regarding wool and chemicals. Now the EEC responded on the poultry front. The first serious trade war had broken out between the United States and the EEC.[37] Many were to follow later.

[35] Ibid., Memorandum from Ball to Kennedy, 23 Aug. 1961, 35–7; ibid., Circular telegram from the Department of State, 5 Sept. 1961, 38–9; ibid., Summary of discussion Kennedy–Macmillan, 28 Apr. 1962, 85–6; NA, Bohlen papers, Secretary's European trip, 18–28 June 1962, 2. See also Winand, *Eisenhower, Kennedy, and the United States of Europe*, 285–94.

[36] *FRUS*, 1961–3: XIII, Summary record of NSC Executive Committee meeting no. 39, 31 Jan. 1963, 162.

[37] Ibid., Circular telegram from the Department of State, 3 Aug. 1963, 213–15; ibid., Telegram from the Department of State to the Mission to the European Communities, 30 Aug. 1963, 216; ibid., Telegram from the Department of State to the Mission to the European Communities, 20 Sept. 1963, 217–18; *FRUS*, 1961–3: IX, Letter from Ball to Freeman, 11 Dec. 1961, 506–9; ibid., Memorandum from Ball to Kennedy, 29 Mar. 1962, 528; ibid., Editorial note, 530; ibid., Memorandum from Ball to Kennedy, 21 Aug. 1962, 532–6; ibid., Memorandum from Rusk to Kennedy, 12 Oct. 1962, 538–9; ibid., Letter from senators Magnuson, Jackson, and Engle to president Kennedy, 20 Feb. 1963, 559–60.

The United States continued to support European integration, but it was increasingly concerned that the EEC was not becoming the outward-looking institution Washington favored. In March 1963 Ball underlined that

Our consistent support for the European Community has been postulated on our assumption that the Community would be outward-looking and that the Common Market and the United States had a common interest in increased trade, lower barriers and economic cooperation. The continuance of our policy of support will depend—to a considerable extent—on a demonstration by the Community and its member countries that this assumption is still valid [emphasis in original].[38]

The concern about the balance of payments situation continued in the Johnson administration. Secretary of the Treasury Henry H. Fowler repeatedly expressed his worries on this point. With reference to the EEC, at an NSC meeting on 3 May 1967, he rhetorically asked whether the US could halt a process which during the last eight years had led to American reserves going down and the EEC's going up. Fowler was also agitated about French measures to restrict US investment: "France is trying either to expel us completely from Europe or at least to diminish our power there."[39] Again, it was assumed that the balance of payments situation would become even worse if Britain joined the EEC and/or devalued the pound. London had to do the latter in November 1967. This set off a wave of speculation against the dollar which in turn forced Johnson to increase taxes, cut spending, and regulate American foreign investment.[40]

Still, Washington's conclusion remained the same as it had always been. While the United States would work hard to open up the EEC, particularly for American agricultural exports, and to reduce US foreign spending and make the Europeans pay more, in offset military outlays, in development assistance, etc. Washington would

[38] Winand, *Eisenhower, Kennedy, and the United States of Europe*, 341; NA, EC/NG EEC, Memorandum of conversation Ball–von der Groeben, 24 Apr. 1963, 2.

[39] *FRUS*, 1964–8: XIII, Notes of National Security Council meeting, 3 May 1967, 572. See also ibid., Memorandum from Fowler to president Johnson, 25 May 1967, 578. For a fine study of French reactions to "Americanization," including US investment in France, see Richard Kuisel, *Seducing the French: The Dilemma of Americanization* (Berkeley: University of California Press, 1993), 154–71, 176–84.

[40] *FRUS*, 1964–8: XIII, Memorandum from Solomon and Stoessel to Ball, 19 July 1966, 437–8; Brands, *The Wages of Globalism*, 117–18.

continue to support the further development of the EEC. This certainly continued to include membership for Britain.[41] The fact that the United States was still running a surplus in its balance of trade reduced the economic worries somewhat. The problem was thus not primarily trade, but all the "extra" expenses involved in being a great power with global commitments.

The internal disputes in the Kennedy and Johnson administrations about America's economic response to the EEC/EC, though growing, were softened by four factors. First, although the economic issues continually increased in importance, they were still generally seen as less important than the political ones.[42] Second, the economic picture was far from one-dimensional. On the positive side, the conclusion that trade creation was more important than trade diversion was still widespread. This presumably applied even to agriculture. Total US farm sales to the EEC countries increased, although they declined as a percentage even of EEC imports. Only exports of certain products, particularly those affected by protectionist levies, such as chicken, fell dramatically.[43] The number of American corporations establishing themselves inside the EEC increased rapidly, and these corporations on the whole had a very positive attitude to the Common Market. An integrated market obviously made their operations much easier than did a fragmented one.[44]

Third, the United States and the EEC were making good progress in establishing that multilateral framework so strongly desired by Washington. The Kennedy round of negotiations in GATT (1964–8), greatly facilitated by the Trade Expansion Act, was the crucial element in this context. Naturally, the final agreement represented a compromise, and the EEC, which for the first time negotiated as one unit, played a substantial role in shaping this compromise. No longer could the United States dominate GATT negotiations in the way it had previously done. Nevertheless, again

[41] *FRUS*, 1964–8: XIII, Memorandum from Solomon and Stoessel to Ball, 19 July 1966, 438; ibid., Telegram from Rusk to the embassy in Switzerland, 23 Apr. 1968, 691.

[42] For a rather dramatic—probably too dramatic—expression of this view, see Eckes, *Opening America's Market*, 178–218.

[43] Zeiler, *American Trade and Power in the 1960s*, 130–9; *FRUS*, 1961–3: XIII, Memorandum of conversation Johnson–Erhard, 28 Dec. 1963, 245–6. For good statistics on US trade with the EC, see US Department of State, *U.S. Trade with the European Community 1958–1980*, 1–7.

[44] Wilkins, "U.S. Multinationals and the Unification of Europe," 352–9.

with the exception of agriculture, the GATT compromise was clearly acceptable to the United States as well.[45]

Fourth, and related particularly to the first factor mentioned, American foreign policy was still formulated primarily by the State Department. The economic departments, Treasury, Commerce, and Agriculture, naturally paid much more attention to domestic economic interests than did State. But presidents, normally backed by their national security advisers, still tended to support State, particularly since the economic departments were often divided. Agriculture took the narrow view which the name suggests; Commerce supported broader American business interests, especially those of an industrial nature; Treasury was primarily interested in promoting multilateral trade.

If all these economic interests, inside the administration and in Congress, would come together, they would represent a most powerful coalition. All of them were clearly more skeptical of the EC than was the State Department: Agriculture and Commerce for the harm done to their respective business clients, Treasury for the break with multilateralism which regional economic integration represented.[46]

This coming together of the economic interests was to take place during the Nixon administration. This Republican administration was considerably more protectionist in its basic attitude than the previous Democratic ones.[47] For a decade de Gaulle had represented the main challenge to the American policy on European integration. With de Gaulle's resignation in 1969, with the EC relatively unified on tariff matters, and with the American economic situation increasingly strained, this was now changing.

The President's foreign policy report for 1970 stated, in tune with traditional US policy, that "We consider that the possible economic price of a truly unified Europe is outweighed by the gain in the political vitality of the West as a whole." The three economic departments expressed disagreement with this statement. They wanted instead to emphasize the problems created by the EC, problems that would only become greater with membership for Britain and other EFTA countries supplemented by the association of the former British colonies. Congress was weighing in more and

---

[45] Zeiler, *American Trade and Power in the 1960s*, 183–256. See also *FRUS*, 1964–8: XIII, Memorandum of conversation Johnson–Hallstein, 19 Mar. 1965, 192–3.

[46] Romero, "Interdependence and Integration in American Eyes," 155–81.

[47] Eckes, *Opening America's Market*, 210–14.

more on the side of the economic departments. In November 1970 Nixon sent Kissinger a note which expressed the new mood: "K— It seems to me that we "protest" and continue to get the short end of the stick in our dealings with the Community." Agriculture was the prime example. "The Congress is simply not going to tolerate this too passive attitude on the part of our representatives in the negotiations."[48]

This pressure from the economic departments and from Congress had to be reflected in Nixon's foreign policy report for 1971. Compared to the 1970 report, in 1971 there was a noticeable shift toward underlining the many problems the EC would create for the United States: for years it had been uncritically believed that a unified Western Europe would automatically lift burdens from the shoulders of the United States. "The truth is not so simple. European unity will also pose problems for American policy, which it would be idle to ignore." Agriculture and preferential trading arrangements were given special mention.[49]

In 1971 the United States was for the first time in decades running a deficit not only in its balance of payments, but also in its balance of trade. These problems in turn led to the Nixon–Connally economic measures of August 1971. The convertibility of the dollar into gold was suspended, the equivalent of a dollar devaluation, and a 10 per cent surtax was added on imported goods. These measures signaled that the United States was paying much more attention to its more narrowly defined economic interests than it had done earlier.

The 1972 foreign policy report attempted to strike some sort of balance, probably partly in response to much of the outside world's disappointment over the August measures. On the one hand, the report reiterated Washington's strong support for the geographical enlargement of the Community represented by the possible membership of Britain, Ireland, Denmark, and Norway. On the other hand, the problems posed for the United States by the enlarged EC were also prominently mentioned. And, as we shall shortly see, these problems were not only economic.[50]

[48] Kissinger, *White House Years*, 425–8. The 1970 foreign policy report is found in *Public Papers of the Presidents. Richard M. Nixon, 1970*, 116–90, particularly 127–9.

[49] *Public Papers of the Presidents. Richard M. Nixon, 1971*, 219–345, particularly 229–33; quotation from 232.

[50] *Public Papers of the Presidents. Richard M. Nixon, 1972*, 194–346, particularly 222–4.

8

THE NIXON–KISSINGER
REAPPRAISAL, 1969–1976

For more than two decades the United States had provided
strong support for European integration. Despite the preoccupation with Vietnam, even the Johnson administration seemed
to operate under the assumption that the more supranational the
integration, the better it apparently was. In the 1960s, however,
the United States had become more and more insistent not only
on European integration taking place within an Atlantic context,
but also on American economic interests being safeguarded. Considerable tension thus existed in the American policy.

Some of this tension was to be resolved by the Nixon administration. This was done despite European affairs not coming very
high on the administration's list of priorities. Most of its attention
was focused on détente with the Soviet Union, the opening to China,
and the ending of the war in Vietnam. Thus, in Nixon's memoirs
neither the EC nor any related item even appears in the index. What
he writes about his conversations with Western European leaders
also deals largely with the Soviet Union, China, and Vietnam.[1]

In their European policy Nixon and his national security adviser
Henry Kissinger gave strong priority to the Atlantic framework for
European integration. US leadership in the Atlantic alliance was
taken for granted even in what the administration saw as a period
of American decline. Europe's support was to strengthen Washington in its dealings with the Soviet Union. With determination
Nixon and Kissinger fought powerful Congressional pressure to

---

[1] Richard M. Nixon, *RN: The Memoirs of Richard Nixon* (New York: Simon &
Schuster, 1978), 370–5 (Europe and de Gaulle), 1095–1122 (index).

reduce the number of American troops in Europe.[2] The administration continued to push for a more open and Atlantic EC, and therefore wanted Britain to "join Europe."

In principle little of this was new. The new element was that, because of this Atlantic priority, Washington was no longer to push for the most supranational forms of European integration. The formal rationale for the new policy was that the Europeans had to decide on their own what they wanted. The real rationale was that the United States had clearly become rather ambivalent about the whole objective of a united Europe.

The new attitude was evident immediately. It flowed from reflections Kissinger had made before assuming office. This fact was obvious from his recommendations to Nixon on American policy towards Western Europe as early as 22 February 1969, i.e. only one month after the inauguration. The first two points were traditional: "1. Affirm our commitment to NATO; 2. Affirm our traditional support of European unity, including British entry into the Common Market." The somewhat newer point was the third one: "3. Make clear that we will not inject ourselves into intra-European debates on the form, methods and timing of steps toward unity." Earlier administrations, particularly Johnson's, had said even this, but they had still favored European supranationalism. The Nixon administration did not.[3]

The Nixon administration generally adhered to its stated policy of leaving the initiative on European integration to the Europeans, with Washington stressing the overall Atlantic framework. Nixon and Kissinger did not directly oppose further integration or pursue a policy of divide-and-rule. Good reasons still existed for the United States to be sympathetic to European integration. As we have seen, in his writings Kissinger was particularly concerned about the evils of European dependence. Dependence could only be avoided if the Europeans developed greater unity. Yet the conclusion was clear: the United States should "leave the internal evolution of a united Europe to the Europeans and use its ingenuity and influence in devising new forms of *Atlantic* cooperation" (emphasis in original).[4]

The administration's ambivalence to the EC showed in the fact that it continued to meet with the national leaders and resisted pressure to meet also with the joint EC Commission, although

[2] Kissinger, *White House Years*, 393–6, 400.   [3] Ibid. 88–9.
[4] Kissinger, "What Kind of Atlantic Partnership?," 32.

some lower-level contacts were established even with the latter. Kissinger explained that although the United States supported the idea of European unity, "if the price for this is that we cannot talk with our traditional European friends, then over time this could create a massive change in our relations."[5]

J. Robert Schaetzel, US ambassador to the EC in the years from 1966 to 1972 and a true believer in European integration, became very frustrated with the new Nixon–Kissinger policy. He later complained about the Nixon years that "in its isolation in Brussels the United States Mission to the European Communities might as well have been located on the upper reaches of the Orinoco."[6]

There were four main reasons for Nixon and Kissinger's change of attitude. These reasons also further illustrate the nature of the change in policy. First, in Kissinger's analysis the earlier policy had allegedly overestimated the American influence on European integration. As he wrote before he became national security adviser, "the future of a united Europe depends more on developments in London, Paris and Bonn than to [sic] strictures from Washington."[7] The American policy might even have led to stalemate: "While not sufficient to bring about our preferred solution, our influence is strong enough to block approaches with which we disagree."[8]

The impact of this point had to be considerably reinforced by the Nixon administration's analysis that the United States was declining and that various regional power centers were rising, particularly on the economic side. Thus, in 1971 the president himself referred to the earlier American domination and alluded to Soviet domination and then stated that instead of there being just two superpowers, "when we think in economic terms and economic potentialities, there are five great power centers in the world today" [the United States, the Soviet Union, Western Europe, China, and Japan].[9] With reduced relative American strength, there had to be more cooperation and less American dictation.

Even for Nixon and Kissinger basic reasons allegedly existed for promoting European integration. Yet, important as these reasons

[5] Kissinger, *Years of Upheaval*, 701–2.
[6] J. Robert Schaetzel, *The Unhinged Alliance: America and the European Community* (New York: Harper & Row, 1975), 60–1.
[7] Kissinger, "What Kind of Atlantic Partnership?," 32.   [8] Ibid. 29.
[9] *Public Papers of the Presidents. Richard M. Nixon, 1971*, 804. For a fine study of Nixon's perception of relative decline and some of the consequences of this, see Litwak, *Detente and the Nixon Doctrine*.

may have been, a tactical side was obviously creeping into the US support, since the remaining three points indicate that Nixon and Kissinger actually disagreed with much of the earlier policy.

Second, the Nixon administration felt that the basic assumption underlying the previous policy—that the United States and Western Europe shared all basic interests—was simply not true. An integrated Europe might well adopt policies which the United States did not favor. Again, as Kissinger stated in his early analysis of the previous policy, "We have sought to combine a supranational Europe with a closely integrated Atlantic Community under American leadership. These objectives are likely to prove incompatible." The differences between the two sides of the Atlantic had already been reflected in monetary and trade policies. "A politically united Europe was more likely to articulate its own conceptions in other areas as well." On the political side Kissinger was undoubtedly influenced by the growing differences between the United States and Western Europe, including West Germany's emerging *Ostpolitik*. These differences were more central to him than economic issues, which he tended to regard as rather pedestrian.[10]

On the economic side, however, it had been illustrated on many occasions that the two sides of the Atlantic did not have identical interests. The joint EC policy, as reflected in for instance the Kennedy round negotiations, enhanced already existing doubts in Washington about the wisdom of the established policy. These doubts now involved not only the economic departments, but more and more members of Congress and clearly, as we have seen, even the president himself.

In the Nixon–Kissinger analysis, Atlantic cooperation worked well in the security field, but not in the economic one. On several occasions this discrepancy led the president to ask whether "Atlantic unity in defense and security [can] be reconciled with the European Community's increasingly regional economic policies." He gave the answer himself: the Europeans could not have it both ways. "They cannot have the United States participation and cooperation on the security front and then proceed to have confrontation and even hostility on the economic and political front."[11] The conclusion was obvious: in return for the security provided by the United

[10] Kissinger, "What Kind of Atlantic Partnership?," 30, also 22; Kissinger, *White House Years*, 390.

[11] *Public Papers of the Presidents. Richard M. Nixon*, 1973, 404–5 (the question); 1974, 276 (the answer). See also 1972, 222–4.

States, the Europeans ought really to become more conciliatory on the economic front. Alternatively, the United States would do less on the security front.

Washington supported the British initiative to establish a Eurogroup within NATO. This group remained firmly Atlantic in its approach and on this basis it could strengthen American–European cooperation in defense, the area—as opposed to the economic one —where it counted the most and where, at least in Kissinger's mind, it was most natural.[12]

Third, in promoting an integrated Europe, Washington might actually push its best friends in Europe away from it. An integrated Europe might come to be dominated by Gaullist ideas, clearly a negative possibility for the Nixon administration. A scenario somewhat less dramatic, but more likely than the Gaullist one, was this: several countries in Europe were following the American lead rather closely, but if their policies were to be submerged in a European community, the result could easily be greater distance from the United States. In Kissinger's words, "A confederal Europe would enable the United States to maintain influence at many centers of decision rather than be forced to stake everything on affecting the views of a single, supranational body."

In line with this argument, Nixon again started referring to the "special relationship" with Britain, a term generally frowned upon by earlier administrations in Washington. For Nixon and Kissinger there was no point in ending the "special relationship." Quite the contrary: the objective should be to bring as many countries as possible into special relationships with Washington.[13] Like previous US governments, the Nixon administration definitely wanted to bring Britain into the EC, but a close relationship with the UK could still be maintained in a confederal structure while this would be impossible in a federal structure. The British were also skeptical of supranationalism, an additional reason for Washington to be the same.

The paradox was that now, when the United States finally took a strong interest in the "special relationship," Britain was not really interested. Edward Heath was more committed to British membership in the EC than any of his predecessors. He was ready to

---

[12] Kissinger, *White House Years*, 385–6; Cromwell, *The United States and the European Pillar*, 42–56.

[13] Kissinger, "What Kind of Atlantic Partnership?," 33; Kissinger, *White House Years*, 89–91.

accept the EC pretty much as it stood. His strategy to acquire membership for Britain included putting some distance between the US and the UK. In large part for this reason, the Nixon–Heath relationship remained rather distant.[14]

Heath did succeed, however, in bringing Britain into the EC. He was himself clearly more pro-European than his predecessors as prime minister. British industrialists were becoming ever more European. Even more important were the changes on the other side of the English Channel. After de Gaulle had lost a referendum on changes in regional institutions in France, he resigned on 28 April 1969. His successor Georges Pompidou held a more flexible position on British membership in the EC. This reflected the new president's more pragmatic personality, but also his uneasiness over West Germany's growing independence. At the EC Hague summit on 1–2 December 1969, it was more or less agreed to let Britain and its closest associates in as the five EC members had long wanted, to settle the question of the finances of the Common Agricultural Policy in the way France wanted, and to develop further cooperation in the fields of monetary and even foreign policy After detailed negotiations Ireland and Denmark followed Britain into the Community on 1 January 1973, while Norway, after a referendum, decided to stay out. The Six had become the Nine.[15]

Finally, the new American policy was undoubtedly also influenced by the complex attitude Nixon and Kissinger had towards France in general and towards de Gaulle in particular. They were actually both great admirers of the French president, especially of his personal qualities, though they had less admiration for his attitude to the United States. As we have seen, the Johnson administration had pursued a relatively calm policy in the face of de Gaulle's challenge to American leadership, but Nixon and Kissinger wanted to take this policy one step further.

A lower American profile on European integration could help improve relations with de Gaulle and with the new French president Pompidou. (De Gaulle retired only three months after Nixon had taken office.) Pushing for a supranational Europe clearly disturbed relations with de Gaulle and Pompidou since they were

[14] Kissinger, *White House Years*, 89–91, 964.

[15] Young, *Britain and European Unity*, 104–19; Denman, *Missed Chances*, 227–42: Dobson, *Anglo-American Relations in the Twentieth Century*, 137–43. Pompidou told Kissinger directly that fear of Germany had caused him to reverse the French position: see Kissinger, *White House Years*, 422. See also ibid. 404, 411, 529–34, 966.

against it and wanted a loose confederal structure. Nixon's initiation of secret American assistance to the French nuclear weapons project certainly also helped improve relations.[16]

The Kennedy and particularly the Johnson administration had expected that the problems between the United States and Western Europe would largely disappear when de Gaulle left the scene. The Nixon administration similarly assumed that its new policy would help improve relations. In some respects relations did improve. The difficult issue of British membership in the EC was solved. Problems remained, however. This was to be most clearly shown in connection with the so-called Year of Europe (1973).

The Year of Europe was Nixon and Kissinger's most ambitious attempt to redefine and strengthen relations with Europe within the crucial Atlantic framework. After the heavy emphasis on the Soviet Union, China, and Vietnam, Europe was again to be at the center of Washington's attention. In the speech launching the scheme Kissinger stated that "The alliance between the United States and Europe has been the cornerstone of all postwar foreign policy." In the agenda for the future, the national security adviser affirmed that the United States would continue to support the unification of Europe. "We have no intention of destroying what we worked so hard to build." For the United States, "European unity is what it has always been: not an end in itself but a means to the strengthening of the West." Washington would "continue to support European unity as a component of a larger Atlantic partnership."[17] The Atlantic framework was essential, but Kissinger's emphasis on European unity was really putting it a bit strong in view of the administration's re-evaluation of this point.

---

[16] Schaetzel, *The Unhinged Alliance*, 50–2; Kissinger, *White House Years*, 104–11; Stephen E. Ambrose, *Nixon: The Triumph of a Politician 1962–1972* (New York: Simon and Schuster, 1989), 23–4; Frédéric Bozo, *Deux stratégies pour l'Europe: de Gaulle, les États-Unis et l'Alliance Atlantique 1958–1969* (Paris: Plon, 1996), 208–12. For atomic cooperation, see Richard H. Ullman, "The Covert French Connection," *Foreign Policy*, Summer 1989, 3–33; Marcel Duval and Pierre Melandri, "Les États-Unis et la prolifération nucléaire: le cas francais," *Revue d'histoire diplomatique* (1995), 193–220.

At the time of de Gaulle's resignation, Nixon sent him an effusive personal letter since "The message I sent to you through official channels could not convey adequately my deep sense of personal loss when you announced your retirement." Nixon went on to write that "I believe history will record that your resignation was a great loss to France and to the cause of freedom and decency in the world." De Gaulle was highly pleased. See Nixon, *RN: The Memoirs of Richard Nixon*, 385–6.   [17] US Department of State, *Bulletin*, 14 May 1973, 593, 595.

The new Atlantic Charter that Kissinger proposed irked the Europeans, and not only the French, by pointing out that while the United States had global responsibilities, the Europeans only had more regional ones, and by emphasizing the "linkage" between the maintenance of the American security guarantee and a European quid pro quo in the economic sphere and with regard to military burden-sharing. In response the EC's draft agreement stressed the political equality of the EC and the US. The Europeans also refused to recognize any linkage between security and political/economic problems.

It was in this context that Nixon presented his warning that "the Europeans could not have it both ways." The Atlantic Declaration, signed on 26 June 1974, was consensus-oriented, but still largely based on American ideas. The American security guarantee to Europe was tied to the Europeans assuming a fair share of the defense burden. The linkage so urgently requested by the United States was also vaguely recognized by an expression of intent that the American–European security relationship "be strengthened through harmonious relations in the political and economic fields." Washington's fear that the Europeans would "gang up" on the Americans was to be avoided by the Europeans consulting the Americans *before* they reached decisions on important matters of common interest.[18]

Still, the Year of Europe came to rather little. French–American differences were substantial, even after de Gaulle. Washington disagreed with most European capitals on the right policy towards the Middle East, a crucial issue in 1973, the Year of Europe. Under Heath even the British were skeptical of the scheme since they wanted to prove themselves good Europeans. American leverage was rapidly being reduced as the growing Watergate scandal weakened the Nixon administration.[19]

After Nixon's resignation in August 1974, president Ford had more pressing matters to deal with than American–European relations. In his very few statements on Europe he tended to emphasize the

[18] This account is based on Miles Kahler and Werner Link, *Europe & America: A Return to History* (New York: Council on Foreign Relations Press, 1996), 79–85. See also Kissinger, *Years of Upheaval*, 151–62.

[19] Kissinger, *Years of Upheaval*, 151–62, 183–94. See also Wilfrid L. Kohl, "The Nixon-Kissinger Foreign Policy System and U.S.-European Relations: Patterns of Policy Making," *World Politics*, Oct. 1975–July 1976, 15–19, and Cromwell, *The United States and the European Pillar*, 79–100.

role of NATO, not the EC. The EC, on its side, was preoccupied with breaking in its three new members. A regular system of consultation was, however, set up between Washington and the capital of the country holding the EC presidency.[20]

[20] *Public Papers of the Presidents. Gerald M. Ford, 1974,* 756; 1975, 714, 719; Anthony Laurence Gardner, *A New Era in US–EU Relations? The Clinton Administration and the New Transatlantic Agenda* (Aldershot: Avebury, 1997), 9.

9

THE US AND EUROPEAN
INTEGRATION FROM CARTER
TO CLINTON, 1977–1997

NIXON and Kissinger thus placed some overall priorities on the sometimes contradictory elements that had developed in the US policy on European integration. As a result, not only did they take the United States out of Europe's quarrels about the various forms of integration; in the process they also changed the American policy. Only if the Europeans themselves pushed directly for further integration would the United States support this goal. Washington's all-important task was to protect American concerns even more forcefully than before, whether they be the supremacy of NATO or concrete economic interests.

The Carter administration came to power believing in "trilateralism" between the United States, Western Europe, and Japan. The new president had criticized Nixon and Kissinger for their concentration on relations with the Soviet Union and China at the expense of loyal allies such as the Europeans. And the new administration did adopt an outwardly favorable attitude to the European Community. In April 1977 Carter proclaimed that "I strongly favor, perhaps more than my predecessors, a close interrelationship among the nations of Europe, the European Community, in particular."[1]

Ford and Kissinger had agreed to consult regularly only with the chairman of the European Council, representing the national governments, not with the supranational Commission president. In January 1978 Carter visited the European Commission in Brussels,

---

[1] *Public Papers of the Presidents. Jimmy Carter, 1977,* 776–7.

in fact the first such visit by a US president. He promised that Washington would give "unqualified support" to what the Community was trying to accomplish, welcomed the participation of the Commission president in the G-7 summits of the leading industrialized countries, and somewhat lowered the American opposition to the Common Agricultural Policy of the (now) Nine. The Tokyo round in GATT was successfully completed in 1979, thereby improving the basic commercial climate between the US and the EC.[2]

All these elements were important, and not only as symbols. There were relatively few trade disputes between the United States and the EC under Carter. The most significant one concerned textiles.[3] Yet the Carter years were also quiet times in the EC. In fact, the whole decade from 1973 to 1983 has been described, with only slight exaggeration, as "the stagnant decade" in EC developments.[4] In part for this reason the Carter administration actually spent little time on EC questions, as witnessed by the fact that in their memoirs the leading policymakers have left these matters virtually unnoticed.[5] A certain cooling of Washington's attitude to the EC could even be noticed after the EC's declaration of June 1980 calling for a Palestinian homeland and Palestinian participation in Arab–Israeli peace talks. This diverged sharply from America's pro-Israeli policy. The Carter administration also felt that the Europeans responded too timidly to Iran's taking of the American hostages in Tehran.[6]

[2] *Public Papers of the Presidents. Jimmy Carter, 1978*, 34; Schwok, *U.S.–EC Relations in the Post-Cold War Era*, 32–3. From 1977 to 1981 Roy Jenkins was president of the European Commission. For his own lively account of his efforts to enhance the status of the Commission in meetings with the Carter administration and with the G-7, see his *European Diary 1977–1981* (London: Collins, 1989), 20–2, 82–7, 96–100, 203–4, 293–4.

[3] *Public Papers of the Presidents. Jimmy Carter, 1980*, 1824–6; Kevin Featherstone and Roy H. Ginsberg, *The United States and the European Union in the 1990s: Partners in Transition* (London: Macmillan, 1996), 169.

[4] Keith Middlemas, (ed.), *Orchestrating Europe: The Informal Politics of European Union 1973–1995* (London: Fontana Press, 1995), 73–110.

[5] Schwok, *U.S.–EC Relations in the Post-Cold War Era*, 32–3. For the memoirs, see Jimmy Carter, *Keeping Faith: Memoirs of a President* (Toronto: Bantam Books, 1982); Cyrus Vance, *Hard Choices: Critical Years in American Foreign Policy* (New York: Simon and Schuster, 1983); Zbigniew Brzezinski, *Power and Principle: Memoirs of a National Security Adviser, 1977–81* (New York: Farrar, Straus, Giroux, 1983).

[6] Brzezinski, *Power and Principle*, 480; Gardner, *A New Era in US–EU Relations?*, 5.

During the first few years of the Reagan administration this lull of interest in the EC continued, but then the EC took on new life, with the adoption of the Single European Act (SEA) of 1985–6 as the crucial new measure. The SEA aimed to establish by the end of 1992 the free flow of persons, goods, capital, and services. in other words a fully integrated market. Although the Reagan administration continued some of the pro-integrationist rhetoric and thus welcomed the Single European Act, it apparently did not take the Act very seriously at first, reflecting the previous decade's experience with an EC of considerable talk, but little action.

As the Act was actually being ratified in the national parliaments and fleshed out, articles about the danger of a "Fortress Europe" began to appear in the American press. The administration now expressed concern on several points. Agriculture remained the single most difficult issue and came up in ever-new variations, as for instance in the harm caused to US agriculture by the inclusion of Spain and Portugal in the EC in 1986. (Greece had been included in 1981, so the EC now had twelve members.) Washington saw many of the SEA directives implementing the integrated market as protectionist and disputes broke out over banking, the standardization question, public procurement preferences for the EC members, etc.[7]

The more critical attitude was stimulated by the fact that the United States, which had consistently been running a surplus in its trade with the EC, began in 1984 to run a deficit.[8] There were protectionist elements on the European side. The fact that the Reagan administration combined free trade arguments with a growing protectionism of its own did not help matters much. Economic disputes between the United States and the EC proliferated not only over the SEA directives, but also about current trade practices. Many

[7] *Public Papers of the Presidents. Ronald Reagan*, 1986, 506; Schwok, *U.S.–EC Relations in the Post-Cold War Era*, 51–8, 63–72, 85–97, 99–120; Alan W. Cafruney, "Economic Conflicts and the Transformation of the Atlantic Order: The USA, Europe and the Liberalization of Agriculture and Services," in Stephen Gill (ed.), *Atlantic Relations: Beyond the Reagan Era* (New York: St. Martin's, 1989), 111–38.

[8] See for instance US Department of State, *Current Policy* (Washington, DC: Department of State, 1980–), US Foreign Policy and Agricultural Trade, Current Policy no. 535, 10 Jan. 1984; ibid., Structural Adjustment and the Trading System: Europe's Role, Current Policy no. 804, 7 Mar. 1986; ibid., US–EC Relations and the International Trading System, Current Policy no. 889, 8 Oct. 1986.

of these disputes were commented upon by the president himself, and usually in rather negative terms.[9]

In 1984 the French presented plans to revitalize the Western European Union. In June the defense ministers of the seven members—France, Germany, the Benelux countries, Britain, and Italy —met for the first time since 1973. In October the foreign and defense ministers adopted a Rome declaration underlining their determination "to make better use of the WEU framework in order to increase cooperation between the member states in the field of security policy and to encourage consensus." This was to be done "bearing in mind the importance of transatlantic relations."

The reactivation of the WEU received the public approval of the Reagan administration. More privately the administration was clearly afraid that the French-led initiative could impact negatively on the supremacy of NATO. In late March 1985 Richard Burt, the assistant secretary of state for European and Canadian affairs, therefore sent a letter to the seven WEU governments cautioning them that in particular they should not seek a common position on arms control matters outside the NATO framework. There was to be no "ganging up" on the United States. The American concern was only partly alleviated by the fact that the reactivation of the WEU did not go as far as the French had hoped.[10]

All these developments, combined with numerous transatlantic quarrels about East–West issues, including arms control, and the close relationship between Reagan and Euroskeptic Margaret Thatcher made relations between the United States and the European Community the coolest ever.[11] US support for the EC seemed largely ritualistic.

The atmosphere between the US and the EC was to improve under George Bush, despite the general continuity between the Reagan and the Bush administrations. An inter-agency study from

[9] Featherstone and Ginsberg, *The United States and the European Union in the 1990s*, 168; *Public Papers of the Presidents. Ronald Reagan, 1982*, 1480; *1983*, 31; *1985*, 796–8, 809–10, 1053–4; *1986*, 417, 506, 610, 904, 1650; *1987*, 37, 1548–0; *1988*, 814.

[10] *Keesing's Contemporary Archives: Record of World Events, 1985* (Cambridge: Longman, 1985), 33879–80; telephone interview with senior US State Department official, 7 Feb. 1997.

[11] For my own earlier analysis of the relationship between the United States and Western Europe under Reagan, see my "The United States and Western Europe under Ronald Reagan," in David E. Kyvig (ed.), *Reagan and the World* (New York: Greenwood, 1990), 39–66.

the summer of 1989 concluded that the "accelerated political integration within the EC was unstoppable and that US opposition to the process would be both futile and counterproductive."[12] Thus, in part the Bush policy consisted of adapting to the inevitable in the form of further integration, but in part it also represented a real change of heart.

While Reagan had tended to get personally involved in the economic disputes between the two sides of the Atlantic, Bush was much more focused on the overall political relationship. His statement about "what an absurdity it would be if future historians attribute the demise of the Western alliance to disputes over beef hormones and wars over pasta" could be seen as an indirect slap at his predecessor.[13]

The change of heart under Bush had not only personal, but also deeper political and economic reasons. On the political side, the Cold War was coming to an end, although the Bush administration was rather slow to declare it over. The end of the Cold War resulted in the liberation of Central and Eastern Europe in 1989 and the unification of Germany in 1990. Both developments reinforced Washington's sympathy for European integration. The liberation of Eastern Europe had to be buttressed financially and commercially and with the Reagan administration having run up huge budget and trade deficits, Washington now left much of the initiative for economic dealings with Eastern Europe to the EC.

A strong EC was seen as even more useful in integrating a reunited Germany in Europe. The United States encouraged German unification, but with a united Germany bound to become the leading Western European power, its further integration in the EC, as well as in NATO of course, was seen as essential for continued stability. The EC was also valuable in a general burden-sharing perspective. The American desire for burden-sharing was underlined

---

[12] John Peterson, *Europe and America in the 1990s: The Prospects for Partnership* (Aldershot: Elgar, 1993), 48.

[13] *Public Papers of the Presidents. George Bush, 1989,* 584. Bush's statement received a response from Jacques Delors, head of the EC Commission, who said that "for the free world, it is a necessity to have a good understanding between the US and the EC." This was "more important than soybeans and hormones . . . than the vanity of heads of states; it's the model for freedom, for liberty, for the future of the world." See Featherstone and Ginsberg, *The United States and the European Union in the 1990s,* 90. See also Ginsberg, "EC–U.S. Political/Institutional Relations," 392; James A. Baker, III, with Thomas M. DeFrank, *The Politics of Diplomacy: Revolution, War & Peace, 1989–1992* (New York: Putnam, 1995), 44.

by developments such as the Gulf War and the reduction of American troops in Europe to 150,000. Starting in 1989 Washington encouraged the Europeans to play a larger role even in such a sensitive area for the US as Central America, but with rather limited success in this case.[14]

On the economic side, the situation was improved by the working out of US–EC compromises on some of the many disputes related to the SEA, such as the banking directive, certain standardization procedures, etc. The fact that by the first quarter of 1990 the United States was again enjoying a surplus in its trade with the EC was important, particularly in view of the much larger trade problems the US was facing with Japan. It must also have helped that detailed analysis of the effects of the EC on American trade once more seemed to indicate that trade creation had considerably exceeded trade diversion during the enlargements of the EC. (Certain agricultural products appear to have been the major losers.) If the SEA generated the expected growth, the assumption was that trade creation would continue to compensate for the diversion losses. American investment in the EC had increased from 18 per cent of total US investment abroad in 1960 to 38 per cent in 1988. And for this investment the single market was undoubtedly a great advantage.[15]

Still, economic disputes continued to arise between the United States and the EC. Even Bush had to protect American economic interests, as witnessed by his early statement that "We're not to disarm unilaterally in agriculture." Agriculture remained the greatest bone of contention between the US and the EC.[16] Some of the economic issues could be addressed in the Uruguay round in GATT. The Bush administration, like all previous administrations

[14] *Public Papers of the Presidents. George Bush, 1989*, 1644–5, 1647, 1651; *1990*, 558; *1991*, 359; Ginsberg, "EC–U.S. Political/Institutional Relations," 388–92; Peterson, *Europe and America in the 1990s*, 48–51, 111; Schwok, *U.S.–EC Relations in the Post-Cold War Era*, 164, 170–4, 192–4; Frank Costigliola, "An 'Arm around the Shoulder': The United States, NATO, and German Reunification, 1989–90," *Contemporary European History*, Mar. 1994, 87–110; Margaret Thatcher, *The Downing Street Years* (New York: HarperCollins, 1993), 792–6.

[15] Gary Clyde Hufbauer (ed.), *Europe 1992: An American Perspective* (Washington, DC: Brookings, 1990), particularly 23–6; Michael Calingaert, *European Integration Revisited: Progress, Prospects, and U.S. Interests* (Boulder, Colo.: Westview, 1996), 152–75.

[16] *Public Papers of the Presidents. George Bush, 1989*, 437; *1992*, 6, 10, 19, 77, 1464, 1468, 2007.

since Eisenhower, hoped that successful GATT negotiations would ensure easier access for American goods to the EC market. Under Bush good progress was made in these negotiations, although the agreement itself was only completed under Clinton.[17]

To facilitate an improved climate the Bush administration, in close cooperation with the German government, proposed the setting up of additional machinery for regular consultations, a proposal which was then formally adopted in the November 1990 Transatlantic Declaration. The point of the Declaration was for the US and the EC to reaffirm their determination to strengthen their partnership. In more direct terms, the US objective was to establish "a more united European Community, with stronger, more formal links with the United States." In the end common goals were indeed stated, although again in rather vague terms.[18] The Declaration represented another attempt to contain structural changes and political and economic differences within new formulations and intricate new machinery for consultations.[19]

In Washington the assumption was still that the United States would act as the undisputed leader, despite the growing strength of Western Europe. This assumption could be expressed with surprising bluntness—at least as much bluntness as in the heyday of US domination—as when under-secretary of state Lawrence Eagleburger stated in 1989 that regardless of how big the EC got, or what issues European governments devolved to common decision-making, the need for a strong American voice in Western affairs would not be diminished. In fact, "the President will remain the preeminent spokesman for the free world in the decade ahead."[20]

---

[17] Baker, *The Politics of Diplomacy*, 605; John Croome, *Reshaping the World Trading System: A History of the Uruguay Round* (Geneva: World Trade Organization, 1995), 6–12, 174–5, 338–45.

[18] Schwok, *U.S.–EC Relations in the Post-Cold War Era*, 222–8. The quotation is from USIS, Speech by ambassador to the European Community James Dobbins, 22 Nov. 1991, 3. My account in based partly on an interview with the former German foreign minister, Hans-Dietrich Genscher, 8 and 9 April, 1997.

[19] USIS, Baker speech, 12 Dec. 1989, particularly 5, 8; Ginsberg, "EC–US Political/Institutional Relations," 394–8; Schwok, *U.S.–EC Relations in the Post-Cold War Era*, 170–4; Michael Smith and Stephen Woolcock, *The United States and the European Community in a Transformed World* (London: Pinter Publishers, 1993), 59–63.

[20] Peterson, *Europe and America in the 1990s*, 150–2. The president himself addressed the leadership issue more diplomatically. See *Public Papers of the Presidents. George Bush, 1990*, 208, 280, 323, 507; *1991*, 367, 1429; *1992*, 128, 625, 1066–7.

When the Bush administration felt that the supreme role of NATO, and of the United States, was threatened it spoke out forcefully. Thus, on 21 February 1991 it presented the so-called Dobbins démarche to European capitals. Through the various US embassies, deputy assistant secretary of state for European affairs James Dobbins made it plain that while the United States would welcome a stronger European voice in NATO, it was most uneasy about the development of a WEU which was not closely connected to NATO. This was the same issue that had made Richard Burt intervene in 1985, and it was the dispute from 1973–4 all over again. A European security "caucus" within the alliance, a caucus possibly based on the WEU, was not acceptable. No "ganging up" against the United States would be tolerated. Indeed, on important matters the United States had to be consulted *before* the Europeans reached agreement.[21] In November 1991, in a statement vaguely reminiscent of Dulles's "agonizing reappraisal," the president himself expressed these feelings in public when he declared that the American premise was that the American role in the "defence and affairs" of Europe would not be made superfluous by a European union. "If our premise is wrong—if, my friends, your ultimate aim is to provide independently for your own defence, the time to tell us is today."[22]

On more concrete defense issues, the strong words occasionally being used by the Bush administration could not hide the fact that it often had difficulties in coming up with clear-cut positions. In principle the administration favored an invigorated WEU, but only as long as the WEU was NATO's European "pillar" and not part

[21] The Dobbins démarche is apparently still classified. My account is based largely on a telephone interview with a senior State Department official on 7 Feb. 1997. The démarche was not supposed to be presented in written form to the European governments. In several countries this was nevertheless done. In France president Mitterrand himself became involved in the discussion of the démarche, and the French president reacted very negatively to it.

For a newspaper report of the démarche, see Jim Hoagland, "America is Coming Home from Europe Too," *Washington Post*, 25 Apr. 1991, A15. It has been argued that under-secretary of state Reginald Bartholomew also presented a note to certain capitals, possibly in 1992. For this, see Paul Cornish, "European Security: The End of Architecture and the New NATO," *International Affairs*, 72:4 (1996), 755. More likely this is a confusion with the Dobbins démarche, since Bartholomew participated in drawing up the Dobbins démarche.

[22] Beatrice Heuser, *Transatlantic Relations: Sharing Ideals and Costs* (London: Royal Institute of International Affairs, 1996), 96–7; David Schoenbaum and Elizabeth Pond, *The German Question and Other German Questions* (London: Macmillan, 1996), 196.

of a European Community "bloc". The good side about the WEU was that it could help in burden-sharing, particularly outside the NATO area. The bad side was that a strong WEU could lead to greater European independence and even threaten the supreme role of NATO. Fortunately for Washington there was opposition to such independence even inside the WEU/EC. On a related issue, the Eurocorps, where France and Germany actually established a joint military unit, the administration was not really able to develop a unified position. The military leaders tended to see the corps in a more favorable light than did the diplomats, who again feared for the pre-eminence of NATO, and of the United States. Washington did, however, give its approval to the talks that were going on between Britain and France about military nuclear cooperation, although it is unclear what this meant since the talks were top secret and not only the British, but even the French were cooperating with the United States in this field.[23]

On the Maastricht agreements of 1991–2 formally proclaiming a European Union (EU), with an Economic and Monetary Union (EMU) to be set up by 1997–9, the Bush administration indicated strong support for further integration. After the Maastricht meeting the president welcomed "the historic steps toward economic and political union" and proclaimed that

The United States has long supported European unity because of our strong conviction that it was good for Europe, good for the Atlantic partnership, and good for the world. I have made clear from the very outset of this administration my view that a strong, united Europe is very much in America's interest. A more united Europe offers the United States a more effective partner, prepared for larger responsibilities.[24]

Again, the administration calculated that developments toward a monetary union were probably inevitable. Washington should in no way be seen as obstructing further progress on this point. In matters of substance, good arguments could be found on both

[23] Stanley R. Sloan, "West European–U.S. Relations and Europe's Future," *Congressional Research Service: The Library of Congress*, 20 Feb. 1992, 2; Peterson, *Europe and America in the 1990s*, 159–64; George Ross, *Jacques Delors and European Integration* (Cambridge: Polity Press, 1995), 137–8, 147; Philip H. Gordon, *France, Germany, and the Western Alliance* (Boulder, Colo.: Westview, 1995), 42, 46, 104; Robert J. Art, "Why Western Europe Needs the United States and NATO," *Political Science Quarterly*, 111:1 (1996), 1–39, particularly 25–9; Stuart Croft, "European Integration, Nuclear Deterrence and Franco-British Nuclear Cooperation," *International Affairs*, 72:4 (1996), 771–87, particularly 779.

[24] *Public Papers of the Presidents. George Bush, 1991*, 1591–2. See also ibid. 1427–8.

sides of the issue. Thus, a monetary union would undoubtedly help American companies inside the EU and greatly alleviate the troublesome problem of competitive devaluations, but it could also threaten the central role of the dollar in international finance. This conflict led to a rather low American profile on the concrete issues involved. For Washington, the EU's Common Foreign and Security Policy (CFSP), even more distant a construction than the EMU, had to be reconciled, as always, with the pre-eminent role of NATO.[25]

Under Clinton the president at first almost seemed to make a point of stressing his lack of interest in foreign affairs. Bush had allegedly lost the election because he had been too preoccupied with the outside world. To Clinton the domestic side was what counted and only those parts of foreign policy which directly affected the state of the American economy were to be given priority. In this respect the importance of the booming Asian markets was often emphasized.

The overall tone of the Clinton administration towards Europe was only to be firmly set by the president himself in Brussels in January 1994. There he proclaimed his support for the European Union and for Europe's development of stronger institutions of common action. The US not only encouraged the EMU; in principle it also looked favorably on the EU's commitment to develop a Common Foreign and Security Policy and on the Western European Union's intention to assume a more vigorous role.[26] Thus, Clinton soon saw himself as more pro-European than his predecessors. In the president's own words, his administration, unlike earlier ones, has "not viewed with alarm . . . the prospect that there could be greater European security cooperation between the French and the Germans and between others as well."[27]

While definitely leaving the initiative almost entirely to the Europeans, the administration did express support for both the widening

[25] Ibid. 1418, 1427–8, 1591–2; Peterson, *Europe and America in the 1990s*, 121–2, 155; C. Randall Henning, "Europe's Monetary Union and the United States," *Foreign Policy*, Spring 1996, 84–85.

[26] *Public Papers of the Presidents. William J. Clinton, 1994*, 20. There was little chance that the CFSP would become "too effective." Washington's concern was rather that no effective foreign policy would be established, that the member states would be referring to a CFSP which did not exist in reality. For this, see Gardner, *A New Era in US–EU Relations?*, 23–32.

[27] *Public Papers of the Presidents. William J. Clinton, 1994*, 1185. Richard Holbrooke describes the Clinton administration as the "most supportive of European integration" of any American administration in thirty years. See Clifford Hackett, *Cautious Revolution: The European Union Arrives* (Westport, Conn.: Praeger, 1995), 190 n. 6.

and the deepening of the European Union. Washington strongly favored the inclusion of the Central and Eastern European countries in the EU. The prospect of membership would "help lock in democratic and market reforms" in these countries. The US distanced itself from the British view of stressing only the widening and largely opposing the deepening. Secretary of state Warren Christopher thus proclaimed that president Clinton "has been a strong supporter of deeper European integration, reaffirming the commitment made, in earlier years, by President John Kennedy." Clinton was thus the only one of Kennedy's successors to have kept the pro-integrationist faith whole and undefiled.[28]

The Clinton administration's support for further European integration was important as such. But how was this approach reconciled with the traditional emphasis on the supremacy of the NATO framework? Under Clinton the Europeans were given more leeway in defining their own posture than had been the case under Bush. The shift was seen in the Eurocorps question. After agreement had been reached in January 1994 that NATO would have "first call" on all units for missions under article 5 of the NATO Treaty—the heart of the treaty—Washington's fears of the corps subsided substantially.[29]

The Bush administration had reluctantly come to support the concept of a "European defense identity." In July 1990 in London NATO had taken the position that such an identity would in principle contribute to the solidarity of the alliance. This position was then largely restated in Copenhagen in June 1991. The NATO summit in Rome on 7–8 November 1991 endorsed the idea somewhat more strongly, although it, too, clearly underlined the essential role of NATO.[30]

[28] The quotations are from USIS, Speech by Secretary of State Warren Christopher, Stuttgart, 6 Sept. 1996, 5, 7. See also Stuart E. Eizenstat, "The US Relationship with the EU and the Changing Europe," in Norman Levine (ed.), *The US and the EU: Economic Relations in a World of Transition* (Lanham, Mass.: University Press of America, 1996), 23–44; Stuart E. Eizenstat, "The United States and the IGC," *Challenge: IGC Intelligence Service*, Jan. 1996, 12–13; Reginald Dale, "Why Washington Wants a Strong EU," *International Herald Tribune*, 29 Nov. 1994, 9.

[29] Author's interviews with US ambassador to NATO Robert E. Hunter, 5 Feb. and 31 Oct. 1996. See also John Gerard Ruggie, *Winning the Peace: America and World Order in the New Era* (New York: Columbia University Press, 1996), 86–7.

[30] *Public Papers of the Presidents. George Bush, 1991*, 1418, 1427, 1591. The "European defence identity" was endorsed in point 22 in the communiqué from the Rome NATO meeting. The formulation read: "Other European institutions such

The Clinton administration was willing to go further. At the NATO meeting in Brussels in January 1994 the alliance members gave their

full support to the development of a European Security and Defence Identity which, as called for in the Maastricht Treaty, in the longer term perspective of a common defence policy within the European Union, might in time lead to a common defence compatible with that of the Atlantic Alliance. The emergence of a European Security and Defence Identity will strengthen the European pillar of the Alliance while reinforcing the transatlantic link and will enable European Allies to take greater responsibility for their common security and defence. The Alliance and the European Union share common strategic interests.[31]

Although the stronger formulation was in part due to the more determined input of the EU, it also reflected the change on the American side from Bush's traditional Cold War insistence on NATO's supremacy to Clinton's added focus on the Europeans doing more for their own defense. The most striking result of the administration's more positive attitude to European defense was the American proposal for Combined Joint Task Forces (CJTF) within NATO. The CJTF concept was first discussed by the NATO defense ministers in Travemünde, Germany in October 1993. It was endorsed in principle by the alliance in Brussels in January 1994 and spelled out in more detail and approved by the NATO members in Berlin in early June 1996.

CJTF meant that specifically designated forces from some (or all) of the NATO countries, or possibly even from the wider Partnership for Peace states (as is now being discussed), could be put together for operations, particularly outside the NATO area ("nonarticle 5 missions," in NATO parlance) while still drawing upon

as the EC, WEU and CSCE also have roles to play, in accordance with their respective responsibilities and purposes, in these fields. The creation of a European identity in security and defence will underline the preparedness of the Europeans to take a greater share of responsibility for their security and will help to reinforce transatlantic solidarity. However, the extent of its membership and of its capabilities gives NATO a particular position in that it can perform all four core security functions. NATO is the essential forum for consultation among the Allies and the forum for agreement on policies bearing on the security and defence commitments of its members under the Washington Treaty." See also Art, "Why Western Europe Needs the United States and NATO," 29–30.

[31] This is point 4 in the communiqué from the Brussels meeting. See also points 5–6 and 9.

NATO infrastructure. As the saying went, these forces would be "separable, but not separate" from NATO. In more understandable terms, under such an arrangement WEU forces could be put into action without any American contribution of troops, while still making use of NATO assets, such as command-and-control systems, and possibly even national assets such as US transport aircraft etc.[32]

The Clinton administration's more forthcoming attitude could be explained by the fact that the Cold War was now definitely over. Washington could then be more relaxed about the forms of European integration. The EU could do a useful job in integrating the Central and Eastern European countries in a democratic and market-oriented system. The administration's initial concentration on domestic affairs and its ensuing desire to take some of the traditional load off the United States certainly also counted. If America was to do less, and it was, it was natural to encourage the Europeans to do more. The American forces in Europe were to be reduced by an additional 50,000 to 100,000. In line with this the Clinton administration initially left most of the initiative in the complex situation in ex-Yugoslavia to the Europeans. This attitude was reinforced by the Republicans after they took control of both houses of Congress after the 1994 elections.[33]

In part the Clinton administration's flexibility reflected a desire to forestall even greater independence on the part of the EU/WEU. The administration was sympathetic to the WEU, especially after it came to clearly accept the supremacy of NATO. Washington was opposed to the WEU being fused with the EU. In Washington's own words, this could easily lead to European "caucusing" or "ganging up" against the United States. In practice it could also result in NATO guarantees being given to "neutral" EU countries that were not members of the WEU. (The United States still supported with "enthusiasm" membership for Sweden, Finland, and Austria in the EU, since the new and open orientation of these three

[32] Interviews with Robert E. Hunter. CJTF is mentioned in point 9 in the communiqué from the Brussels meeting. For the Berlin meeting, see Joseph Fitchett, "U.S. and Europe Clash over New NATO Roles," *International Herald Tribune*, 31 May 1996, 1, 10; Rick Atkinson, "NATO Broadens Combat Flexibility," *International Herald Tribune*, 4 June 1996, 1.

[33] Dale, "Why Washington Wants a Strong EU," 9; Stanley R. Sloan, "US Perspectives on NATO's Future," *International Affairs*, 71:2 (1995), 217–31.

countries could enable them to serve as US allies in liberalizing the EU's markets and trade.[34] The three countries entered the EU as of 1 January 1995, and made it the EU of the Fifteen. Norway again said no in a referendum.) If, on the other hand, all the EU members joined NATO, such a fusion of the EU and the WEU might be acceptable to Washington.[35]

Time and again even the Clinton administration emphasized the supreme role of NATO. In the words of Warren Christopher, "The first principle is that NATO is and will remain the anchor of America's engagement in Europe and the core of transatlantic security."[36] The administration's proposal, first, of a Partnership for Peace for all interested countries, including Russia, and, then, of full membership in NATO for at least some of the Central and Eastern European countries could also strengthen the American influence. The implication was that these countries would be admitted to American-dominated NATO before they entered the European Union.[37]

In reality it was difficult to foresee how any CJTF mission could be undertaken without American backing. Naturally NATO was to have first call on NATO resources if NATO wanted to undertake some action. If for some reason it did not want to do this and the WEU were then to act using NATO resources, the necessary decision would have to be taken by the NATO Council and the NATO chain of command had to be respected. Of course the US had full control over its national resources, such as transport aircraft. Since all this clearly meant many different forms of American approval, it was difficult to see how the Europeans could really act alone. In the more relaxed international climate the Europeans had great difficulties in building up their own national resources, such as satellites, transport aircraft, etc. In fact they were all reducing their defense forces considerably, and were therefore in some respects coming to rely even more on the Americans than before.[38]

---

[34] Gardner, *A New Era in US–EU Relations?*, 20–2, 32–9.
[35] Interviews with Robert E. Hunter.
[36] USIS, Christopher's speech, 1 Dec. 1994, 6.
[37] Madeleine Albright, "Enlarging NATO: Why Bigger is Better," *The Economist*, 15 Feb. 1997, 20.
[38] Philip H. Gordon, "'Europeanization' of NATO: A Convenient Myth," *International Herald Tribune*, 7 June 1996, 8; Art, "Why Western Europe Needs the United States and NATO," 30. See also *The Economist*, 25 Feb. 1995, 23–5; US

After the initial period of hesitation, it became increasingly clear that the United States certainly did not want to be left out of European decision-making. Sometimes a considerable discrepancy existed between what the administration said and what it actually did. This was best illustrated in the case of the former Yugoslavia. After having indicated that it would leave the solution of that conflict largely to the Europeans, Washington actually undercut the European peace effort in February 1993 by turning down the Vance–Owen plan which formed the heart of the European effort. The Clinton administration argued that the plan rewarded Serbian aggression and encouraged ethnic cleansing. In the summer of 1995 Washington took the lead itself in Yugoslavia both militarily and diplomatically, and, through the Dayton accords of November–December 1995, it was able to establish a framework for peace, one which with regard to the division of territory among Serbs, Croats, and Bosnians was not much different from the Vance–Owen plan. The administration had amply demonstrated that there could be no Europe-only solution to Europe's problems.[39]

On 5 December 1995, France proclaimed that it would be joining much of NATO's military structure again. This could be seen as a triumph for the United States, both in terms of a revenge on de Gaulle and of French recognition of a crucial role for the US in Europe even after the end of the Cold War. In return, however, Paris insisted on a stronger role for Europe, and for France, in NATO. The resulting disputes between the Clinton administration and the government of Jacques Chirac about the new command structure for NATO revealed a firm American position. America would not yield its hold on NATO's Southern Command, which supervises US ground forces in Bosnia and the sixth Fleet in the

Department of Defense, *United States Security Strategy for Europe and NATO* (June 1995), particularly 8–9; Luisa Vierucci, "The Role of the Western European Union in the Maintenance of International Peace and Security," *International Peacekeeping*, 2:3 (1995), 309–29; Cornish, "European Security," 751–69; Anand Menon, "Defence Policy and Integration in Western Europe," *Contemporary Security Policy*, 17:2 (1996), 264–83; author's interviews with Norwegian ambassador to NATO Leiv Mevik, 24 Aug. 1995, and Robert E. Hunter, 5 Feb. and 31 Oct. 1996.

[39] The peace effort in Yugoslavia is chronicled in David Owen, *Balkan Odyssey* (New York: Harcourt Brace, 1995). For an excellent review of some of the literature on this point, see Michael Ignatieff, "The Missed Chance in Bosnia," *The New York Review of Books*, 29 Feb. 1996, 8–10. Interview with Robert E. Hunter, 5 Feb. 1996.

Mediterranean. Washington was also skeptical of French–German satellite cooperation, at least in part for business reasons.[40]

On the economic side, Washington insisted that the markets of Eastern Europe be kept open for American goods and not more or less taken over by the West Europeans.[41] Under Clinton, too, numerous trade disputes disturbed relations between the United States and the European Union. These disputes concerned agriculture, as always, but also telecommunications; movie and television quotas; financial services; arms sales; US dislike of the EU's preferential trade agreements with former colonies, particularly the banana agreement; compensation to the US for the enlargement of the EU to include Austria, Finland, and Sweden; etc. Washington also signed "open skies" airline agreements with the separate countries, and not with the EU Commission as the latter wanted.[42] In 1996–7 the attempts by Congress, half-heartedly supported by the Clinton administration, to apply US economic sanctions against foreign companies, including European firms, doing trade with Cuba (the Helms–Burton Act) led to harsh comments from the European side. The same applied to Washington's attempts to apply sanctions against trade with Iran and Libya (the D'Amato Act). The Americans, on the other hand, objected to the EU's "critical dialogue" with Iran.[43]

However, with the significant exception of the extraterritoriality effects of the two acts, on the whole these economic disputes now played less of a role in determining the overall climate than they had done even under Bush. Despite considerable disagreement, especially between the United States and France, the US and the EU were able to complete the crucial Uruguay GATT round, thereby also establishing a new World Trade Organization (WTO). This fact overshadowed lingering disputes about various products, at least temporarily. And with Washington now concentrating on opening up the Japanese market, and to some extent even the

[40] Jim Hoagland, "The Uniting Europe Can Have Interests of its Own to Further", *International Herald Tribune*, 17 Oct. 1996, 10; Philip H. Gordon, "France Fully in NATO? Maybe Not," *International Herald Tribune*, 22 Nov. 1996, 8; Heuser, *Transatlantic Relations*, 90–104; Anne-Marie Le Gloannec, "Europe by Other Means?," *International Affairs*, 73:1 (1997), 83–98.

[41] Tom Buerkle, "U.S. Tells EU it Wants Eastern Europe Kept Open," *International Herald Tribune*, 26 Apr. 1995, 11.

[42] Gardner, *A New Era in US–EU Relations?*, 18–19, 39–43.

[43] Ibid. 92–7. See also Tom Buerkle, "A Stay in EU–U.S. Trade Spat," *International Herald Tribune*, 13 Feb. 1997, 12.

Chinese market, it could ill afford major disputes with the EU as well.[44] Despite Congress's ratification of the WTO and the North Atlantic Free Trade Area (NAFTA), Washington was also becoming less free-trade oriented, as could be witnessed in the follow-up negotiations to the GATT agreement between the US and the EU on the liberalization of services.

At first the Americans had not taken the prospects of a European monetary union very seriously. Even in Europe there was great uncertainty as to who would be able to live up to the strict criteria laid down at Maastricht and thereby qualify as members of EMU from the start in 1999. As the time for a common European currency approached, Washington and the American business community were waking up. The administration was "marginally positive" towards the EMU. The tentative conclusion appeared to be that despite the challenge the euro might come to represent to the dollar, the new currency could stimulate growth and thereby also further American economic interests.[45]

Christopher's speech on 2 June 1995, urging the development of "a broad-ranging transatlantic agenda for the new century," could be seen as the Clinton administration's attempt to reformulate the basic creed of cooperation and to develop a machinery of consultations even beyond that of the Transatlantic Declaration of 1990.[46] It led to the New Transatlantic Agenda, including the Joint US–EU Action Plan signed by Clinton, Spanish prime minister Felipe Gonzalez—on behalf of the European Council—and president Jacques Santer of the EU's Commission at the half-yearly US–EU summit in Madrid on 3 December.

There was one marked difference, however, between this New Transatlantic Agenda and Kennedy's, Kissinger's, and Baker's earlier initiatives. Now the Europeans, not the Americans, had clearly taken most of the lead. This had been done by Helmut Kohl as early as November 1992, and the German chancellor was quickly supported by many prominent EU politicians. The Europeans wanted to guard against the domestic emphasis of the Clinton administration after the end of the Cold War, the signs of the United States reducing its role in Europe, and Washington's apparent concen-

[44] Croome, *Reshaping the World Trading System*, 367–81.

[45] Gardner, *A New Era in US–EU Relations?*, 22–3; Henning, "Europe's Monetary Union and the United States," 84–5; Alan Friedman, "U.S. is Waking Up to EU Monetary Union," *International Herald Tribune*, 30 Sept. 1996, 1.

[46] USIS, Christopher's speech, 2 June 1995, 1.

tration on Asia.[47] The New Transatlantic Agenda committed the US and the EU to working together in about one hundred policy areas. The system of consultation was patterned after that of the EU's Common Foreign and Security Policy. It remained to be seen how effective the new scheme would prove.

The most striking new concept being discussed was the idea of a transatlantic free trade agreement (TAFTA), based on the model of the NAFTA agreement with Canada and Mexico. The Clinton administration first stated that it intended to give this idea "the serious study it deserves."[48] It faced serious obstacles, however: growing protectionism in the United States, Washington's new emphasis on the markets in Asia, divided opinions in Europe with France in particular being opposed, the unresolved relationship between such a vast free trade area and global trade liberalization. So, just a few months later, at the December 1995 summit, the free trade agreement was largely dropped in favor of a more loosely worded joint US–EU study "on ways of facilitating trade in goods and services and further reducing or eliminating tariff and non-tariff barriers."[49]

[47] For a fine account of the origins of the New Transatlantic Agenda, see Gardner, *A New Era in US–EU Relations?*, particularly 13–14, 61–8. See also United States Mission to the European Union, *US–EU: Facts and Figures* (Brussels, 1996), 13–15; Stephen Woolcock, "EU–US Commercial Relations and the Debate on a Transatlantic Free Trade Area," in Jarrod Wiener (ed.), *The Transatlantic Relationship* (London: Macmillan, 1996), 172–8.

[48] USIS, Christopher's speech, 2 June 1995, in particular 5 and 9.

[49] Woolcock, "EU–US Commercial Relations," 172–82; USIS, The New Transatlantic Agenda: Joint US–EU Action Plan, 3 Dec. 1995, 11; Tom Buerkle, "Free-Trade Talks Fail," *International Herald Tribune*, 31 Oct. 1995, 15; Calingaert, *European Integration Revisited*, 202–4.

10

WHAT DIFFERENCE DID US SUPPORT MAKE TO EUROPEAN INTEGRATION?

THE question of what difference the American attitude made to the development of European integration cannot be fully answered without going into the archives of the many countries involved in this process. This I have not done. Some tentative reflections may nonetheless be offered on the American role, reflections based on the existing literature, primarily American sources, and simple reasoning.

European integration developed for numerous reasons, certainly including many that had little or nothing to do with Washington's role.[1] With different forces all pulling in the same direction, it is difficult to isolate the American influence. Nevertheless, the combined facts that, on the one hand, a more or less continuous deepening and widening of European integration has taken place and, on the other, the United States supported this process, and rather strongly supported it until the 1960s, have led many historians to assume there was a connection between these two phenomena. For what we may call "traditionalists," the American impulse was a most important driving force—for a few of the traditionalists even the most important force behind European integration.[2]

---

[1] See references in Ch. 2 n. 1.

[2] These "traditionalists" are different from the traditionalists in the debate on the origins of the Cold War. In this debate both traditionalists and revisionists actually see a strong American influence on Western Europe. The first see this influence as largely beneficial; the latter view it much more negatively. For my own analysis of the Cold War debate, see *America, Scandinavia, and the Cold War*,

Traditionalist viewpoints of one kind or another dominate most general accounts of European integration. Van der Beugel and Ellwood offer clear-cut examples of traditionalism; more moderate versions are found in Vaughan, Urwin, and even Loth.[3] Among specialized studies of the United States and European integration, as reflected in accounts of specific periods or of American relations with specific countries, Camps, Rappaport, Melandri, Bossuat, Wall, Gillingham, Schwartz, and Schwabe may all be categorized as traditionalists.[4]

In an extraordinarily explicit traditionalist statement about the European Coal and Steel Community, Gillingham writes that "without American backing, the coal-steel negotiations would not have gotten off the ground; and, in fact, major U.S. intervention would subsequently save them from utter collapse."[5] In his most recent

particularly 7–35 and *The American "Empire,"* 11–29. On the other hand, among scholars in international relations it has been argued that the so-called (neo-) realists are generally "revisionist" in the sense that they emphasize the specific security considerations of each state. In their opinion, this, and not any American influence, was also really the basis for European integration. For this argument, see Featherstone and Ginsberg, *The United States and the European Union in the 1990s,* 16–25, 58–71.

[3] Van der Beugel, *From Marshall Aid to Atlantic Partnership,* passim; David W. Ellwood, *Rebuilding Europe: Western Europe, America and Postwar Reconstruction* (London: Longman, 1992), 168–72, 226–40; Vaughan, *Post-War Integration in Europe,* 1–10; Vaughan, *Twentieth-Century Europe,* 80–1, 152–4; Urwin, *The Community of Europe,* 12–25, 48–9, 60–7, 118–19. In the conclusion of his *Der Weg nach Europa,* Loth plays down the American influence rather more than his treatment of the American role in the rest of the book would seem to justify. For the conclusion, see 140; for his more general treatment of the United States, see particularly 37–43, 60–8, 76–84, 106–10.

[4] Camps, *European Unification in the Sixties,* 236–57; Armin Rappaport, "The United States and European Integration: The First Phase," *Diplomatic History,* Spring 1981, 121–49; Melandri, *Les États-Unis face à l'unification de l'Europe,* passim; Bossuat, *L'Europe occidentale à l'heure américaine,* particularly 305–16; Irving M. Wall, *The United States and the Making of Postwar France 1945–1954* (Cambridge: Cambridge University Press, 1991), particularly 192–204; Gillingham, *Coal, Steel, and the Rebirth of Europe,* 228–34, 264–6, 297–300, 340–2, 367–8; John Gillingham, "From Morgenthau Plan to Schuman Plan: America and the Organization of Europe," in Jeffery M. Diefendorf, Axel Frohn, and Hermann-Josef Rupieper (eds.), *American Policy and the Reconstruction of West Germany, 1945–1955* (Washington, DC: German Historical Institute, 1993), 111–33, particularly 132; Schwartz, *America's Germany,* particularly 187, 210–34, 298–301; Schwartz, "Victories and Defeats in the Long Twilight Struggle," 115–48, particularly 115–16; Schwabe, "The United States and European Integration," 115–36.

[5] Gillingham, "From Morgenthau Plan to Schuman Plan," 132.

analysis, Schwabe appears to argue that the American influence was predominant only until 1954. After the defeat of the EDC

The supranational ideal was discredited; the United States had lost much of its previous leverage and prestige as Europe was no longer dependent on American economic assistance and, under the auspices of detente, no longer felt immediately threatened by the Soviet Union. What we know of European integration today—the common market and the Brussels European Commission—was the result of European initiatives, Dutch and French in particular, rather than American nudges.[6]

Michael Hogan's position in his crucial *The Marshall Plan* is complex. With respect to the American influence, however, Hogan is rather traditionalist, as when he writes about the Schuman plan: "Although not the by-product of American initiative, the plan had been inspired in part by American policy and brought to fruition with the help of American intervention."[7]

In her recent *Eisenhower, Kennedy, and the United States of Europe*, Pascaline Winand gives a detailed presentation of the evolving American attitude, but she does not really offer many explicit comments on the importance this attitude had for the development of European integration as such. Still, the tone of her book is traditionalist. What she calls "the Euro-American intelligentsia for the uniting of Europe" was decisive on both sides of the Atlantic, and differences between the European and the American members of this intelligentsia were "somehow secondary."[8]

The traditionalist interpretation has thus received strong support on both sides of the Atlantic. What we may term the "revisionist" case can be seen as a European reaction against the traditionalist focus on the American role, although even most Europeans remain traditionalists.[9] European revisionism has been presented with the greatest vigor by Alan S. Milward. Milward sees the American influence as relatively unimportant both for European reconstruction, which is at the focus of attention in his *The Reconstruction of Western Europe 1947–51*, and for European integration. European

[6] Schwabe, "The United States and European Integration," 129.

[7] Hogan, *The Marshall Plan*, 378.

[8] Winand, *Eisenhower, Kennedy, and the United States of Europe*, pp. xiv–xv.

[9] A similar reaction against American-dominated interpretations, whether traditionalist, revisionist, or post-revisionist, can also be found in the debate on the origins of the Cold War. For a collection of European interpretations on this question, see Reynolds, *The Origins of the Cold War in Europe*.

integration as it actually developed was based not on American ideas, not even on the influence of the European "saints" (Monnet, Schuman, Adenauer, Spaak, etc.), but on practical, largely economic considerations in the various European nation states: "the process of integration was a Western European solution to a Western European problem . . ." The objective of this European process was not at all to replace the nation state, but rather, as the title of Milward's second major work in this field makes clear, *The European Rescue of the Nation-State*.

Furthermore, in Milward's analysis, the Americans were pro-integrationist only until 1958, and even from 1945 to 1958 their support was ineffective because it was too abstract-federalist and too defense-oriented. Washington was pushing for a federal Europe and for the EDC, and neither this federal Europe nor the EDC ever developed. Still, the United States had *some* influence, if only because the Europeans had to develop their own ideas in response to the American pressure: "without the drive of the United States to impose integration to suit its own strategic goals Western Europe would perhaps not have discovered its own different route to a settlement." (One might of course turn the tables on Milward and argue that even such *indirect* influence was important indeed.) Milward's general downplaying of the American influence seems more pronounced in *The Reconstruction of Western Europe 1947–51* than in *The European Rescue of the Nation-State*.[10] Although Milward is definitely in a minority among historians, his interpretation has received some support.[11]

We should keep in mind that the different positions of the historians concerned clearly depend not only on the nature of the specific topics they have analyzed, but also on their analytical starting

[10] Milward, *The Reconstruction of Western Europe*; Milward, *The European Rescue of the Nation-State*; Milward, "Conclusions: The Value of History." The quotations are from *The Reconstruction of Western Europe*, 502. See also ibid. 168–72, 320–34, 380–400, 465–77, 491–502.

[11] See the other contributions in Milward et al., *The Frontier of National Sovereignty*, particularly Romero's. See also Gunther Mai, "American Policy toward Germany and the Integration of Europe, 1945–1955," in Diefendorf, Frohn, and Rupieper, *American Policy and the Reconstruction of Germany, 1945–1955*, 85–109, particularly 96–8; Martin J. Dedman, *The Origins and Development of the European Union 1945–95: A History of European Integration* (London: Routledge, 1996), particularly 48–54; and even Richard T. Griffiths, "The European Historical Experience," in Middlemas, *Orchestrating Europe*, 1–70, particularly 3, where he sees "American hegemony theory" as quite outdated.

points. Thus, Milward is an economic historian and therefore tends to give weight to economic explanations, while I, like many others, will tend to highlight the importance of Great Power considerations, my own area of expertise. To some extent this is another version of the old debate of *Primat der Innenpolitik* versus *Primat der Aussenpolitik*. So, while appearing contradictory, the different perspectives can instead be seen at least in part as supplementary.[12]

It is easy to demonstrate that there were clear limits to the American influence on European integration. Thus, the United States was never able to develop the kind of cooperation it wanted in the OEEC. The EDC was defeated by France, despite the strong American threats to Paris. Initially at least, Washington was pushing for EURATOM while providing less leadership on the much more important and much more successful EEC. Britain could not be brought into the Community until after de Gaulle had left the scene. The widening and deepening of European integration that took place in the 1980s and 1990s happened in a period when both the US role in general and America's support for European integration had declined a great deal compared to the heyday of the 1950s and early 1960s.

Yet Milward clearly exaggerates the impractical nature of the American ideas, especially in the Truman years, thereby overstating the extent to which American and European versions of European integration were at odds with each other. True, many, particularly in the Eisenhower administration and in Congress, wanted to create a federal Europe on the American model, but this was clearly a long-term objective. Short-term objectives were much more limited. A pragmatic attitude almost always prevailed. This was evident from the very beginning, during the Marshall Plan discussions, as when acting secretary Robert Lovett told under-secretary William Clayton, "We are all here in agreement with you on the point that a customs union is a desirable long-term objective," but continued by stating "that to attempt to work it out now would bog Europe down in details and distract from the main effort."[13] Later under the Marshall Plan, the Truman administration did not even

---

[12] For an excellent review of Milward's books which stresses this very point, see Perry Anderson, "Under the Sign of the Interim," *London Review of Books*, 4 Jan. 1996, 13–17.

[13] *FRUS*, 1947: III, Secretary of State to the consulate in Geneva, 10 July 1947, 325. A similar conclusion had been drawn in the American debate on the loan to Britain in 1945–7. In his *Sterling-Dollar Diplomacy: The Origins and the Prospects*

propose to the Europeans the institution modeled after the US Interstate Commerce and Federal Trade Commission to which it had given such serious consideration. To override the jurisdiction of the separate states to enforce pro-competitive practices was simply too dramatic.[14] The overall recovery of Europe was the main effort.

Not even Congress was as enthusiastic in its support of European federation as is often believed. Thus, the Fulbright–Boggs Resolution of 1947 in favor of a United States of Europe was never brought to a vote; it was not even debated in Congress.[15] When the Truman administration felt that Congress had gone too far, it told the lawmakers that "it would not be feasible for most of them [the European states] at this time formally to accept political federation as their policy especially where it appeared to be under compulsion from us."[16]

Some key policymakers, such as secretary of state Dean Acheson, were lukewarm at best to the whole idea of a United States of Europe even at some indefinite point in the future. The objective was generally to promote "*greater* European economic and political unification" (emphasis mine). Acheson told his NATO colleagues that the United States was perhaps "more aware than we are given credit for, of the enormous obstacles of tradition, distinct national economies, etc."[17] When Washington on occasion showed its impatience with the European "national states" too clearly, one or more US ambassadors in Western Europe tended to intervene to "explain" the attitude in question.[18]

of our International Economic Order (New York: McGraw-Hill, 1969) Richard N. Gardner writes about this loan that "when it came to a choice, American opinion subordinated the immediate enforcement of multilateralism to the political and economic interests of the Western world" (345–6).

[14] Immanuel Wexler, *The Marshall Plan Revisited: The European Recovery Program in Economic Perspective* (Westport, Conn.: Greenwood, 1983), 157–8.

[15] Ferrell, "The Truman Era and European Integration," 34–7.

[16] *FRUS*, 1950: III, Acting Secretary Webb to the Secretary of State, 10 May 1950, 654.

[17] The quotations are from Cees Wiebes and Bert Zeeman, "Eine Lehrstunde in Machtpolitik," *Vierteljahrshefte für Zeitgeschichte*, July 1992, 421. See also Hogan, *The Marshall Plan*, 371, 429–30; John Lamberton Harper, *American Visions of Europe: Franklin D. Roosevelt, George F. Kennan, and Dean G. Acheson* (Cambridge: Cambridge University Press, 1994), 286–9.

[18] *FRUS*, 1950: III, Acting Secretary to certain diplomatic offices, 5 Oct. 1950, 674–5; ibid., Chargé Bohlen to the Secretary of State, 14 Oct. 1950, 676–8; ibid., Ambassador Douglas to the Secretary of State, 17 Oct. 1950, 678–81; ibid., Ambassador Murphy to the Secretary of State, 20 Oct. 1950, 681–2.

Under the Eisenhower administration Washington was clearly willing to push much harder for supranationalism in the form of the EDC. But after the threat of the "agonizing reappraisal" had failed to persuade the French, even this administration left more of the initiative with the Europeans.

My own position on the question of the American influence on European integration is rather traditionalist. However, I shall not primarily emphasize the effects of the American position on integration as such, important as that was at least through the early 1960s. Rather, I shall stress the great influence that flowed from the American role in Germany and from the more general position of the United States in Europe. While Europeans on the whole decided the forms European integration was to take, the United States could of course encourage some Europeans over others. And all Europeans had to take the overall role of the US into account.

Washington promoted European integration in three main ways. The first, and most obvious one, was by explicitly pushing the Europeans in the direction of integration. The second was by insisting, first, on the reconstruction of West Germany, and then on the equality of West Germany in European affairs. How could Germany be both equal and controlled at the same time? European integration was the obvious solution. The third way in which the United States promoted European integration was through its role as Europe's ultimate arbiter.[19] The Europeans could undertake their integration on the premise that the United States was the overall balancer in Europe in general and the guarantor against anything going seriously wrong in West Germany in particular. While most earlier studies of European integration have focused

---

[19] I generally prefer the term "arbiter" for the American role in Western Europe after 1945. Its connotation of "umpire" or "judge" may convey a meaning of too much objectivity on the part of the United States concerning Europe's affairs, but its meaning of "one who has supreme control" seems to be just the right one. For the definitions, see *New Webster's Dictionary and Roget's Thesaurus* (New York: Basic Books, 1992), 30. The term "pacifier" could also be used, but "pacify" also has the meaning of "appease" or "tranquilize," neither of which is right. For a good article using this term, see Josef Joffe, "Europe's American Pacifier," *Foreign Policy*, Spring 1984, 64–82. The most important way in which the United States kept the peace was by being the overall "balancer" in Europe against the Soviet Union, but also *vis-à-vis* West Germany. The US thus became the "guarantor" of European security. I am grateful to professor Douglas Eden for having discussed these terms with me.

only on the first two ways, I shall deal with all three, but especially with the last one.

First, it did of course matter that the United States, the leading Western power and also the leading power in Western Europe, pushed as hard for European integration as long as it did. The Europeans did not go so far as the Americans wanted, but they had to deal with a consistent American pressure to move towards integration. The OEEC and even the EPU fell short of Washington's expectations, but they strengthened the habit of cooperation in Western Europe and weakened protectionism. The crucial European initiatives, the ECSC, EURATOM, and the EEC, were taken against a background of American insistence that this was the direction in which Europe had to move. It is simply artificial, then, to conclude, as revisionists tend to do, that the American role was rather insignificant since the concrete initiatives to establish these organizations were primarily European.

The American influence was greatly enhanced by the fact that powerful forces in most of continental Europe shared the US objective. European integrationists both worked closely with the Truman and Eisenhower administrations and favored close ties with the US. This was most definitely the case with Jean Monnet in France, Konrad Adenauer in West Germany, Paul-Henri Spaak in Belgium, and the Dutch in general. The cooperation between these persons on the European side and, on the American side, equally crucial representatives such as John McCloy, David Bruce, John Foster Dulles, and for that matter, Dwight D. Eisenhower was frequently virtually symbiotic.

The importance of Monnet's very extensive network has been demonstrated time and again, in this study as elsewhere. Less frequently noted is the fact that Monnet became a committed European integrationist quite late in the course of events—in the spring of 1948—and that this happened under considerable American influence.[20] Gillingham, Schwartz, and Schwabe have indeed shown how the American influence on Adenauer was crucial at several points on the road leading to the ECSC and EURATOM. Spaak and the Dutch were reluctant to proceed with the ECSC and the EDC without Britain being included and, at least indirectly, the Americans being committed as well. Even the strongly pro-European foreign

---

[20] Roussel, *Jean Monnet*, 484–9; Milward, *The European Rescue of the Nation-State*, 335–7; Lankford, *The Last American Aristocrat*, 208–10, 220–3.

minister Johan Willem Beyen, who Milward has shown played such a fundamental role in working out the EEC, clearly appreciated the American support for European integration, although, after the EDC failure, he too encouraged a lower American profile.[21]

More concretely, I would argue that, despite the lower American profile after the defeat of the EDC, Washington had rather substantial direct influence on the overall process of integration until 1957–8. Thus, EURATOM could not have been established without Washington's strong backing. After 1958 the US had less influence on the overall process, although it could still affect important *elements* of the integration process, as was seen for instance in the British application for membership.

When in 1961 Britain finally decided to apply for membership in the EEC, the American attitude appears to have been one of the most important factors behind this reappraisal on Britain's part. London's plans for a free trade area and the establishment of EFTA had not met with the response Macmillan had hoped for, either in Washington or on the continent. The Kennedy administration favored the EEC and stressed Britain's need to accept the treaties of Rome. If it did join, however, London could work with Washington to provide stability and to open up the EEC more to the outside world. Macmillan's conclusion was that the "special relationship" with the US was probably better maintained inside the EEC than outside it.[22]

Although de Gaulle vetoed the British application, the American influence on important elements of the integration process continued. The most striking example was the way in which Bonn

[21] Gillingham, *Coal, Steel, and the Rebirth of Europe*, 231–4, 274–80, 297–300; Schwartz, *America's Germany*, 104–5, 134–42, 153, 187, 192–8, 202–3, 298–301; Schwabe, " 'Ein Akt konstruktiver Staatskunst,' " 228–39. For his most recent analysis, see Klaus Schwabe, "Do Personalities Make a Difference? Washington Working with Europeans," unpub. paper presented to the Commonwealth Conference, London University, 16–17 Feb. 1996. *FRUS*, 1955–7: IV, Chargé Durbrow to the Department of State, 17 June 1957, 300–1; ibid., Memorandum of conversation Merchant–van Voorst, 13 Dec. 1955, 364–5. For an analysis of Holland's and Beyen's role in the integration process, see also Milward, *The European Rescue of the Nation-State*, 173–96; Wiebes and Zeeman, "Benelux," in Reynolds, *The Origins of the Cold War in Europe*, 186–92.

[22] Kaiser, *Grossbritannien und die Europäische Wirtschaftsgemeinschaft*, 146–7, 186–92; Young, *Britain and European Unity*, 76–7; Storeheier, *US Policy towards the European Free Trade Association*, 116–22. In her early study Miriam Camps did not regard the American influence on Britain's decision as important. See her *Britain and the European Community 1955–1963* (Oxford: Oxford University Press, 1964), 336.

was forced in 1963 to emphasize Washington over Paris in the ratification of the Franco–German treaty. After the mid-1960s American influence declined further. Even then, however, the US maintained some influence over those elements that touched directly on America's own interests, whether these elements were the Atlantic framework for the EC/EU's foreign and security policy, various EC/EU economic directives, etc. And, as we shall soon see, America's more indirect influence as Europe's ultimate arbiter remained important long after the mid-1960s.

Occasionally the American influence could also be negative, in the sense that some Europeans also wanted to strengthen Europe vis-à-vis the United States. In 1956 the US thoroughly humiliated Britain and France, two of its most important allies, in the Suez affair. Particularly in France, the Suez humiliation magnified support for European integration, in part to make it easier for France and Europe to stand up even to the US.[23]

Although they wanted the two sides of the Atlantic to cooperate closely, in a more general sense it was probably also the desire of most European policymakers to strengthen Western Europe vis-à-vis the United States. This could be done economically by supporting the Common Market and politically by working more closely together on the European side.

Second, as we saw in Chapter 4, the effects of the American policy in Germany probably meant even more for European integration than did the formal American position on integration as such. Washington insisted that the western part of Germany be reconstructed. On this point London agreed on the whole. Together the Americans and the British established the Bizone in December 1946, incorporated the western zones of Germany in the Marshall Plan in July 1947, introduced currency reform in the three zones in June 1948, and convened a parliamentary council to set up the new West German state in September 1948.[24]

If this policy was not to disrupt Western Europe, the economic and political reconstruction of Germany had to be balanced with

---

[23] Pierre Guillen, "Europe as a Cure for French Impotence? The Guy Mollet Government and the Negotiation of the Treaties of Rome," in Ennio Di Nolfo (ed.), *Power in Europe? Vol. II: Great Britain, France, Germany and Italy and the Origins of the EEC, 1952–1957* (Berlin and New York: Walter de Gruyter, 1992), 513–16; Young, *Britain and European Unity*, 49–56. For a different emphasis, see Milward, *The European Rescue of the Nation-State*, 214–15.

[24] Eisenberg, *Drawing the Line*, particularly 485–6.

assistance and sympathy for France. The French complained incessantly that the western zones were rebuilt too quickly and that the Germans received too much from the US and they too little. Slowly Paris had to yield, although it always tried to get something in return. In a letter from Bidault to Marshall on 13 April 1948, the French foreign minister in fact told his American counterpart that French acceptance of a West German state depended on America's willingness to ally itself militarily with Western Europe.[25] The balance between Germany and France was clearly one major dimension both in the Marshall Plan and the formation of NATO, although Gimbel and Ireland exaggerate the importance of this dimension—Gimbel for the Marshall Plan, Ireland for NATO—at the expense of more traditional Cold War concerns.[26] In April 1949 NATO was formed; the Federal Republic was established in May.

Washington could do something to allay French fears about Germany, but with the country's continued reconstruction and rehabilitation Paris needed more direct control. The US strongly indicated that European integration was the way in which to solve the German problem. After London had failed to take the lead on this issue, the Truman administration instead began pushing the French to lead. There was no way around the reconstruction of Germany, economically, politically, and, ultimately, even militarily. Washington still left it to Paris to decide exactly *how* Germany's equality with other states was to be accomplished. Yet the answer seemed so obvious: European integration. Germany could then be equal with others and under control at the same time. Paris had hoped that the United States could in some mysterious way solve the German problem. Washington insisted, however, that the French had to do it. In May 1950, after considerable hesitation, Paris finally made the "plunge" in the form of the Schuman plan. This seemed to provide Paris with a semblance of control over its German problem.

The ECSC flowed from many sources. These certainly included the French desire to protect its privileged access to German coal.

---

[25] Soutou, "France," in Reynolds, *The Origins of the Cold War in Europe*, 106–7. See also Schwabe, "The Origins of the United States' Engagement in Europe," 174–5.

[26] Gimbel, *The Origins of the Marshall Plan*; Ireland, *Creating the Entangling Alliance*. For criticism of Gimbel, see my "Der Marshall-Plan und Osteuropa," in Othmar Nikola Haberl and Lutz Niethammer (eds.), *Der Marshall-Plan und die europäische Linke* (Frankfurt: Athenäum, 1986), 59–74.

In a way, the Schuman plan was to rescue the Monnet plan for the modernization of France.[27] In this context, however, it has to be stressed that the ECSC was formed in close cooperation with the United States. This applied both to the background of the French initiative, as described earlier, and to the detailed negotiations in 1950–2 on the formation of the community.

In the 1950s and early 1960s Washington continued to press for Germany's basic equality with other countries. The French had their doubts, particularly on the defense side, but for them too it became increasingly evident that security against Germany could best be provided by integrating it with its neighbors. The ECSC in turn set the pattern for future continental integration. It was to be supranational, based on the centrality of French–German cooperation, and, for more than two decades, exclude Great Britain and Scandinavia.

There can really be little doubt about the significance of Germany's position for European integration. No country had greater influence on West Germany than did the United States. Milward too recognizes the essential role of Germany in European integration when he writes that the single greatest problem of European interdependence has been political: the future of Germany, as in 1848, in 1864, in 1870, in 1914, and since 1933. "No European rescue of the nation-state was of any validity, unless it also offered a solution to this problem." And, Milward continues, "What, after all, was personal security for Europeans in 1945 without personal security against Germany?" The economic rescue of the nation state was only one dimension of European integration, as Milward himself so clearly recognizes in the quotation above, but makes so little allowance for in the rest of his analysis.[28]

Third, the discussion of Germany's position leads naturally to America's role as Europe's ultimate arbiter. The American position in the world after 1945 was stronger than that of any earlier Great Power. Naturally, this position was particularly strong within the American sphere of influence, which certainly included Western Europe. Thus, one would tend to expect a considerable degree of American influence on European integration as well. More concretely, with the kind of pre-eminent position the United States

---

[27] Milward, *The Reconstruction of Western Europe*, 474–7; Lynch, "Resolving the Paradox of the Monnet Plan," 242.

[28] Milward, *The European Rescue of the Nation-State*, 44–5.

had in several European countries, including the crucial nation of Germany, at least through the 1950s, it is difficult to believe that European integration could actually have taken place without American backing.[29]

The balancing of Germany in Europe, and of Japan in Asia for that matter, was one of America's most important functions within its "empire." The United States was not only to contain the Soviet Union; it was also to contain Germany and even to provide a framework for peaceful developments in Western Europe in general. This was the backdrop against which European integration took place.

History cannot be played backwards and there are many problems with counterfactual history. Yet, the effective way in which West Germany was integrated in European politics, compared with the preceding eighty years of Franco–German conflict, clearly suggests, although it does not prove, the centrality of the American role. When we consider France's traumatic experience with the EDC and German rearmament, one can imagine many different horror scenarios as to how Western Europe would have handled the German problem without the American involvement.

Again, this wider role for the United States is one which Milward appears to admit that the US did indeed play, but he seems to think it relevant only for the Atlantic path of integration, not for the European one as well.[30] Although there is certainly something to this, as witnessed by the fact that defense integration was to take place primarily within the Atlantic framework, Milward's distinction is too simple. The United States was *a*, sometimes *the* central actor in European politics, and European integration occurred within the American–Atlantic framework. European and Atlantic integration were not two separate worlds; they were in fact closely connected.

The fact that in the end the French did make the "plunge" on European integration brings up the question of why they now felt that they could do so. The French hand was certainly forced by the events in Germany and by the pressure from Washington. Yet, without the risk being manageable in some way, Paris still might not have agreed to the full reconstruction of Germany, much less taken the crucial first steps on the road to European integration.

---

[29] Lundestad, *The American "Empire,"* particularly 39–54; Schwartz, *America's Germany,* particularly 298–301.

[30] Milward, *The European Rescue of the Nation-State,* 425–6, 431, 444.

When Schuman launched his Coal and Steel Initiative, the French still hoped to include Britain, but they were clearly prepared to proceed without it. They also wanted to enhance the American position in Europe further, at least through a stronger role in the OEEC.[31] When Pleven proposed the EDC, Britain was expected to remain outside, although the British forces in Germany could help in the control of Germany. Nevertheless, the French did proceed even on defense, admittedly rather hesitantly, but proceed they did. In a deeper sense it may be argued that the French initiatives represented a shift in the French focus, away from the United Kingdom and to the United States.

With the strong American role in Europe, which was similar to the role the French had wanted the United States to play even after the First World War, and with NATO not only in place, but also becoming an integrated organization after the outbreak of the Korean War, the United States was clearly the ultimate guarantor in case anything should go wrong with the integration of Germany.[32] The ECSC was established. EURATOM and the EEC were to follow.

On the defense side the risks were higher and France was even more divided than on the economic side. Germany had to be controlled, but what if the Germans came to dominate even the European organization that was to be set up to control them? As early as December 1950 defense minister Pleven and foreign minister Schuman indicated that their EDC project might have to develop closer ties to NATO to get it through the French national assembly.[33] This was clearly a sign that France was already doubting that it would be able to control West Germany in the EDC, particularly when Washington would not permit Paris to discriminate as strongly against West Germany as was obvious in the initial French plan.

The fact that in the final EDC agreement the connection with Britain and even with the United States and NATO did not become as close as some French Socialists and even centrists wanted was indeed one element in the ultimate rejection of the EDC by the

---

[31] Edmund Dell, *The Schuman Plan and the British Abdication of Leadership in Europe* (Oxford: Oxford University Press, 1995), 110–70; *FRUS, 1950: III*, Acheson to the Acting Secretary of State, 16 May 1950, 659–60.

[32] Duchêne, *Jean Monnet*, 204–5. See also Joffe, "Europe's American Pacifier," 64–82; Uwe Nerlich, "Western Europe's Relations with the United States," *Daedalus*, Winter 1979, 87–111.

[33] *FRUS, 1950: III*, Spofford to the Secretary of State, 2 Dec. 1950, 512.

French national assembly. After a meeting with the French prime minister before the EDC vote in the national assembly on 30 August 1954, Churchill told Dulles that Mendès-France was really much keener about NATO than about the EDC since France would not want to be boxed up alone with a more active and powerful West Germany, "whereas in the NATO system, the UK and US counterbalance Germany to proper proportions." Then, when NATO and the Americans were brought in more directly, the French national assembly did, still reluctantly, consent to German rearmament through NATO and the WEU.[34]

While the United States could remain more in the background on the economic and political sides, it had to be brought in directly on the defense side. It appears unlikely that the French would have played the role they did in the 1950s, but also later, without the United States having been there both to insist on West Germany's rearmament and to serve consistently as the ultimate guarantor in case anything should go wrong in Germany.

In the perspective of the United States as the guarantor against Germany and arbiter in Europe, Charles de Gaulle seems to represent a special case. True, de Gaulle was strongly opposed to supranationality, but the paradox in his position was that he favored close European cooperation based on the Paris–Bonn axis but with a minimum of ties to the United States, Britain, and NATO. How, then, was Germany to be controlled if anything went wrong? Kissinger, with his keen understanding of *realpolitik*, commented thus to de Gaulle after having heard the French president develop his views on Europe: "I do not know how the President will keep Germany from dominating the Europe he has just described." De Gaulle simply responded: "Par la guerre" (through war).[35]

So, it would appear that the direct relationship between European integration and the need for the United States to balance Germany can be overstated. De Gaulle's attitude would seem to show, if proof were needed, that it was possible to pursue forms of European integration without basing them on an explicit Atlantic framework.

[34] Fursdon, *The European Defence Community*, 292; Dedman, *The Origins and Development of the European Union*, 74–5, 80–2, 87–8; Wilfried Loth, "The French Socialist Party, 1947–1954" and Denis Lefebvre, "The French Socialist Party, 1954–1957," both in Richard T. Griffiths (ed.), *Socialist Parties and the Question of Europe in the 1950's* (Leiden: E. J. Brill, 1993), 36–42 and 43–6 respectively.
[35] Kissinger, *White House Years*, 110.

In the new Europe from the Atlantic to the Urals which de Gaulle allegedly wanted to create, Germany could be controlled by France in cooperation with the Soviet Union. Yet this was at best a vision for the long-term future even for de Gaulle. In the foreseeable future, his rhetoric notwithstanding, de Gaulle did not actually want to push the United States out of Europe. In their opposition to the EDC, de Gaulle and his Gaullists in fact supported a German contribution to NATO. The general made this point in a letter to Washington in January 1951.[36] While in his opinion supranationality and American domination were wrong, there was nothing wrong with the American military association with Europe, in the form of the NATO guarantee as such and American atomic weapons and troops on European, though not on French, soil.

To de Gaulle the American threat to France was primarily economic and cultural, although he supported the Marshall Plan. The American role in Europe represented a form of hegemony, but the general called it a "protective hegemony." The security threat came from the Soviet Union. In good times the need for the American presence declined. When the Soviet threat was most evident, de Gaulle clearly stressed the importance of the American role in Europe. This had been the case in 1945–6 when the Soviet domination of Eastern Europe became even more direct than he had expected and it was to happen again after the Soviet invasion of Czechoslovakia in 1968.[37]

In the end, then, and perhaps to de Gaulle as well, the United States *was* the ultimate balancer in Europe. True, in his analysis the Americans were to balance primarily the Soviets, but, once here, they would also handle the Germans. De Gaulle did not press for

---

[36] Aimaq, *For Europe or Empire?*, 190.

[37] For contemporary American analyses of de Gaulle, see *FRUS*, 1961–3: XIII, Telegram from Bohlen to the State Department, 16 Feb. 1963, 758–60; NA, POL FR-US, Memorandum from Read to McGeorge Bundy, Talking points paper for the president's meeting with Couve de Murville, 1–2, 6; NA, POL FR-US, Memorandum from Bohlen to the Secretary of State, 13 Dec. 1963. For de Gaulle's fears in 1945, see NA, 751.00/5-1245, Telegram from Matthews to Dunn, 1–3. For later historical analyses, see Conze, "Hegemonie Durch Integration?," 307; Lacouture, *De Gaulle. The Ruler: 1945–1970*, 61–3, 363–86, 471–4; Bozo, *Deux stratégies pour l'Europe*, 198–212; Stanley Hoffmann, *Decline or Renewal? France since the 1930s* (New York: Viking, 1974), 308, 310, 312, 350–1, 356–7; Soutou, "France," particularly 98, 100–4; Camilla Elisabeth Lund, "Changing Perceptions of the National Interest in Economic and Defence Policy under Mitterrand, 1981–1989" (Cambridge University Ph.D. diss., 1995), 1–13.

the Americans to leave Germany, only France. If, on the other hand, the United States should really end up leaving Europe, as the general frequently implied but as he probably feared, and as the US had done after the First World War, then it would be best to have the European integrative structure in place before that happened. It might be too late to create it after the Americans had left.

In 1963 de Gaulle had vetoed British membership in the EEC because he felt the "Anglo-Saxon" influence would be too strong at the expense of France. The implicit assumption was that on the economic-political level at least France could still control Germany. Nevertheless, with West Germany's economic strength and political confidence growing, French fears increased. The loss of power of the Christian Democrats in the 1969 elections and the coming to power of the Social Democrats under Willy Brandt (in coalition with the Free Democrats) was significant in this context. The German *Ostpolitik* was viewed with concern not only in Washington, but certainly also in Paris. De Gaulle had just retired when Brandt took over in Germany so it was for his successor, Georges Pompidou, to draw the conclusion from these developments. At the EC Hague summit in 1969 Pompidou agreed to let Britain in and enlarge the EC in return for reforms of the CAP and new initiatives towards monetary union and political coordination. This could all be seen as a way of balancing Germany's enhanced influence.[38]

It is beyond the scope of this study to analyze in any detail the American policy on German unification in the 1940s and 1950s. Formally Washington supported the unification of the western and the eastern parts. In the context of German public opinion it could hardly do otherwise. Even at the level of *realpolitik* it was difficult to foresee exactly the consequences of a permanent division of Germany.

At the practical level, however, the United States did little or nothing to bring about unification. It concentrated entirely on the reconstruction and integration of West Germany. When one considers how laborious this task was, one can imagine how hard the integration of a united Germany would have been. In her recent book Carolyn Eisenberg has argued that US actions "divided

---

[38] Dedman, *The Origins and Development of the European Union*, 119–21; Bozo, *Deux stratégies pour l'Europe*, 171–2, 194, 198–208; Urwin, *The Community of Europe*, 137–40.

Germany." It can be argued with equal force, however, that the actions of France and the Soviet Union, and even of Britain, also divided the country. The Soviet Union controlled the smallest part of the country and would therefore have more reason to support unification, but the policies Moscow actually pursued in the eastern zone undermined any such course. From 1955 the Soviet Union, alone among the occupying powers, openly advocated a two-Germany policy.[39]

If Germany were to be unified, in Washington's opinion this had to take place on Western terms. The united Germany had to be democratic and it had to be free to join the Atlantic and European structure of integration. This was clearly reflected in the American response to the Soviet note of March 1952. And, as high commissioner McCloy told Adenauer, "the Allies would not abandon their powers only to find the Federal Republic taking a neutral position." In the end Washington was quite pleased, as was probably Adenauer, that it only had to deal with the challenge of West Germany, not of a united Germany.[40]

The role of the United States as the ultimate arbiter in Europe remained important long after the American support for integration as such had begun to weaken. The changes in European politics in connection with Germany's eventual unification in 1990 would seem to bear this conclusion out.

Both Britain's Margaret Thatcher and France's François Mitterrand were clearly skeptical of Germany's unification. The two of

[39] In *Drawing the Line* Eisenberg demonstrates the American insistence on reconstructing the western zones of Germany. Whether this, more or less alone, "divided Germany," as she insists, is more debatable. For a more balanced approach, see Melvyn P. Leffler, *The Struggle for Germany and the Origins of the Cold War* (Washington, DC: German Historical Institute, 1996), particularly 71–7. For Soviet policies, see Norman M. Naimark, *The Russians in Germany: A History of the Soviet Zone of Occupation, 1945–1949* (Cambridge, Mass.: Harvard University Press, 1995).

[40] Schwartz, *America's Germany*, 237, 264–6, 282–4. Occasionally Adenauer's lack of interest in German unification could be expressed with rather surprising bluntness. On 17 March 1960, Herter thus reported to Eisenhower that the chancellor had made it clear to him that he (Adenauer) "had no interest in bringing East Germany into reunification with West Germany at all. He said that reunification is not practicable, and referred to the Socialist voting strength in East Germany." For this, see *FRUS*, 1958–60: IX, Memorandum of conversation with Eisenhower, 17 Mar. 1960, 239. For a recent analysis in the German literature on unification, see Wolfram F. Hanrieder, *Deutschland, Europa, Amerika: Die Aussenpolitik der Bundesrepublik Deutschland 1949–1994* (Paderborn: Ferdinand Schöningh, 1995), 151–74.

them tried to find common ground on this crucial transformation in European politics. As Mitterrand explained, at times of great danger France and Britain had always established special relations. "Such a time had come again." However, they could come up with no real alternative and therefore had to flow with the dramatic events.[41]

Only the United States, among the four old occupying powers in Germany, wholeheartedly supported chancellor Helmut Kohl's ever more rapid timetables on unification. President Bush agreed to the hectic pace in part to reduce Soviet leverage on the process, but the choice of strategy probably also made it easier for the United States to secure its most important objectives in Germany. As always, these related to the position of the United States in Europe and the protection of the Atlantic framework: "NATO remained; American troops and nuclear weapons stayed in Europe; and German power continued to be tightly integrated into the postwar structures." Suggestions for the neutralization of all or parts of Germany were rejected. Even the former East Germany was to belong to NATO, although special limitations would apply on the Allied presence there.[42]

The United States was the balancer of the whole process. As Elizabeth Pond has argued, the United States played a crucial role by reassuring Moscow that its "security interests would not be impaired," reassuring "Germany's neighbors that the United States would be on hand as a counterweight to ascendant German power," and uttering "some hard truths about the need for NATO's continuance that the British and the French, by their resistance to unification, had disqualified themselves from saying."[43] In this process, Paris and even Moscow came to agree that the American presence in Europe had a stabilizing function, although they of course disagreed with Washington on many aspects of this presence.[44]

[41] Thatcher, *The Downing Street Years*, 792–9. For a superior study of Germany's unification, although viewed primarily from Washington, see Philip Zelikow and Condoleezza Rice, *Germany Unified and Europe Transformed: A Study in Statecraft* (Cambridge, Mass.: Harvard University Press, 1995).

[42] Zelikow and Rice, *Germany Unified and Europe Transformed*, particularly 147, 160, 165–72, 176, 180, 186–7, 195–6, 207, 211, 214–15, 277–9, 340–2, 368–9. The quotation is from 368.

[43] Elizabeth Pond, *Beyond the Wall: Germany's Road to Unification* (Washington, DC: Brookings, 1993), 164.

[44] Zelikow and Rice, *Germany Unified and Europe Transformed*, 170–1, 205–7, 236–8, 276–8, 300.

Germany's unification had rather immediate effects on French policy. Paris concluded that the new unified Germany had to be even more closely bound up with Europe than before. Kohl, the European federalist, readily agreed. Thus, Germany's unification was undoubtedly one very important factor behind the Maastricht Treaty.[45] France also not only moved closer to Britain and to the United States, but has now resumed its seat on NATO's Military Committee and on several other military bodies.

A great paradox surfaced in French policy. When the Cold War was finally over and the division of Europe had been ended—in other words when de Gaulle's vision of a Europe from the Atlantic to the Urals had actually come true—France had not triumphed. On the contrary, it went back into NATO. True, this was to be a reformed NATO with greater emphasis on the importance of the European defense identity. The French shift still indicated that while the Gaullist rhetoric during the Cold War may in many ways be seen as "revolutionary," France's real desires were rather more oriented to the status quo. In a Europe from the Atlantic to the Urals Germany would most likely be unified. This was certainly no deep desire in France. Instead Germany's unification was to provide the main, though far from the only, explanation for France's rather surprising partial reintegration into NATO.[46]

Thus, it can be argued that even today the United States appears to be the ultimate arbiter of European politics. The unification of Germany provides only one example of this, although a rather dramatic one. Developments in the former Yugoslavia provide another, as we have already seen. A third would be the considerable control the United States has exercised over the process of NATO expansion from the Partnership for Peace idea to the current preparations for the admission of the first three Central European states into NATO.

[45] Middlemas, *Orchestrating Europe*, 156–79; Michael J. Baun, *An Imperfect Union: The Maastricht Treaty and the New Politics of European Integration* (Boulder, Colo.: Westview Press, 1996), 92–7. See also Baun's "The Maastricht Treaty as High Politics: Germany, France and European Integration," *Political Science Quarterly*, 1995–6:4, 605–24; Zelikow and Rice, *Germany Unified and Europe Transformed*, 234–5, 365.

[46] This argument was probably first presented by Stanley Hoffmann. Here it is based in part on Lund, "Changing Perceptions," 1–13, 186–232. See also Art, "Why Western Europe Needs the United States and NATO," 1–39. Other reasons for the reintegration of France into NATO are the French experiences in the Gulf War and in Bosnia, the need to reduce defense spending substantially, the transformation of NATO, the new European defense identity within NATO, etc.

Much more vaguely, on the global scale, the maintenance and further growth of the Western liberal-democratic order, as seen in the so-called "third wave" of democratic rule and many new free trade areas, can also be interpreted as signs of enduring American strength, despite such phenomena of course having many and complex explanations. Today the United States is the only remaining superpower, although it has still declined in certain respects compared to its heyday in the first twenty years after 1945.[47]

---

[47] For my own analysis of the debate about America's possible decline, see my *The American "Empire,"* particularly 85–115. For the "third wave" of democracy. see Samuel P. Huntington, *The Third Wave: Democratization in the Late Twentieth Century* (Norman, Okla.: University of Oklahoma Press, 1991). For the order underlying today's apparent "chaos," see G. John Ikenberry, "The Myth of Post-Cold War Chaos," *Foreign Affairs*, May/June 1996, 79–91.

11

WHY WAS THERE NOT MORE ATLANTIC INTEGRATION?

....

O NE may ask why, if the Atlantic framework was so important to Washington as well as to most European capitals, even more integration did not take place at this Atlantic level. Similarly, if the point was to make absolutely certain that the German influence would be securely balanced, then the most logical conclusion would have been to work for Atlantic, not simply European, integration.

To answer this question, it is important to remember that Atlantic integration did indeed take place through the OEEC–OECD, through the GATT reductions in tariffs, and most important, through NATO. This *was* the essential framework into which European integration was to be fitted, and was indeed fitted.

In the United States there was considerable talk about Atlantic integration going far beyond the OEEC–NATO dimension. An Atlantic Union Committee existed, with senator Estes Kefauver as the main driving force. Throughout the 1950s resolutions were presented in Congress in favor of exploring an Atlantic "union." In the fall of 1951 Kefauver had 28 collaborators in the Senate and 110 in the House on such a resolution. Yet the resolution was never even brought to a hearing, much less a vote. The immediate reason was the rush of more important events in Korea and Europe.[1]

The deeper reason was that neither the Truman nor the Eisenhower administration actually supported the Atlantic union resolutions. In fact, Acheson and Dulles—the latter had been involved

---

[1] Wesley T. Wooley, *Alternatives to Anarchy: American Supranationalism since World War II* (Bloomington, Ind.: Indiana University Press, 1988), 119–20.

in the early work of the Committee—both warned that an American proposal for Atlantic federation would undermine the more immediate objective of bringing about greater integration in Europe. Union Committee appeals to the presidents to overrule their secretaries of state did not help much. Eisenhower in particular emphasized that nothing was to be done which could disturb the further progress of European integration.[2]

In 1959 the State Department withdrew its opposition to the Atlantic resolution. It was then actually passed by the Senate (51 to 44) and the House (288 to 103). This change could be seen as reflecting Washington's increased emphasis on the Atlantic framework to European integration after de Gaulle had come to power. Even more, however, it reflected a combination of Christian Herter, a committed "Atlanticist," having taken over as secretary of state from Dulles; of Senate majority leader Lyndon B. Johnson showing an interest in improving his foreign policy credentials before the 1960 election; and of the very innocuous wording of the 1959 resolution, a wording which made it more broadly acceptable than earlier resolutions. Thus, this resolution contained no reference to federalism. An Atlantic convention of private citizens was simply to "explore means by which greater cooperation and unity of purpose may be developed to the end that democratic freedom may be promoted by economic and political means." Nothing of any substance came out of this.[3]

The deepest reason for the failure of Atlantic integration in general and the Atlantic Union Committee in particular was quite simply that there was virtually no interest in the United States in anything that would reduce American sovereignty. While most Americans saw it as highly desirable that the Europeans abandon old notions of sovereignty, the same clearly did not apply to the United States. In September 1952 David Bruce, at the time undersecretary of state, commented that "While urging others to surrender sovereignty, the US is unwilling to do so itself."[4] Even for many members of the Atlantic Union Committee it was rather unclear what "union" meant. Many of those who actually favored some sort of supranational arrangement gave the US such a com-

---

[2] Ibid.; Winand, *Eisenhower, Kennedy, and the United States of Europe*, 196–7.
[3] Wooley, *Alternatives to Anarchy*, 130–1; Winand, *Eisenhower, Kennedy, and the United States of Europe*, 196–8.
[4] *FRUS*, 1952–4: VI. 1, Summary minutes of the chiefs of mission meeting, London, 24–6 Sept. 1952, 655.

manding position in the voting formula drawn up for the union that it would not have meant much loss of sovereignty after all.[5]

As with the British arguments against European integration, the American ones against Atlantic integration represented an apparent mixture of internationalism and nationalism. The Atlantic area was both too small and too big for integration. On the one hand the United States had global interests and could not give too exclusive a priority to Europe over other parts of the world. On the other hand the US would not give up any real sovereignty to anyone under any circumstance.

President Kennedy presented his largely internationalist version of this mixture when he told Congress, with respect to his ideas for Atlantic cooperation, that he was *not* proposing that America join the Common Market, and thereby "alter our concepts of national sovereignty, establish a 'rich man's' trading community, abandon our traditional most-favored nation policy, create an Atlantic free-trade area, or impair in any way our close economic ties with Canada, Japan, or the rest of the free world."[6]

The more nationalist side of the argument was succinctly summed up by McGeorge Bundy, when he stated that any real Atlantic union was "still constitutionally and psychologically out of range for the people of the United States."[7] It was unthinkable for most Americans to go much beyond the OEEC–NATO model of Atlantic integration. A true Atlantic union, as an alternative to an integrated Europe cooperating closely with the United States, was out of the question.

As the history of US foreign relations clearly indicates, even with its dominant position after 1945 the United States could only take part in international cooperation on an inter-governmental basis. If an organization had elements of supranationality, as for instance the United Nations had in theory, then the United States insisted on having a veto. As witnessed in the UN Military Staff Committee talks in 1946–7, the US insisted on American troops remaining under American control.[8] The mere suspicion of supranationality

---

[5] Wooley, *Alternatives to Anarchy*, 124–5.

[6] *Public Papers of the Presidents. John F. Kennedy*, 1961, 782.

[7] Winand, *Eisenhower, Kennedy, and the United States of Europe*, 196–8; US Department of State, *Bulletin*, 12 Mar. 1962, 423.

[8] Jonathan Soffer, "All for One and One for All: The UN Military Staff Committee and the Contradictions within American Internationalism," *Diplomatic History*, Winter 1997, 45–69.

could prevent Congressional approval. Despite the efforts, first, of the Truman and, then, of the Eisenhower administration, Congress refused to ratify respectively the International Trade Organization (ITO) and the Organization for Trade Cooperation (OTC) to administer GATT.[9] When NATO in fact developed supranational features, as on the strategy side, Washington took it for granted that American strategy would also constitute NATO strategy. When Washington adopted "massive retaliation," NATO quickly followed; when Washington then moved on to "flexible response," NATO, after some delay, did the same.[10]

Even today, when the United States has become so much more economically dependent on the outside world than it used to be, few countries are as sovereignty-conscious as the United States. (Perhaps the recent surge in unilateralism can in fact be seen at least in part as a reaction against this new fact of interdependence.) Washington's attitude, especially that of Congress, both to the UN (membership dues, American troops fighting under foreign commands, etc.) and to the WTO (enforcing rulings against the US) illustrates the point.[11]

So the United States pushed European integration for the Europeans, though in an Atlantic framework, not really Atlantic integration for both Europe and the United States. Atlantic union was, however, precluded not only because of the American attitude. The Europeans did not want to go anywhere as far as a union in their support of Atlantic cooperation, either. Britain often used Atlantic-oriented language, but it had no desire to make even Atlantic cooperation supranational. London kept balancing its three circles of interest, the United States, Europe, and the Commonwealth, even after some preference was given to the European circle when in 1961 Britain applied for membership in the EEC. A "special relationship" with the United States was one thing; giving up sovereignty

---

[9] The question of US sovereignty was far from the only issue in these rejections, but it was certainly part of the picture. For a short study of this, see Wendy Asbeek Brusse, "The Americans, GATT, and European Integration, 1947–1957: A Decade of Dilemma," in Heller and Gillingham, *The United States and the Integration of Europe*, 221–49, particularly 229–30, 241–3.

[10] For the changes in NATO strategy, see Stromseth, *The Origins of Flexible Response*; Haftendorn, *NATO and the Nuclear Revolution*.

[11] For a fine short article, among an almost endless number of others, on the recent mood in America, see Martin Walker, "The New American Hegemony," *World Policy Journal*, Summer 1996, 13–21. For a longer study, see Ruggie, *Winning the Peace*.

to a far bigger country was something entirely different.[12] In Europe Britain could hope to play a leading role. It could hardly do the same *vis-à-vis* the United States.

On the continent the Dutch were the most Atlantic-oriented. They strongly supported both the Marshall Plan and the creation of NATO, and while they also favored European integration they wanted to link this firmly with the wider Atlantic framework. Thus, until Washington came round to support the EDC, the Dutch government only participated in these negotiations as observers. Even for the Hague, however, the important thing was to work closely with Britain and the United States, not to promote a high degree of Atlantic integration. When the more European-oriented Johan Willem Beyen replaced Atlanticist Dirk Stikker as foreign minister in 1952, Beyen and Belgium's Paul-Henri Spaak in turn came to take the initiatives which were to lead to the treaties of Rome. The new course did not conflict with the Atlantic framework, but the emphasis was now more on Europe.[13]

In France Georges Bidault in particular was highly sympathetic to the Atlantic framework, but even his emphasis was on France playing a leading role in NATO, not on Atlantic integration in any supranational form, at least not for France. The French plans for a tripartite directorate in NATO go back to 1949, long before de Gaulle.[14] From 1950 European integration was France's main concern. For one thing, since an Atlantic form of integration had to be rather loose, Germany could never be as closely bound up here as it could under the European form. For another, obviously France could lead only under a European formula. In the Atlantic setting France was easily relegated to a secondary, if not a tertiary role. This de Gaulle clearly understood and he therefore took France out of NATO's military structure.

In Germany Ludwig Erhard had an Atlantic-oriented attitude on trade, but for Adenauer and Kohl in particular it was essential to combine the American security guarantee with French–German reconciliation. The integration which could give Germany the equality it craved could in practice only take place through European, not Atlantic integration.

---

[12] Charmley, *Churchill's Grand Alliance*, 248–51.

[13] For a good short account of the policies of the Benelux countries, see Wiebes and Zeeman, "Benelux."

[14] Pierre Melandri's comment in Paxton and Wahl, *De Gaulle and the United States*, 221; Schwartz, *America's Germany*, 251–2.

The Atlantic framework was crucial to European integration as it actually developed. What would have happened if this framework had not been in place? To introduce an intriguing counterfactual note, John Foster Dulles, certainly one of the strongest American proponents of European integration, actually stated in a reflective moment that "it is possible that the historian may judge that the Economic Recovery Act and the Atlantic Pact were the two things which *prevented* a unity in Europe which in the long run may be more valuable than either of them" (emphasis mine).[15]

By establishing the Marshall Plan and NATO, the United States allegedly did the job for Western Europe. As a result, Western Europe had to transform itself much less radically than would otherwise have been the case. Dulles's implication was that if the United States had not intervened, Western Europe could have created the United States of Europe which he so strongly desired.

Of course, no one can tell what would have happened if the United States had not played the role it actually did. History is what has happened; it cannot be played backwards. This book, like history writing in general, has attempted to describe what happened and explain why it happened. Still, by way of counterfactual speculation, there is reason to doubt Dulles's argument. I have seen little evidence that European leaders thought a dramatically reduced American role would have brought about greater European integration. Several European complaints can, however, be found about the United States not pushing European integration even harder than it did. Thus, in 1954 Spaak blamed the US for not having done enough to push European integration *vis-à-vis* the Europeans. The Americans "had missed a golden opportunity when at the outset of the Marshall Plan they did not make all Marshall aid contingent upon the creation of a unified political community in Europe."[16]

I have implied here that without the American role and the Atlantic framework, it is more likely that history would have repeated itself, in the sense that the traditional rivalry among the West European states, especially between Germany and France,

[15] Lawrence S. Kaplan, *The United States and NATO: The Formative Years* (Lexington, Ky.: University of Kentucky Press, 1984), 102. See also ibid. 185–6. For a similar argument, see Dell, *The Schuman Plan and the British Abdication of Leadership*, 106–9.

[16] *FRUS*, 1952–4: VI. 1, Ambassador Dillon to the Department of State, 26 Apr. 1954, 385.

would have continued. Integration was something dramatically new in European history. There was certainly no automatic change to integration after the Second World War. In 1945-6 French policy towards Germany seemed to represent a basic repetition of the old pattern. American, and British, reconstruction of their zones and Soviet opposition to French plans for division and decentralization of Germany, as well as the Cold War in general, more or less forced Paris to change.[17] Even then, we have seen how slowly French leadership on European integration emerged in 1949-50.

With the slow pace of German rearmament in 1950-5, despite the strong leadership exerted by Washington starting in September 1950, it is difficult indeed to agree with Dulles that anything approaching the United States of Europe could have been the outcome. The Soviet threat may possibly have led to some sort of initial balancing in Western Europe,[18] but would this have included German rearmament? If it had not, what would Germany's role then have been? One clear finding of the present analysis has been the remarkably durable fear in Washington and elsewhere of what the Germans might be up to at some point in the future. If this was the case with Germany included in an integrated Western Europe within an Atlantic framework, what would the situation have been without this framework? No one can really answer such questions. My guess is that the Atlantic framework was an important requirement not only for stability in Western Europe, but also for "the long peace" in Europe in general.[19]

[17] Willis, *France, Germany and the New Europe*, 15-19.

[18] "Balancing" and "band-wagoning" are key terms in Stephen M. Walt, *The Origins of Alliances* (Ithaca, NY: Cornell University Press, 1987).

[19] John Lewis Gaddis, *The Long Peace: Inquiries into the History of the Cold War* (New York: Oxford University Press, 1987), 215-45.

12

AMERICA'S "EMPIRE": THE COMPARATIVE DIMENSION

THUS, the United States supported the integration of Western Europe, very strongly up to the mid-1960s, somewhat less strongly later. As a result of the negative balance of payments and the challenge from de Gaulle, US support for European integration had to be balanced more and more by the protection both of American economic interests and the crucial NATO framework. Then under Nixon and Kissinger Washington largely took itself out of the integration question and concentrated on the wider framework. Later administrations, especially Clinton's, might again become more positive towards European integration, but now the American position counted for less than it had done earlier. Washington never supported a really independent "third force" in Western Europe. Western Europe was definitely meant to belong within the American "empire."

The United States, like other Great Powers (or small powers too for that matter), wanted to exert maximum influence, but it did so in its own way. In a comparative context, the most surprising element in the American way remains not the qualifications in the support given to an integrated Western Europe, but rather that such strong support was given for so long to a politicical unit that had at least the potential to become an alternative political center.

Why did the United States pursue a course so different from that of other Great Powers? It is impossible to give a definitive answer to such a complex question. Any such answer would have to involve an extended discussion of "the American way" in international politics. This will not be attempted here. Still, some relevant points may be briefly discussed.

The reasons for the American support of European integration have already been presented. The deeper comparative answer, however, has to come in several parts. I shall argue that the United States behaved differently from other Great Powers for two basic reasons, reasons which in turn can be divided into several subgroups. The first set of reasons has to do with the values on which American foreign policy were based; the second set deals with the ways in which Washington interpreted its more traditional Great Power needs.

On the value side, federalism, democracy, and open markets represented core American values. This is what America exported. Other Great Powers exported their systems of government, whether it be French centralism and civilization, British indirect rule and free trade, or Soviet direct control and Communist ideology.

This point can be divided into several subgroups. First, the United States definitely did not consider itself an imperial power. On the contrary, it viewed itself as anti-imperial. The United States had been created in rebellion against British imperial rule. The whole idea of one center formally controlling other territories was imperial. In a sense it was therefore also un-American.

After the Second World War the United States continued to oppose imperial rule by Western European powers, although this opposition was often tempered by various Cold War considerations. And Washington of course opposed Soviet domination. It would have been awkward for the United States to pursue policies which could be seen as resembling too closely those of more traditional Great Powers.

There was the reality of empire without the formal rule. This was most clearly illustrated by the Soviet model. The Soviet Union was even more anti-imperial in its rhetoric than was the United States, but this did not prevent it from establishing an empire of its own in Eastern Europe. In reality Moscow exercised greater control over that region of formally independent countries than did London and even Paris over most of their colonial areas. The United States too could behave in relatively traditional imperial ways. This it sometimes did in Central America and in parts of the Pacific and East Asia. Still, as a starting point, to the extent that the imperial model in general and the Soviet model in particular had any influence on the United States, it was clearly a negative one. Washington should not behave in the way Moscow, or even London, did.

Second, European integration represented the European version of American federalism, democracy, and the free market. Americans considered federalism to be closely related to the other two concepts, and saw it as one of their most beneficial inventions. Again and again American policymakers pointed to the lessons for Europe in the growth of the United States of America from the thirteen colonies to the 48 (and 50) states. Federalism was quite simply the "right" way to run large territorial units (and sometimes even smaller ones like West Germany). Federalism in the American view was probably too closely connected with democracy and open markets, i.e. probably more than reality warranted. The French in particular, and this certainly included American favorite Jean Monnet, thus combined integration with heavy doses of state ownership and *dirigisme*.[1]

Free trade could be combined with considerable political control, as the British imperial example clearly indicated. At least until 1932, Britain was a stronger believer in, and a much more consistent executor of, free trade policies than the United States was ever to be. Under the system of imperial preferences set up at the Ottawa conference in 1932, British political control was actually to diminish, although this fact was more one of coincidence than of cause and effect. Other aspects than free trade versus protectionism determined the degree of independence for the colonies.

On the democracy side, again, of course, American ideals were sometimes corrupted by Great Power practices. Leftist democracies (Czechoslovakia in 1946, Guatemala in 1954, Chile in 1973) were undermined; many a right-wing dictatorship was supported. Yet, as Tony Smith has recently argued so powerfully, America's more general mission *was* to promote democracy.[2] Democratic rule could hardly be combined with formal control over other peoples, at least not in the long run. The American experience in the Philippines was one indication of this.[3] Ultimately the widening of

---

[1] Duchêne, *Jean Monnet*, 370–2; Gillingham, *Coal, Steel, and the Rebirth of Europe*, 229–31.

[2] Smith, *America's Mission*, particularly chs. 2–6. For a similar argument emphasizing the effects of liberalism on cooperation among democracies, see Thomas Risse-Kappen, *Cooperation among Democracies: The European Influence on U.S. Foreign Policy* (Princeton: Princeton University Press, 1995), 24–41. For a different perspective combining the promotion of democracy with world systems theory and the Gramscian concept of hegemony, see William J. Robinson, *Promoting Polyarchy: Globalization, US Intervention and Hegemony* (Cambridge: Cambridge University Press, 1996).   [3] Smith, *America's Mission*, 37–59.

democracy in the metropolitan country stimulated the dissolution of empire, as the history of the British empire clearly suggests, and the histories of the Portuguese and the Soviet empires so amply demonstrate.

The informal American "empire" did not sit well with any form of formal control. Not only that, the core American values of federalism, democracy, and open markets probably made the United States much more comfortable with spontaneity and self-organization than earlier Great Powers had been. Local initiatives were more highly appreciated, particularly when, as in the case of European integration, they fell well within the realm of what Washington wanted anyway.[4]

Of course Europe was not there to be molded by the Americans in ways they wanted regardless of the continent's earlier history. Michael Hogan has argued that "the Marshall Plan had aimed to remake Europe in an American mode", but then goes on to state that "In the end, America was made the European way."[5] While both conclusions seem a bit overstated, it is true that even during the Marshall Plan Washington had to make many concessions to European realities. Integration never went as far as the United States wanted; in the European version of democracy the left was much more important than in America; accordingly the markets never became as open as the Truman administration wanted them.

Third, while there were significant differences between the United States and the countries of Western Europe, the United States felt much closer to Western Europe than the Soviet Union did toward Eastern Europe and than Britain, France, or other imperial powers generally had towards their colonial areas. Because of this closeness, too, Washington had much to gain and little to lose by promoting European integration. The best parallel here would probably be the British attitude to the white dominions. There, as opposed to other areas of the empire, London was prepared to grant early self-government.

The assumption behind the American policy on European integration was that the United States and Western Europe had the most basic interests in common. They had fought together against Germany; now they stood united against the Soviet Union. The

---

[4] On this point I have particularly benefited from conversations with John Gaddis. A similar argument is found in Smith, *America's Mission*.

[5] These are in fact the concluding words in Hogan, *The Marshall Plan*, 445.

two sides of the Atlantic shared democratic ideals. If most Europeans were to the left of most Americans in their economic policies, this was at least in part not only understandable, but perhaps also desirable under the circumstances prevailing in Europe.[6] In their general cultures as in their degrees of development the United States and Western Europe were close. Most Americans were of European descent and race.

The Europeans in fact "invited" the Americans to play the overall role they did in Western Europe after the Second World War.[7] The Americans in turn basically trusted the Europeans. Dulles thus believed it was almost certain that the United States and Western Europe would stay close together for the very good reason that the Western European nations and the United States "were part and parcel of Western civilization, with similar religion, culture, and other fundamental affinities."[8] Or, in McGeorge Bundy's words, in the end America's confidence in Europe rested "on deeper and more solid political ground" since the European peoples are "our cousins by history and culture, by language and religion. We are cousins too in our current sense of human and social purpose."[9]

Again, in other parts of the American "empire" or sphere of influence, where the interests of the United States and the local governments did not coincide to the extent they did in Western Europe, American rule could be more direct. When necessary, the United States was certainly able to act much more imperially than it did in Western Europe.[10]

[6] Lundestad, *America, Scandinavia, and the Cold War*, 110–18, 154–66; Schwartz, *America's Germany*, 51, 80, 85, 91, 205–8, 298–9.

[7] Geir Lundestad, "Empire by Invitation? The United States and Western Europe, 1945–1952," *Journal of Peace Research*, Sept. 1986, 263–77.

[8] Warner, "Eisenhower, Dulles and the Unity of Western Europe," 326.

[9] US Department of State, *Bulletin*, 12 Mar. 1962, 423. In a more recent expression of this point, George Bush put it this way in 1990: "We do not expect perfect agreement between the United States and the EC on every issue, but we do agree that our inherent belief in the value of freedom, democracy, opportunity binds us together and that our mutual cooperation can benefit all" (*Public Papers of the Presidents. George Bush, 1990*, 280). For the wider issue of race in American foreign policy, see Michael H. Hunt, *Ideology and U.S. Foreign Policy* (New Haven: Yale University Press, 1987).

[10] The literature on the United States and "the Third World" is huge and growing rapidly. For good recent reviews of this literature, see the essays by Gary Hess (on the Vietnam War), Mark T. Gilderhus (the US and Latin America), Douglas Little (the Middle East), and Robert J. McMahon (Asia) in Michael Hogan (ed.), *America in the World: The Historiography of American Foreign Relations since*

Fourth, based on the relative coincidence of American and European values, Washington promoted European integration with the expectation that this was a realistic option. Most policymakers assumed that integration was what the Europeans wanted or at least what they would come to want once they were able to see beyond their small national states (and recognize that Germany could not be kept down indefinitely).

The Europeans did not support European integration as strongly as Washington wanted in the 1950s and early 1960s. After that, the picture changed. Under special circumstances, such as with the Franco-German treaty of 1963, integration clearly went too far for Washington. In the larger context, however, Washington appears to have been fundamentally correct in its appraisals of the prospects for integration. The EEC/EC/EU has moved in spurts, with long periods of inactivity, but in a longer-term perspective it has been able to combine a steady geographical widening with a considerable contextual deepening.

The difference with Asia is striking. Because of the widespread hatred of Japan, the liberated colonies' emphasis on national self-determination, and the general complexity of the regional scene, East Asian integration was really out of the question. There it was even impossible for Washington to establish one overall defense organization on the pattern of NATO. Instead a complicated system of regional alliances and bilateral defense treaties was created.[11]

In the British empire, the integration of the far-flung colonies and territories was probably not possible without London's direct control. They had too little in common to make voluntary integration go very far. Integration in the form of for instance Joseph Chamberlain's plans at the turn of the century for an imperial federation was widely perceived as just another form of colonial domination. Even the white dominions, sentimentally so close to

---

1941 (Cambridge: Cambridge University Press, 1995); David S. Painter, "Research Note: Explaining U.S. Relations with the Third World," *Diplomatic History*, Summer 1995, 525–48. For a strong comprehensive attack on US policies—too strong and too comprehensive, many historians will argue—see Gabriel Kolko, *Confronting the Third World: United States Foreign Policy, 1945–1980* (New York: Pantheon Books, 1988).

[11] Leffler, *A Preponderance of Power*, chs. 9–11. For an account of US policies towards Third World neutralism, see H. W. Brands, *The Specter of Neutralism: The United States and the Emergence of the Third World, 1947–1960* (New York: Columbia University Press, 1989).

Britain, but also with the highest degree of autonomy, rejected such a federation.[12] Where the British promoted local federations without direct British participation, as in Central Africa in the 1950s, this was done to strengthen the influence of Britain and/or the white settlers.[13] These efforts too collapsed. Almost without exception the colonies came to want national independence.

The French and the Portuguese attempted to fully integrate the colonies into the mother country and to rule on the basis of a common assimilated French or Portuguese culture. They combined apparent egalitarianism with very real control from Paris and Lisbon. This combination could not prevent independence either. In Indochina, Algeria, and Angola in particular these attempts only made the independence struggle more bloody when it came, although we can now see that in many French colonies in Africa Paris was actually able to lay the foundation for more lasting ties.[14]

In the Soviet case, Tito showed an interest in a Balkan federation, but after some initial vacillation Stalin put a stop to any such effort. No one could be permitted to stand up to Moscow in any way.[15] After the collapse of the Soviet Union, virtually all the Central and Eastern European countries became strongly interested in integration with NATO and the EU, and much less in integration with each other.

Important as the value side was, the United States also had basic Great Power needs. The two aspects were closely related, but for analytical reasons they are more clearly separated here than the reality actually justifies. These Great Power needs certainly also help explain why the United States pursued the kind of integrationist policies it did in Western Europe.

---

[12] Aaron L. Friedberg, *The Weary Titan: Britain and the Experience of Relative Decline, 1895–1905* (Princeton: Princeton University Press, 1988), 45–79.

[13] Prosser Gifford, "Misconceived Dominion: The Creation and Disintegration of Federation in British Central Africa," in Prosser Gifford and William Roger Louis (eds.), *The Transfer of Power in Africa: Decolonization, 1940–1960* (New Haven: Yale University Press, 1982), 387–416.

[14] The literature on the colonial empires is vast. For as good a starting point as any, see D. K. Fieldhouse, *The Colonial Empires: A Comparative Survey from the Eighteenth Century* (London: Macmillan, 1982), which also contains a good bibliography (435–58).

[15] Leonid Gibianski, "The 1948 Soviet-Yugoslav Conflict and the Formation of the "Socialist Camp" Model," in Odd Arne Westad, Sven Holtsmark, and Iver B. Neumann (eds.), *The Soviet Union in Eastern Europe 1945–89* (London: St. Martin's, 1994), 26–46.

First, the United States encouraged integration in Europe because this was seen as the most effective way of organizing the containment of its main enemy, the Soviet Union. As we have seen, this motive was underlined time and again by all administrations in Washington starting with Truman's. America's policy cannot be understood without keeping this factor in mind.

Yet in a comparative perspective this factor is more complicated than it would at first appear. Other Great Powers of course also had enemies and they did not support integration in the way the US did. The effect of the existence of major enemies was sometimes to underline the importance of imperial control. In fact, traditional imperial expansion in the nineteenth century was in many cases at least in part related to Great Power rivalry, whether between Britain and France in Africa or between Britain and Russia in Asia. The Soviet Union was particularly vigilant against "nationalist deviations" during the height of the Cold War; with détente more openness was tolerated.

The short-run effect of the Second World War on British policy in the crucial colony of India was two-sided. On the one hand, the war made any grant of immediate independence impossible. No disturbance of the war effort could be tolerated when the survival of Britain was at stake. Similar considerations made the United States postpone the independence it had promised the Philippines until the war was over. On the other hand, London's promises as to what would follow once the war was over also had to become ever stronger during the war itself.

In the long run the effect of the Second World War was undoubtedly to undermine the control of the traditional imperial powers. The huge significance of the Japanese defeat of the European colonial powers in East Asia is not particularly relevant in this context, but other effects are, such as the promises given to the colonies to encourage their full support and avoid their siding with Japan, the need to draw upon the resources of the various areas as effectively as possible, the idealism on which the struggle against the enemy had to be based, etc.[16]

During the Cold War, unless the nationalist movements were already considered to be under "Communist" control, Washington

---

[16] A good short discussion of the effects of the Second World War on the British empire is found in John Darwin, *The End of the British Empire: The Historical Debate* (Oxford: Blackwell, 1991), 43–5, 117–20.

tended to favor independence for the colonies, at least in the long run. The holding back of independence would strengthen the chances of these movements going "Communist." Thus, the Americans pushed Holland to grant early independence to Indonesia while they supported the French in Indochina.[17]

The conflict with the Soviet Union had striking effects on the American policy towards Western Europe. It underlined the need to use the resources of "the free world" as effectively as possible. European integration in an Atlantic framework was undoubtedly seen as doing exactly that. At the same time, however, the United States could not push this objective too hard against local opposition. If it did, leftist forces could gain at the expense of the centrist governments the United States normally supported in Western Europe. Thus, from the Marshall Plan to the EDC many a French government could secure concessions from the United States by threatening to fall ("the tyranny of the weak").[18]

When the Europeans in the late 1980s and early 1990s took several initiatives to speed up European integration considerably, the Reagan and the Bush administrations were afraid that on the defense side this might violate the supremacy of NATO. As we have seen, the end of the Cold War then became one factor which helped explain why the Clinton administration was somewhat more relaxed about the forms of European defense organization than its two predecessors had been.

Second, the importance of the historic threat from Germany has been repeatedly underlined. With Germany being seen as responsible for two world wars, how could one really trust the Germans? With the Soviets holding such strong cards *vis-à-vis* Germany, how could Washington in the long run prevent a *rapprochement* between the past and the present enemy? Western European integration seemed to be the obvious answer.

In a comparative perspective, it was something new that the victors in the Second World War not only defeated, but also occupied the entire territory of the main enemy. Not even Napoleon, who temporarily controlled such a large part of Europe, had in

---

[17] For good accounts of US policies in Southeast Asia, see Gary R. Hess, *The United States' Emergence as a Southeast Asian Power, 1945–1950* (New York: Columbia University Press, 1987) and Robert J. McMahon, *Colonialism and Cold War: The United States and the Struggle for Indonesian Independence, 1945–1949* (Ithaca, NY: Cornell University Press, 1981).

[18] Lundestad, *The American "Empire,"* 80–1.

the end been able to defeat either of his main antagonists, Britain and Russia. The completeness of the Allied victory in 1945 left a problem unlike those any previous victors had faced. In the short run Germany would be held down, the traditional way of controlling a defeated enemy. But in the long run this approach was untenable for the United States and at least also for Britain, for obvious reasons, most of which have in fact been presented in the discussion of the previous points. Since Germany could not be let loose either, integration seemed the obvious answer. The American experience in Germany in a way resembled the North's experience with the South after the American Civil War. First there would be occupation and control, later there would be integration and equality.

Third, in American eyes an integrated Europe was not only the most efficient way for Europe to run itself, but, as we have seen, it was also widely perceived as resulting in the smallest expense for the United States. Other Great Powers presumably also tried to run the areas they controlled much more directly than the United States controlled Western Europe, in ways they considered efficient and inexpensive.[19]

Finally, but certainly not least important, one is struck by the strength, self-confidence, and success of the American approach. This strength, self-confidence, and success disposed the United States towards European integration as compared with more imperial and more direct ways of rule. It was not only difficult, but quite simply unnecessary for the United States to establish any form of direct rule. It could achieve the kind of control it wanted through more indirect, more American means.

The United States of Truman and Eisenhower was really much stronger, in relative as well as absolute terms, than not only Stalin's Soviet Union, but also Victoria's Britain, Louis XIV's and Napoleon's France, Philip II's Spain, and Charles V's Habsburg empire. The United States was relatively stronger than all of them in every category of power at the same time: military, economic, political, cultural, and structural.[20]

[19] The costs of empire are further discussed in ibid. 107–14.
[20] Ibid. 39–46, 85–7. See also Paul Kennedy, *The Rise and Fall of the Great Powers: Economic Change and Military Conflict from 1500 to 2000* (New York: Random House, 1987); Joseph S. Nye, *Bound to Lead: The Changing Nature of American Power* (New York: Basic Books, 1990); Aaron L. Friedberg, "The End of the Cold War and the Future of American Power," in Lundestad, *The Fall of Great Powers*, 175–96.

Washington had its periods of self-doubt and pessimism. Many American policymakers frequently perceived their country as fragile, as easily threatened, either by infiltration from within or by attack from without. Pearl Harbor had greatly heightened American fears and led to ever-new "windows of vulnerability" being discovered.

Yet even in such pessimistic analyses the United States almost invariably prevailed in the end. In the 1940s George Kennan was grateful to "Providence" which had provided the American people with a Soviet threat and thereby made "their entire security as a nation dependent on their pulling themselves together and accepting the responsibilites of moral and political leadership that history plainly intended them to bear." In the 1980s Ronald Reagan painted the Soviets ten feet tall, but still consigned Marxism-Leninism to the ash-heap of history.[21]

So, despite their doubts, most American policymakers were on the whole rather self-confident. American isolationism, especially in the 1930s, had been a reaction against the dangers of Europe: America must not be contaminated by the evils of the Old World. After the Second World War there was little danger of such contamination. Influence seemed to flow entirely in the other direction, from the New to the Old World.

The American policy was not only quite successful in Western Europe, but also globally. True, the United States was defeated in the back yard of the Soviet Union, in Eastern Europe, and in the world's most populous country, in China. These were significant defeats, but they should not make us overlook the success the United States had in organizing "the free world," or the American "empire," including the traditional power centers of Britain, France, most of Germany, and Japan.

When, in the early 1960s, the Gaullist challenge to the American position in Western Europe really arose and America's relative strength and even its self-confidence eroded somewhat, Washington's support for European integration became more conditional. The domination that was only implicit in the NATO structure was made more explicit and American economic interests had to be protected more directly than before.

---

[21] For a further discussion of optimism versus pessimism in American foreign policy, see my The American "Empire," 138–41.

13

THE PAST, THE PRESENT, AND THE FUTURE

Aᴄᴛᴇʀ 1945 the United States was in a unique position. Never had the world seen a power with such overwhelming strength, in relative as well as in absolute terms. We can now see that the American expansion was really even more striking than the Soviet one. In some ways Washington's influence within the American "empire" surpassed that of more explicitly imperial capitals within their more formal empires.

Today the situation is clearly different from what it was during the first years after the Second World War. The European Union of fifteen countries has a population that is substantially larger than that of the United States (approximately 370 million as opposed to 265 million). In 1945 the United States produced almost as much as the rest of the world put together, a truly unique moment in history. Today the gross national product of the EU is larger than that of the United States. The new-found economic strength of the EU is reflected in many ways. For example, the countries of the EU, not the United States, are now the major contributors of economic assistance to the countries of the South and to Central and Eastern Europe, as well as to the area of the former Soviet Union.[1]

The EU, however, still has a long way to go to reach the military strength and political organization of the United States. As we have seen so clearly in the Gulf War and in the former Yugoslavia, only the United States can undertake really large-scale military

---

[1] For a further discussion of this, see my *The American "Empire,"* 87–93. For the relative development of the US gross national product, see ibid. 202.

action. Despite the impressive deepening of European integration, as expressed most recently in the Maastricht Treaty and in the further work towards the Economic and Monetary Union, most likely there will never be a United States of Europe in any way similar to the United States of America. In that sense the dream of the most optimistic integrationists on both sides of the Atlantic may well fail. In fact, it is still not clear when and how the EU will accomplish its Economic and Monetary Union. The Common Foreign and Security Policy remains a distant hope rather than a present reality.[2]

Since president Kennedy's famous speech on Atlantic interdependence on 4 July 1962, ever-new statements have been issued from both sides of the Atlantic about the need for a new kind of basis for US–European relations. The most striking of these statements have come from the American side, since, on the European side, the French in particular had a rather ambivalent attitude to such declarations. The new basis allegedly had to be one of equality between the two sides of the Atlantic. Thus, even Kennedy explicitly stated that the United States was seeking a partner in Europe "with whom we can deal on a basis of full equality."[3]

Yet such statements ring a little hollow. As we have seen, it is highly doubtful that the United States has ever wanted a Europe really equal to the US. Moreover, there is no politically united Europe. As long as there is a definite, although well-contained, rivalry among the major powers of the EU, there can be no equality between the United States and Western Europe. Were a really united EU to emerge, this would be so strong a unit that there would be virtually no need for the EU to draw upon the military and political resources of the United States.

The United States and Western Europe have never actually had a balanced relationship. Under isolationism the United States feared Europe since it saw itself as weak. When, after the Second World War, it was itself strong, it promoted Europe's integration. When America's position began to weaken in the 1960s, its support for European integration faltered too. Nixon saw the US as declining; he stopped America pushing the Europeans towards some sort of federal structure.

---

[2] For a presentation of the CFSP, see for instance Martin Westlake, *The Council of the European Union* (London: Cartermill, 1995), 211–33.
[3] *Public Papers of the Presidents. John F. Kennedy, 1962,* 538.

The expectation in Washington for a long time was that even a strong and integrated Europe would continue to cooperate closely with the United States. Today this basic assumption may perhaps seem more open to doubt than it used to be, but clearly so does the possibility of the EU really developing into some sort of federal Europe. A truly balanced relationship between the United States and Western Europe would represent a new state of affairs. It would probably also represent a highly challenging state of affairs.

It has been argued that almost without exception alliances do not survive the disappearance of the threat against which they are directed.[4] As Lord Ismay, the first secretary general of NATO, allegedly quipped, "NATO was founded to keep the Russians out, the Germans down, and the Americans in." Now the Americans are greatly reducing the number of troops in Europe, the Germans, though unified, seem to be entirely peaceful, and the Soviet threat disappeared with the dissolution of the Soviet Union itself. NATO is searching for new missions. Economic disputes between the allies are proliferating, particularly between the United States and Japan, but also between the US and the EU.

Yet, it can be argued that in modified form the original rationale for NATO still exists. The Soviet Union is gone, but no one is certain what will happen in the dominant new unit, Russia. Germany remains strongly democratic and less nationalistic than virtually any other Great Power, but concern is nevertheless growing in Europe about the new Germany simply becoming too strong compared to the other powers of the EU. France is moving closer to Britain and to the United States and NATO. The United States is reducing its military presence in Europe, but although the invitations are more ambiguous now, few Europeans want the Americans to leave entirely. Thus, the EU side, more than the US, initiated the newest statement of common interest, the New Transatlantic Agenda, from the Madrid summit of December 1995. If something should go wrong, it is still thought useful to have the Americans

---

[4] This is one of the basic assumptions of the so-called realist school in international relations. The starting point here is Kenneth N. Waltz, *Theory of International Relations* (Reading, Mass.: Addison-Wesley, 1979). For a presentation of the view that the disintegration of NATO is likely, see John J. Mearsheimer, "Back to the Future: Instability in Europe after the Cold War," *International Security*, Summer 1990, 52. For a more moderate interpretation of the changes likely in NATO, see Philip H. Gordon, "Recasting the Atlantic Alliance," *Survival*, Spring 1996, 32–57.

in place. And, finally, the United States, though strongly interested in reducing the burdens of leadership, is "the only remaining super-power" and clearly expects to remain Number One in the fore-seeable future. Such a role for the US is much facilitated by a close relationship with Western Europe (and Japan).

The American–European relationship will be redefined. The redefinition will probably result in the further weakening of what remains of the American "empire", although it must be said that the unification of Germany, recent events in the former Yugoslavia related to the signing and implementation of the Dayton accords, the process towards the expansion of NATO eastwards, and France's partial reintegration in NATO's military structure have all under-lined the continued role of the US as the ultimate arbiter in Europe.

Despite the opening words of the Madrid statement that "We, the United States and the European Union, affirm our conviction that the ties which bind our people are as strong today as they have been for the past half century," the US does not loom as large for the Europeans as it did in the Cold War years. And Washington is definitely focusing less on Western Europe than it did during the first Europe-centered decades after 1945. There is a strong tend-ency in America to stress domestic matters over foreign affairs. The basic feeling appears to be that Western Europe should now manage more on its own. Other parts of the world have become increasingly important, especially on the economic side. The share of Americans of European ancestry is falling while the percentages of Hispanics and Asians are growing. (On the other hand, the significance of the fact that three out of four Americans are still of European descent should not be underestimated.)

With the Reagan years the striking correspondence between America's strength and its support for European integration began to break down. Reagan indeed saw America as strong, but his administration was still less positive towards European integration than any earlier or later one. Despite America's strength, the Rea-gan administration feared the economic and political consequences of Europe's renewed push towards integration in the form of the Single Market.

Both the history of the Clinton years and simple logic would seem to indicate that perhaps an opposite correspondence might now be developing, i.e. that a weaker and less Europe-centred United States will in fact be more, rather than less interested in a strong EU. If the United States is to do less in Europe, the Europeans will have to do more. This would particularly be the case with the Cold War over. Then the United States could be somewhat more relaxed about the forms of European integration even on the defense side. Such a line of reasoning would indeed appear to be the major reason for the increased American sympathy for European integration which we have seen in the Clinton years.

The relative strengths of the United States and of the European Union are important for relations between the two, although in ways more complicated than would appear at first glance. So is the existence of major threats which can bind Europe and America closer together. An additional consideration of overriding significance will be the following: the closer Washington feels the Europeans are to the US, the greater the chance of continued or even increased American support for European integration.

The present study has demonstrated Washington's general support for European integration, but this support has always been conditioned on Europe being fitted into a wider Atlantic framework. If this framework is questioned, Washington's response can be dramatic, as we have seen especially in connection with the Franco–German treaty of 1963, but also in connection with the discussions surrounding the Year of Europe, the Burt letter of 1985, and the Dobbins démarche of 1991. So once the Atlantic framework is seriously questioned, it seems likely that US support for European integration will falter rather quickly. The end of the Cold War may have widened the perimeters of the Atlantic framework, but there are still limits to how far Washington will permit a "friendly" EU to move.

For the historian it is time to stop. We are good at proclaiming matters "inevitable" once they have happened. We are rather bad at predicting matters *before* they happen.

Bibliography

Unpublished documents

Declassified Documents Reference Service, 1975– (Woodbridge, Conn.: Research Publications International, 1975–).

General Records of the Department of State, National Archives (NA), Washington, DC, Record Group 59

(1) Central Decimal Files 1945–1962, particularly the following:

711.51	US Relations with France, 1945–1949
751	France: International Political Relations, 1945–1949
396.1	LO Council of Foreign Ministers, 1949–1950
611.51	US Relations with France, 1950–1954
611.62	US Relations with Germany, 1950–1954
651	France: International Political Relations, 1950–1954
662	Germany: International Political Relations, 1950–1954
751	France: Political/Defense Affairs, 1950–1954
762	Germany: Political/Defense Affairs, 1950–1954
850.33	European Coal and Steel Community
375	NATO, 1959–1962
375.42	EEC-EFTA, 1960–1962
396.1	Council of Foreign Ministers, 1959–1962
611.41	US Relations with Britain, 1959–1962
611.51	US Relations with France, 1959–1962
611.62	US Relations with Germany, 1959–1962
651.62	Relations between France and West Germany, 1959–1962
110.11-RU	The records of Dean Rusk, 1961–1963

(2) The following Alpha-Numeric Files, 1963:

ECIN 3 and ECIN 6, Organizations and Conferences

Pol W EUR

Pol UK-US

Pol FR-UK

Pol FR-US

Pol FR-WGER

Pol WGER-US

(3) Lot Files

Records of Charles E. Bohlen, 1952–1963, Lot 74D379

Papers from the presidential libraries (Truman, Eisenhower, Kennedy, and Johnson) available on microfilm and upon request by mail.

Interviews

Hans-Dietrich Genscher, former German foreign minister, 8 and 9 April, 1997.

Richard C. Holbrooke, former US assistant secretary of state for European and Canadian affairs, 5 Sept. 1996.

Robert E. Hunter, US ambassador to NATO, 5 Feb. and 31 Oct. 1996.

Leiv Mevik, Norwegian ambassador to NATO, 24 Aug. 1995.

Senior US State Department official, telephone interview, 7 Feb. 1997.

Published documents

Akten zur Auswärtigen Politik der Bundesrepublik Deutschland, 1949–1952, 1963–1965 (Munich: Herausgegeben im Auftrag des Auswärtigen Amts vom Institut für Zeitgeschichte, Oldenbourg Verlag, 1989–96).

American Foreign Policy 1950–1955: Basic Documents. Volumes I and II (Washington, DC, Government Printing Office, 1957).

Economic Report of the President 1996 (Washington, DC: Government Printing Office, 1996).

Galambos, Louis (ed.), *The Papers of Dwight David Eisenhower. XII: NATO and the Campaign of 1952* (Baltimore: Johns Hopkins University Press, 1989).

Public Papers of the Presidents of the US, all volumes from Harry S. Truman to William J. Clinton (Washington, DC: Government Printing Office, 1946–96).

US Department of Defense, *United States Security Strategy for Europe and NATO* (Washington, DC: US Department of Defense, 1995).

US Department of State, *A Decade of American Foreign Policy: Basic Documents, 1941–49* (Washington, DC: Government Printing Office, 1950).

—— *Bulletin* (Washington, DC: Government Printing Office, 1947–96).

—— *Current Policy* (Washington, DC: Department of State, 1980–).

—— *Foreign Relations of the United States (FRUS)*, particularly these volumes, all published by the Government Printing Office in Washington, DC:

1946: V, *The British Commonwealth; Western and Central Europe* (1969)

1947: II, *Council of Foreign Ministers; Germany and Austria* (1972)

1947: III, *The British Commonwealth; Europe* (1972)

1948: II, *Germany and Austria* (1973)

1948: III, *Western Europe* (1974)

1949: III, *Council of Foreign Ministers; Germany and Austria* (1974)

1949: IV, *Western Europe* (1975)

1950: I, *National Security Affairs; Foreign Economic Policy* (1977)

1950: III, *Western Europe* (1977)

1950: IV, *Central and Eastern Europe; The Soviet Union* (1980)

1951: I, *National Security Affairs; Foreign Economic Policy* (1979)

1951: III, parts 1 and 2, *European Security and the German Question* (1981)

1952-1954: II, parts 1 and 2, *National Security Affairs* (1984)

1952-1954: V, parts 1 and 2, *Western European Security* (1983)

1952-1954: VI, parts 1 and 2, *Western Europe and Canada* (1986)

1952-1954: VII, parts 1 and 2, *Germany and Austria* (1986)

1955-1957: IV, *Western European Security and Integration* (1986)

1955-1957: IX, *Foreign Economic Policy; Foreign Information Program* (1987)

1955-1957: XXVI, *Central and Southeastern Europe* (1992)

1955-1957: XXVII, *Western Europe and Canada* (1992)

1958-1960: IV, *Foreign Economic Policy* (1992)

1958-1960: VII, parts 1 and 2, *Western European Integration and Security; Canada; Western Europe* (1993)

1958-1960: IX, *Berlin Crisis 1959-1960; Germany; Austria* (1993)

1961-1963: IX, *Foreign Economic Policy* (1995)

1961-1963: XIII, *West Europe and Canada* (1994)

1964-1968: XIII, *Western Europe Region* (1995).

United States Mission to the European Union, *US-EU: Facts and Figures* (Brussels, 1996).

USIS (United States Information Service), news sheets, issued on a very frequent basis, of official speeches etc.

Books and articles

This list of books and articles has been confined to works referred to in the text. Newspaper articles are not included.

Acheson, Dean, *Present at the Creation: My Years in the State Department* (New York: Norton, 1969).

Aimaq, Jasmine, *For Europe or Empire? French Colonial Ambitions and the European Army Plan* (Lund, Sweden: Lund University Press, 1996).

Aldrich, Richard J., "European Integration: An American Intelligence Connection," in Anne Deighton (ed.), *Building Postwar Europe: National Decision-Makers and European Institutions, 1948–63* (London: Macmillan, 1995), 159–79.

Ambrose, Stephen E., *Eisenhower: The President* (New York: Simon and Schuster, 1984).

—— *Nixon: The Triumph of a Politician 1962–1972* (New York: Simon and Schuster, 1989).

Anderson, Perry, "Under the Sign of the Interim," *London Review of Books*, 4 Jan. 1996, 13–17.

Arkes, Hadley, *Bureaucracy, the Marshall Plan, and the National Interest* (Princeton: Princeton University Press, 1972).

Art, Robert J., "Why Western Europe Needs the United States and NATO," *Political Science Quarterly*, 111:1 (1996), 1–39.

Baker, James A., III, with Thomas M. DeFrank, *The Politics of Diplomacy: Revolution, War & Peace, 1989–1992* (New York: Putnam, 1995).

Ball, George W., *The Past has Another Pattern: Memoirs* (New York: Norton, 1982).

Baun, Michael J., *An Imperfect Union: The Maastricht Treaty and the New Politics of European Integration* (Boulder, Colo.: Westview Press, 1996).

—— "The Maastricht Treaty as High Politics: Germany, France and European Integration," *Political Science Quarterly*, 110:4 (1995–6), 605–24.

Beloff, Max, *The United States and the Unity of Europe* (Washington, DC: Brookings, 1963).

Borden, William, "Defending Hegemony: American Foreign Economic Policy," in Thomas G. Paterson (ed.), *Kennedy's Quest for Victory: American Foreign Policy, 1961–1963* (London: Oxford University Press, 1989), 57–85.

Bossuat, Gérard, *L'Europe occidentale à l'heure américaine 1945–1952* (Paris: Éditions Complexe, 1992).

Bozo, Frédéric, *Deux stratégies pour l'Europe: de Gaulle, les États-Unis et l'Alliance Atlantique 1958–1969* (Paris: Plon, 1996).

Brands, H. W., *The Specter of Neutralism: The United States and the Emergence of the Third World, 1947–1960* (New York: Columbia University Press, 1989).

—— *The Wages of Globalism: Lyndon Johnson and the Limits of American Power* (New York: Oxford University Press, 1995).

Brinkley, Douglas, *Dean Acheson: The Cold War Years, 1953–71* (New Haven: Yale University Press, 1992).

Brusse, Wendy Asbeek, "The Americans, GATT, and European Integration, 1947–1957: A Decade of Dilemma," in Francis H. Heller and John

R. Gillingham (eds.), *The United States and the Integration of Europe: Legacies of the Postwar Era* (New York: St. Martin's, 1996), 221–49.

Brzezinski, Zbigniew, *Game Plan: How to Conduct the U.S.-Soviet Contest* (New York: Atlantic Monthly Press, 1986).

—— *Power and Principle: Memoirs of a National Security Adviser, 1977–81* (New York: Farrar, Straus, Giroux, 1983).

Cafruney, Alan W., "Economic Conflicts and the Transformation of the Atlantic Order: The USA, Europe and the Liberalization of Agriculture and Services," in Stephen Gill (ed.), *Atlantic Relations: Beyond the Reagan Era* (New York: St. Martin's, 1989), 111–38.

Calingaert, Michael, *European Integration Revisited: Progress, Prospects and U.S. Interests* (Boulder, Colo.: Westview, 1996).

Calleo, David P., *Beyond American Hegemony: The Future of the Western Alliance* (New York: Basic Books, 1987).

Camps, Miriam, *Britain and the European Community 1955–1963* (London: Oxford University Press, 1964).

—— *European Unification in the Sixties: From the Veto to the Crisis* (London: Oxford University Press, 1967).

Carter, Jimmy, *Keeping Faith: Memoirs of a President* (Toronto: Bantam Books, 1982).

Charmley, John, *Churchill's Grand Alliance: The Anglo-American Special Relationship 1940–1957* (London: Hodder & Stoughton, 1995).

Collins, Robert M., "The Economic Crisis of 1968 and the Waning of 'The American Century'," *American Historical Review*, Apr. 1996, 396–422.

Conze, Eckart, "Hegemonie durch Integration? Die amerikanische Europapolitik und de Gaulle," *Vierteljahrshefte für Zeitgeschichte*, Apr. 1995, 297–340.

Cornish, Paul, "European Security: The End of Architecture and the New NATO," *International Affairs*, 72:4 (1996), 751–69.

Costigliola, Frank, "An 'Arm around the Shoulder': The United States, NATO, and German Reunification, 1989-90," *Contemporary European History*, Mar. 1994, 87–110.

—— *France and the United States* (New York: Twayne, 1992).

—— "Kennedy, de Gaulle, and the Challenge of Consultation," in Robert O. Paxton and Nicholas Wahl (eds.), *De Gaulle and the United States: A Centennial Reappraisal* (Oxford: Berg, 1994).

—— "Kennedy, the European Allies, and the Failure to Consult," *Political Science Quarterly*, Winter 1995, 105–23.

—— "Lyndon B. Johnson, Germany, and 'the End of the Cold War'," in Warren I. Cohen and Nancy Bernkopf Tucker (eds.), *Lyndon Johnson*

Confronts the World: American Foreign Policy, 1963–1968 (Cambridge: Cambridge University Press, 1994), 173–210.

—— "The Failed Design: Kennedy, de Gaulle, and the Struggle for Europe," *Diplomatic History*, Summer 1984, 227–51.

Croft, Stuart, "European Integration, Nuclear Deterrence and Franco-British Nuclear Cooperation," *International Affairs*, 72:4 (1996), 771–87.

Cromwell, William C., *The United States and the European Pillar: The Strained Alliance* (London: Macmillan, 1992).

Croome, John, *Reshaping the World Trading System: A History of the Uruguay Round* (Geneva: World Trade Organization, 1995).

Darwin, John, *The End of the British Empire: The Historical Debate* (Oxford: Blackwell, 1991).

Dedman, Martin J., *The Origins and Development of the European Union 1945–95: A History of European Integration* (London: Routledge, 1996).

Dell, Edmund, *The Schuman Plan and the British Abdication of Leadership in Europe* (Oxford: Oxford University Press, 1995).

Denman, Roy, *Missed Chances: Britain and Europe in the Twentieth Century* (London: Cassell, 1996).

Dimbley, David, and Reynolds, David, *An Ocean Apart: The Relationship between Britain and America in the Twentieth Century* (New York: Random House, 1988).

Dobson, Alan P., *Anglo-American Relations in the Twentieth Century* (London: Routledge, 1995).

Dockrill, Saki, *Britain's Policy for West German Rearmament 1950–55* (Cambridge: Cambridge University Press, 1991).

—— "Cooperation and Suspicion: The United States' Alliance Diplomacy for the Security of Western Europe, 1953–54," *Diplomacy and Statecraft*, Mar. 1994, 138–82.

Dore, Sally, "Britain and the European Payments Union: British Policy and American Influence," in Francis H. Heller and John R. Gillingham (eds.), *The United States and the Integration of Europe: Legacies of the Postwar Era* (New York: St. Martin's, 1996), 167–97.

Duchêne, Francois, *Jean Monnet: The First Statesman of Interdependence* (New York: Norton, 1994).

Dutton, David, *Anthony Eden: A Life and Reputation* (London: Arnold, 1997).

Duval, Marcel, and Melandri, Pierre, "Les États-Unis et la prolifération nucléaire: Le cas francais," *Revue d'histoire diplomatique* (1995), 193–220.

Eckes, Alfred E., Jr., *Opening America's Market: U.S. Foreign Trade Policy since 1776* (Chapel Hill, NC: University of North Carolina Press, 1995).

Eisenberg, Carolyn Woods, *Drawing the Line: The American Decision to Divide Germany, 1944–1949* (Cambridge: Cambridge University Press, 1996).

Eizenstat, Stuart E., "The United States and the IGC," *Challenge: IGC Intelligence Service*, Jan. 1996, 12–13.

—— "The US Relationship with the EU and the Changing Europe," in Norman Levine (ed.), *The US and the EU: Economic Relations in a World of Transition* (Lanham, Mass.: University Press of America, 1996), 23–44.

Ellwood, David W., *Rebuilding Europe: Western Europe, America and Postwar Reconstruction* (London: Longman, 1992).

Featherstone, Kevin, and Ginsberg, Roy H., *The United States and the European Union in the 1990s: Partners in Transition* (London: Macmillan, 1996).

Ferrell, Robert H., "The Truman Era and European Integration," in Francis H. Heller and John R. Gillingham (eds.), *The United States and the Integration of Europe: Legacies of the Postwar Era* (New York: St. Martin's, 1996), 25–44.

Fieldhouse, D. K., *The Colonial Empires: A Comparative Survey from the Eighteenth Century* (London: Macmillan, 1982).

Friedberg, Aaron L., "The End of the Cold War and the Future of American Power," in Geir Lundestad (ed.), *The Fall of Great Powers: Peace, Stability, and Legitimacy* (Oslo and Oxford: Scandinavian University Press, 1994), 175–96.

—— *The Weary Titan: Britain and the Experience of Relative Decline, 1895–1905* (Princeton: Princeton University Press, 1988).

Fursdon, Edward, *The European Defence Community: A History* (London: Macmillan, 1980).

Gaddis, John Lewis, *The Long Peace: Inquiries into the History of the Cold War* (New York: Oxford University Press, 1987).

Gardner, Anthony Laurence, *A New Era in US-EU Relations? The Clinton Administration and the New Transatlantic Agenda* (Aldershot: Avebury, 1997).

Gardner, Lloyd, "Lyndon Johnson and de Gaulle," in Robert O. Paxton and Nicholas Wall (eds.), *De Gaulle and the United States: A Centennial Reappraisal* (Oxford: Berg, 1994), 257–78.

Gardner, Richard N., *Sterling-Dollar Diplomacy: The Origins and Prospects of our International Economic Order* (New York: McGraw-Hill, 1969).

Gerber, Pierre, "European Integration as an Instrument of French Foreign Policy," in Francis H. Heller and John R. Gillingham (eds.), *The United States and the Integration of Europe* (New York: St. Martin's, 1996), 57–77.

Geyelin, Philip, *Lyndon B. Johnson and the World* (New York: Praeger, 1966).

Gibianski, Leonid, "The 1948 Soviet-Yugoslav Conflict and the Formation of the 'Socialist Camp' Model," in Odd Arne Westad, Sven Holtsmark, and Iver B. Neumann (eds.), *The Soviet Union in Eastern Europe 1945–89* (London: St. Martin's, 1994), 26–46.

Gifford, Prosser, "Misconceived Dominion: The Creation and Disintegration of Federation in British Central Africa," in Prosser Gifford and William Roger Louis (eds.), *The Transfer of Power in Africa: Decolonization, 1940–1960* (New Haven: Yale University Press, 1982), 387–416.

Gillingham, John, *Coal, Steel, and the Rebirth of Europe, 1945–1955: The Germans and the French from the Ruhr Conflict to Economic Community* (Cambridge: Cambridge University Press, 1991).

—— "From Morgenthau Plan to Schuman Plan: America and the Organization of Europe," in Jeffery M. Diefendorf, Axel Frohn, and Hermann-Josef Rupipier (eds.), *American Policy and the Reconstruction of West Germany, 1945–1955* (Washington, DC: German Historical Institute, 1993), 111–33.

Gimbel, John, *The Origins of the Marshall Plan* (Stanford, Calif.: Stanford University Press, 1976).

Ginsberg, Roy H., "EC-US Political/Institutional Relations," in Leon Hurwitz and Christian Lequesne (eds.), *The State of the European Community: Policies, Institutions and Debates in the Transition Years* (Boulder, Colo.: Lynne Rienner, 1991), 387–402.

Goodman, S. F., *The European Union* (London: Macmillan, 1996).

Gordon, Philip H., *France, Germany and the Western Alliance* (Boulder, Colo.: Westview, 1995).

—— "Recasting the Atlantic Alliance," *Survival*, Spring 1996, 32–57.

Grabbe, Hans-Jürgen, "Konrad Adenauer, John Foster Dulles, and West German-American Relations," in Richard H. Immerman (ed.), *John Foster Dulles and the Diplomacy of the Cold War* (Princeton: Princeton University Press, 1990), 109–32.

Griffiths, Richard T., "The European Historical Experience," in Keith Middlemas (ed.), *Orchestrating Europe: The Informal Politics of European Union 1973–1995* (London: Fontana Press, 1995), 1–70.

Guillen, Pierre, "Europe as a Cure for French Impotence? The Guy Mollet Government and the Negotiation of the Treaties of Rome," in Ennio Di Nolfo (ed.), *Power in Europe? Vol. II: Great Britain, France, Germany and Italy and the Origins of the EEC, 1952–1957* (Berlin and New York: Walter de Gruyter, 1992), 505–16.

Hackett, Clifford, *Cautious Revolution: The European Union Arrives* (Westport, Conn.: Praeger, 1995).

—— *Monnet and the Americans: The Father of a United Europe and his U.S. Supporters* (Washington, DC: Jean Monnet Council, 1995).

Haftendorn, Helga, *NATO and the Nuclear Revolution: A Crisis of Credibility, 1966–1967* (Oxford: Clarendon Press, 1996).

Hanrieder, Wolfram F., *Deutschland, Europa, Amerika: Die Aussenpolitik der Bundesrepublik Deutschland 1949–1994* (Paderborn: Ferdinand Schöningh, 1995).

Harper, John Lamberton, *American Visions of Europe: Franklin D. Roosevelt, George F. Kennan, and Dean G. Acheson* (Cambridge: Cambridge University Press, 1994).

Heller, Francis H., and Gillingham, John R. (eds.), *NATO: The Founding of the Atlantic Alliance and the Integration of Europe* (London: Macmillan, 1992).

—— —— (eds.), *The United States and the Integration of Europe: Legacies of the Postwar Era* (New York: St. Martin's, 1996).

Helmreich, Jonathan E., "The United States and the Formation of EURATOM," *Diplomatic History*, Summer 1991, 387–410.

Hennesy, Peter, *Never Again: Britain 1945–51* (London: Jonathan Cape, 1992).

Henning, C. Randall, "Europe's Monetary Union and the United States," *Foreign Policy*, Spring, 1996, 83–100.

Hentschel, Volker, *Ludwig Erhard: Ein Politikerleben* (Munich: Olzog, 1996).

Herz, Martin F., *David Bruce's "Long Telegram" of July 3, 1951* (Lanham, Mass.: University Press of America, 1978).

Hess, Gary, *The United States' Emergence as a Southeast Asian Power, 1945–1950* (New York: Columbia University Press, 1987).

Heuser, Beatrice, *Transatlantic Relations: Sharing Ideals and Costs* (London: Royal Institute of International Affairs, 1996).

Hoffmann, Stanley, *Decline or Renewal? France since the 1930s* (New York: Viking, 1974).

Hogan, Michael, *The Marshall Plan: America, Britain, and the Reconstruction of Western Europe, 1947–1952* (Cambridge: Cambridge University Press, 1987).

—— (ed.), *America in the World: The Historiography of American Foreign Relations since 1941* (Cambridge: Cambridge University Press, 1995).

Hufbauer, Gary Clyde (ed.), *Europe 1992: An American Perspective* (Washington, DC: Brookings, 1990).

Hunt, Michael H., *Ideology and U.S. Foreign Policy* (New Haven: Yale University Press, 1987).

Huntington, Samuel P., *The Third Wave: Democratization in the Late Twentieth Century* (Norman, Okla.: University of Oklahoma Press, 1991).

Ignatieff, Michael, "The Missed Chance in Bosnia," *The New York Review of Books*, 29 Feb. 1996, 8–10.

Ikenberry, G. John, "The Myth of Post-Cold War Chaos," *Foreign Affairs*, May/June 1996, 79–91.

Ireland, Timothy P., *Creating the Entangling Alliance: The Origins of the North Atlantic Treaty Organization* (Westport, Conn.: Greenwood, 1981).

Jackson, Scott, "Prologue to the Marshall Plan: The Origins of the American Commitment for a European Recovery Program," *Journal of American History*, Mar. 1979, 1043–68.

Jenkins, Roy, *European Diary 1977–1981* (London: Collins, 1989).

Joffe, Josef, "Europe's American Pacifier," *Foreign Policy*, Spring 1984, 64–82.

Kahler, Miles, and Link, Werner, *Europe & America: A Return to History* (New York: Council on Foreign Relations Press, 1996).

Kaiser, Wolfram, *Grossbritannien und die Europäische Wirtschaftsgemeinschaft 1955–1961: Von Messina nach Canossa* (Berlin: Akademie Verlag, 1996).

—— "The Bomb and Europe: Britain, France, and the EEC Entry Negotiations 1961–1963," *Journal of European Integration History*, 1:1 (1995), 65–85.

—— *Using Europe, Abusing the Europeans: Britain and European Integration, 1945–63* (London: Macmillan, 1996).

Kaplan, Lawrence S., *The United States and NATO: The Formative Years* (Lexington, Ky.: University of Kentucky Press, 1984).

Kelleher, Cathrine McArdle, *Germany and the Politics of Nuclear Weapons* (New York: Columbia University Press, 1975).

Kennedy, Paul, *The Rise and Fall of the Great Powers: Economic Change and Military Conflict from 1500 to 2000* (New York: Random House, 1987).

Kissinger, Henry A., "What Kind of Atlantic Partnership?," *The Atlantic Community Quarterly*, 7 (1969), 18–38.

—— *White House Years* (Boston: Little, Brown and Company, 1979).

—— *Years of Upheaval* (Boston: Little, Brown and Company, 1982).

Kocs, Stephen A., *Autonomy or Power? The Franco-German Relationship and Europe's Strategic Choices, 1955–1995* (Westport, Conn.: Praeger, 1995).

Kohl, Wilfrid L., "The Nixon-Kissinger Foreign Policy System and U.S.-European Relations: Patterns of Policy Making," *World Politics*, Oct. 1975–July 1976, 1–43.

Kolko, Gabriel, *Confronting the Third World: United States Foreign Policy, 1945–1980* (New York: Pantheon Books, 1988).

Krause, Lawrence B., *European Economic Integration and the United States* (Washington, DC: Brookings, 1968).

Kuisel, Richard, *Seducing the French: The Dilemma of Americanization* (Berkeley: University of California Press, 1993).

Kunz, Diane B., "Cold War Dollar Diplomacy: The Other Side of Containment," in Diane B. Kunz (ed.), *The Diplomacy of the Crucial Decade: American Foreign Relations during the 1960s* (New York: Columbia University Press, 1994), 80–114.

Kyvig, David E. (ed.), *Reagan and the World* (New York: Greenwood, 1990).

Lacey, Michael J. (ed.), *The Truman Presidency* (Cambridge: Cambridge University Press, 1989).

Lacouture, Jean, *De Gaulle. The Ruler: 1945–1970* (London: Harvill, 1991).

Lankford, Nelson D., *The Last American Aristocrat: The Biography of Ambassador David K.E. Bruce* (Boston: Little, Brown and Company, 1996).

Large, David Clay, *Germans to the Front: West German Rearmament in the Adenauer Era* (Chapel Hill, NC: University of North Carolina Press, 1996).

Lee, Sabine, "Staying in the Game? Coming into the Game? Macmillan and European Integration," in Richard Aldous and Sabine Lee (eds.), *Harold Macmillan and Britain's World Role* (London: Macmillan, 1996), 123–36.

Lefebvre, Denis, "The French Socialist Party, 1954–1957," in Richard T. Griffiths (ed.), *Socialist Parties and the Question of Europe in the 1950's* (Leiden: E. J. Brill, 1993), 43–56.

Leffler, Melvyn P., *A Preponderance of Power: National Security, the Truman Administration, and the Cold War* (Stanford, Calif.: Stanford University Press, 1992).

—— *The Struggle for Germany and the Origins of the Cold War* (Washington, DC: German Historical Institute, 1996).

Le Gloannec, Anne-Marie, "Europe by Other Means?," *International Affairs*, 73:1 (1997), 83–98.

Lerner, Daniel, and Aron, Raymond (eds.), *France Defeats EDC* (New York: Praeger, 1957).

Levine, Norman (ed.), *The US and the EU: Economic Relations in a World of Transition* (Lanham, Mass.: University Press of America, 1996).

Lipgens, Walter, *A History of European Integration, 1945–47. Vol. 1: The Formation of the European Unity Movement* (London: Oxford University Press, 1982).

Litwak, Robert S., *Detente and the Nixon Doctrine: American Foreign Policy and the Pursuit of Stability, 1969–1976* (Cambridge: Cambridge University Press, 1984).

Loth, Wilfried, "The French Socialist Party, 1947–1954," in Richard T. Griffiths (ed.), *Socialist Parties and the Question of Europe in the 1950's* (Leiden: E. J. Brill, 1993), 25–42.

Loth, Wilfried, *Der Weg nach Europa: Geschichte der europäischen Integration 1939–1957* (Göttingen: Vandenhoeck & Ruprecht, 1982).

Lund, Camilla Elisabeth, "Changing Perceptions of the National Interest in Economic and Defence Policy under Mitterrand, 1981–1989" (Cambridge University Ph.D. diss., 1995).

Lundestad, Geir, *America, Scandinavia, and the Cold War, 1945–1949* (New York: Columbia University Press, 1980).

—— "Der Marshall-Plan und Osteuropa," in Othmar Nikola Haberl and Lutz Niethammer (eds.), *Der Marshall-Plan und die europäische Linke* (Frankfurt: Athenäum, 1986), 59–74.

—— "Empire by Invitation? The United States and Western Europe, 1945–1952," *Journal of Peace Research*, Sept. 1986, 263–77.

—— *The American "Empire" and Other Studies of US Foreign Policy in a Comparative Perspective* (Oxford and Oslo: Oxford University Press, 1990).

—— *The American Non-Policy towards Eastern Europe 1943–1947* (Oslo: Universitetsforlaget, 1975).

—— "The United States and Western Europe under Ronald Reagan," in David E. Kyvig (ed.), *Reagan and the World* (New York: Greenwood, 1990), 39–66.

—— (ed.), *The Fall of Great Powers: Peace, Stability, and Legitimacy* (Oslo and Oxford: Scandinavian University Press, 1994).

Lynch, Frances, "Resolving the Paradox of the Monnet Plan: National and International Planning in French Reconstruction," *Economic History Review*, 37:2 (1984), 229–43.

—— "The Role of Jean Monnet in Setting up the European Coal and Steel Community," in Klaus Schwabe (ed.), *Die Anfänge des Schuman-Plans 1950/51* (Baden-Baden: Nomos, 1988), 229–43.

Mai, Gunther, "American Policy toward Germany and the Integration of Europe, 1945–1955," in Jeffery M. Diefendorf, Axel Frohn, and Hermann-Joseph Rupipier (eds.), *American Policy and the Reconstruction of West Germany, 1945–1955* (Washington, DC: German Historical Institute, 1993), 85–109.

Maier, Charles S., "Alliance and Autonomy: European Identity and U.S. Foreign Policy Objectives in the Truman Years," in Michael J. Lacey (ed.), *The Truman Presidency* (Cambridge: Cambridge University Press, 1989), 273–98.

—— "Analog of Empire: Constitutive Moments of United States Ascendancy after World War II", unpub. paper presented at the Woodrow Wilson Center, Washington, DC, 30 May 1989.

Martin, Laurence W., "The American Decision to Rearm Germany," in Harold Stein (ed.), *American Civil-Military Decisions: A Book of Case*

Studies (Birmingham Ala.: University of Alabama Press, 1963), 643–65.

May, Ernest R., "The American Commitment to Germany, 1949–1955," in Lawrence S. Kaplan (ed.), *American Historians and the Atlantic Alliance* (Kent, Oh.: Kent State University Press, 1991), 52–80.

Mayer, Frank A., *Adenauer and Kennedy: A Study in German-American Relations, 1961–1963* (London: Macmillan, 1996).

McGeehan, Robert, *The German Rearmament Question: American Diplomacy and European Defense after World War II* (Urbana, Ill.: University of Illinois Press, 1971).

McMahon, Robert J., *Colonialism and Cold War: The United States and the Struggle for Indonesian Independence, 1945–1949* (Ithaca, NY: Cornell University Press, 1981).

Mearsheimer, John J., "Back to the Future: Instability in Europe after the Cold War," *International Security*, Summer 1990, 5–56.

Melandri, Pierre, *Les États-Unis face à l'unification de l'Europe 1945–1954* (Lille: Université de Lille III, 1979).

Menon, Anand, "Defence Policy and Integration in Western Europe," *Contemporary Security Policy*, 17:2 (1996), 264–83.

Middlemas, Keith (ed.), *Orchestrating Europe: The Informal Politics of European Union 1973–1995* (London: Fontana Press, 1995).

Milward, Alan S., "Conclusions: The Value of History," in Alan S. Milward *et al.*, *The Frontier of National Sovereignty: History and Theory 1945–1992* (London: Routledge, 1993), 182–201.

—— *The European Rescue of the Nation-State* (London: Routledge, 1992).

—— *The Reconstruction of Western Europe 1945–51* (Berkeley: University of California Press, 1984).

—— Lynch, Frances M. B., Romero, Federico, Ramieri, Ruggero, and Sørensen, Vibeke, *The Frontier of National Sovereignty: History and Theory 1945–1992* (London: Routledge, 1993).

Monnet, Jean, *Memoirs* (London: Collins, 1978).

Naimark, Norman M., *The Russians in Germany: A History of the Soviet Zone of Occupation, 1945–1949* (Cambridge, Mass.: Harvard University Press, 1995).

Nerlich, Uwe, "Western Europe's Relations with the United States," *Daedalus*, Winter 1979, 87–111.

Nixon, Richard M., *RN: The Memoirs of Richard Nixon* (New York: Simon & Schuster, 1978).

Nunnerly, David, *President Kennedy and Britain* (London: Bodley Head, 1972).

Nye, Joseph S., *Bound to Lead: The Changing Nature of American Power* (New York: Basic Books, 1990).

Owen, David, *Balkan Odyssey* (New York: Harcourt Brace, 1995).

Painter, David S., "Research Note: Explaining U.S. Relations with the Third World," *Diplomatic History*, Summer 1995, 525–48.

Peterson, John, *Europe and America in the 1990s: The Prospects for Partnership* (Aldershot: Elgar, 1993).

Paxton, Robert O., and Wahl, Nicholas (eds.), *De Gaulle and the United States: A Centennial Reappraisal* (Oxford: Berg, 1994).

Plowden, Edwin, *An Industrialist in the Treasury: The Post-War Years* (London: André Deutsch, 1989).

Poidevin, Raymond, *Histoire des débuts de la construction Européenne/ Origins of European Integration* (Brussels: Bruylant, 1986).

Pond, Elizabeth, *Beyond the Wall: Germany's Road to Unification* (Washington, DC: Brookings, 1993).

Pruessen, Ronald W., "Cold War Threats and America's Commitment to the European Defense Community: One Corner of a Triangle," *Journal of European Integration History*, Spring 1996, 51–69.

—— *John Foster Dulles: The Road to Power* (New York: Free Press, 1982).

—— "Mixed Messages: U.S.-E.U. Relations in the 1990s and Traditional Patterns of Transatlantic Ambivalence," unpub. paper presented at the Conference on Decision-Making in US-EU Relations, Brussels, May 1996.

Rappaport, Armin, "The United States and European Integration: The First Phase," *Diplomatic History*, Spring 1981, 121–49.

Reid, Escott, *Time of Fear and Hope: The Making of the North Atlantic Treaty 1947–1949* (Toronto: McClelland and Stewart, 1977).

Reynolds, David (ed.), *The Origins of the Cold War in Europe: International Perspectives* (New Haven: Yale University Press, 1994).

Risse-Kappen, Thomas, *Cooperation among Democracies: The European Influence on U.S. Foreign Policy* (Princeton: Princeton University Press, 1995).

Robinson, William J., *Promoting Polyarchy: Globalization, US Intervention and Hegemony* (Cambridge: Cambridge University Press, 1996).

Romero, Federico, "Interdependence and Integration in American Eyes: From the Marshall Plan to Currency Convertibility," in Alan S. Milward *et al.*, *The Frontier of National Sovereignty: History and Theory 1945–1992* (London: Routledge, 1993), 155–81.

—— "U.S. Attitudes to Integration and Interdependence: The 1950s," in Francis H. Heller and John R. Gillingham (eds.), *The United States and the Integration of Europe* (New York: St. Martin's, 1996).

Ross, George, *Jacques Delors and European Integration* (Cambridge: Polity Press, 1995).

Rostow, Walt W., "Jean Monnet: The Innovator as Diplomat," in Gordon A. Craig and Francis L. Loewenheim (eds.), *The Diplomats 1939–1979* (Princeton: Princeton University Press, 1994), 257–88.

—— *The Diffusion of Power: An Essay in Recent History* (New York: Macmillan, 1972).

Roussel, Eric, *Jean Monnet* (Paris: Fayard, 1996).

Ruggie, John Gerard, *Winning the Peace: America and World Order in the New Era* (New York: Columbia University Press, 1996).

Schaetzel, J. Robert, *The Unhinged Alliance: America and the European Community* (New York: Harper & Row, 1975).

Schertz, Adrian W., *Die Deutschlandpolitik Kennedys und Johnsons: Unterschiedliche Ansätze innerhalb der amerikanischen Regierung* (Cologne: Böhlau, 1992).

Schlesinger, Arthur M., Jr., *A Thousand Days: John F. Kennedy in the White House* (Boston: Houghton Mifflin Company, 1965).

Schoenbaum, David, and Pond, Elizabeth, *The German Question and Other German Questions* (London: Macmillan, 1996).

Schröder, Hans-Jürgen, "Deutsche Aussenpolitik 1963/64," *Vierteljahrshefte für Zeitgeschichte*, July 1995, 521–37.

Schwabe, Klaus, "'Ein Akt konstruktiver Staatskunst'—die USA und die Anfänge des Schuman-Plans," in Klaus Schwabe (ed.), *Die Anfänge des Schuman-Plans 1950/51* (Baden-Baden: Nomos, 1988), 211–39.

—— "The Origins of the United States' Engagement in Europe, 1946–1952," in Francis H. Heller and John R. Gillingham (eds.), *NATO: The Founding of the Atlantic Alliance and the Integration of Europe* (London: Macmillan, 1992), 161–92.

—— "The United States and European Integration: 1947–1957," in Clemens Wurm (ed.), *Western Europe and Germany: The Beginnings of European Integration 1945–1960* (Oxford: Berg, 1995), 115–35.

—— "Do Personalities Make a Difference? Washington Working with Europeans," unpub. paper presented at the Commonwealth Fund Conference, London University, 16–17 Feb. 1996.

—— (ed.), *Die Anfänge des Schuman-Plans 1950/51/The Beginnings of the Schuman Plan* (Baden-Baden: Nomos, 1988).

Schwartz, Thomas Alan, *America's Germany: John J. McCloy and the Federal Republic of Germany* (Cambridge, Mass.: Harvard University Press, 1991).

—— "The Berlin Crisis and the Cold War," *Diplomatic History*, Winter 1997, 139–48.

—— "Victories and Defeats in the Long Twilight Struggle: The United States and Western Europe in the 1960s," in Diane B. Kunz (ed.), *The*

Diplomacy of the Crucial Decade: American Foreign Relations during the 1960s (New York: Columbia University Press, 1994), 115–48.

Schwarz, Hans-Peter, *Adenauer. Der Staatsmann: 1952–1967* (Stuttgart: Deutsche Verlags-Anstalt, 1991).

Schwarz, Insa, "The United States and the Creation of the European Atomic Energy Community 1955–58," *Historians of Contemporary Europe Newsletter*, Dec. 1992, 209–224.

Schwok, René, *U.S.-EC Relations in the Post-Cold War Era: Conflict or Partnership?* (Boulder, Colo.: Westview, 1991).

Sherwood, Elizabeth D., *Allies in Crisis: Meeting Global Challenges to Western Security* (New Haven: Yale University Press, 1990).

Sisk, Thomas M., "Forging the Weapon: Eisenhower as NATO's Supreme Allied Commander, 1950–1952," in Günther Bischof and Stephen E. Ambrose (eds.), *Eisenhower: A Centenary Assessment* (Baton Rouge, La.: Lousiana State University Press, 1995), 64–83.

Sloan, Stanley R., "US Perspectives on NATO's Future," *International Affairs*, 71:2 (1995), 217–31.

—— "West European–U.S. Relations and Europe's Future," *Congressional Research Service: The Library of Congress*, 20 Feb. 1992.

Smith, Michael, and Woolcock, Stephen, *The United States and the European Community in a Transformed World* (London: Pinter Publishers, 1993).

Smith, Tony, *America's Mission: The United States and the Worldwide Struggle for Democracy in the Twentieth Century* (Princeton: Princeton University Press, 1994).

Soffer, Jonathan, "All for One and One for All: The UN Military Staff Committee and the Contradictions within American Internationalism," *Diplomatic History*, Winter 1997, 45–69.

Sorensen, Theodore C., *Kennedy* (New York: Bantam Books, 1966).

Soutou, Georges-Henri, "France," in David Reynolds (ed.), *The Origins of the Cold War in Europe* (New Haven: Yale University Press, 1994), 96–120.

Steinbruner, John D., *The Cybernetic Theory of Decision* (Princeton: Princeton University Press, 1974).

Steininger, Rolf, "Grossbritannien und de Gaulle: Das Scheitern des britischen EWG-Beitritts im Januar 1963," *Vierteljahrshefte für Zeitgeschichte*, Jan. 1996, 86–118. English version: "Great Britain's First EEC Failure in January 1963," *Diplomacy & Statecraft*, 7:2 (1996), 404–35.

—— "John Foster Dulles, the European Defense Community, and the German Question," in Richard H. Immerman (ed.), *John Foster Dulles and the Diplomacy of the Cold War* (Princeton: Princeton University Press, 1990), 79–108.

Stent, Angela, *From Embargo to Ostpolitik: The Political Economy of West German-Soviet Relations, 1955–1980* (Cambridge: Cambridge University Press, 1981).

Storeheier, Heidi, *US Policy towards the European Free Trade Association 1959–1963* (Norwegian University of Technology and Science Cand. philol. thesis, 1996).

Strikwerda, Carl, "The Troubled Origins of European Economic Integration: International Iron and Steel and Labor Migration in the Era of World War I," *American Historical Review*, Oct. 1993, 1106–42.

Stromseth, Jane, *The Origins of Flexible Response* (New York: St. Martins, 1988).

Thatcher, Margaret, *The Downing Street Years* (New York: HarperCollins, 1993).

Treverton, Gregory F., *The Dollar Drain and American Forces in Germany: Managing the Political Economies of Alliance* (Athens, Oh.: Ohio University Press, 1978).

Ullman, Richard H., "The Covert French Connection," *Foreign Policy*, Summer 1989, 3–33.

Urwin, Derek W., *The Community of Europe: A History of European Integration since 1945*, 2nd edn. (London: Longman, 1995).

Vance, Cyrus, *Hard Choices: Critical Years in American Foreign Policy* (New York: Simon and Schuster, 1983).

Vandenberg, Arthur H., Jr. (ed.), *The Private Papers of Senator Vandenberg* (Boston: Houghton Mifflin, 1952).

Van der Beugel, Ernst H., *From Marshall Aid to Atlantic Partnership: European Integration as a Concern of American Foreign Policy* (Amsterdam: Elsevier, 1966).

Varsori, Antonio, "Italy's Position towards European Integration (1947–58)," in Christopher Duggan and Christopher Wagstaff (eds.), *Italy in the Cold War: Politics, Culture and Society 1948–58* (Oxford: Berg, 1995), 47–66.

Vaughan, Richard, *Post-War Integration in Europe* (London: Croom Helm, 1976).

—— *Twentieth-Century Europe: Paths to Unity* (London: Croom Helm, 1979).

Vierucci, Luisa, "The Role of the Western European Union in the Maintenance of International Peace and Security," *International Peacekeeping*, 2:3 (1995), 309–29.

Walker, Martin, "The New American Hegemony," *World Policy Journal*, Summer 1996, 13–21.

Wall, Irving M., *The United States and the Making of Postwar France 1945–1954* (Cambridge: Cambridge University Press, 1991).

Walt, Stephen M., *The Origins of Alliances* (Ithaca, NY: Cornell University Press, 1987).

Waltz, Kenneth N., *Theory of International Relations* (Reading, Mass.: Addison-Wesley, 1979).

Warner, Geoffrey, "Eisenhower, Dulles and the Unity of Western Europe, 1955–1957," *International Affairs*, 69:2 (1993), 319–29.

—— "The Labour Governments and the Unity of Western Europe, 1945–51," in Ritchie Ovendale (ed.), *The Foreign Policy of the British Labour Governments, 1945–1951* (Leicester: Leicester University Press, 1984), 61–82.

Watt, D. Cameron, *Succeeding John Bull: America in Britain's Place, 1900–1975—A Study of the Anglo-American Relationship and World Politics in the Context of British and American Foreign-Policy-Making in the Twentieth Century* (Cambridge: Cambridge University Press, 1984).

Westlake, Martin, *The Council of the European Union* (London: Cartermill, 1995).

Wexler, Immanuel, *The Marshall Plan Revisited: The European Recovery Program in Economic Perspective* (Westport, Conn.: Greenwood, 1983).

Wiebes, Cees, and Zeeman, Bert, "Benelux," in David Reynolds (ed.), *The Origins of the Cold War in Europe: International Perspectives* (New Haven: Yale University Press, 1994), 167–93.

—— —— "Eine Lehrstunde in Machtpolitik," *Vierteljahrshefte für Zeitgeschichte*, July 1992, 413–23.

Wiener, Jarrod (ed.), *The Transatlantic Relationship* (New York: St. Martin's, 1996).

Wilkins, Mira, "U.S. Multinationals and the Unification of Europe, 1945–60," in Francis H. Heller and John R. Gillingham (eds.), *The United States and the Integration of Europe* (New York: St. Martin's, 1996), 342–55.

Willis, F. Roy, *France, Germany and the New Europe 1945–1967* (Oxford: Oxford University Press, 1968).

Winand, Pascaline, *Eisenhower, Kennedy, and the United States of Europe* (London: Macmillan, 1993).

—— "European Insiders Working Inside Washington: Monnet's Network, Euratom and the Eisenhower Administration," unpub. paper presented at the Commonwealth Fund Conference, London University, 16–17 Feb. 1996.

Woodhouse, Roger, *British Policy towards France 1945–51* (London: Macmillan, 1995).

Woolcock, Stephen, "EU-US Commercial Relations and the Debate on a Transatlantic Free Trade Area," in Jarrod Wiener (ed.), *The Transatlantic Relationship* (London: Macmillan, 1996), 164–84.

Wooley, Wesley T., *Alternatives to Anarchy: American Supranationalism since World War II* (Bloomington, Ind.: Indiana University Press, 1988).

Young, John, *Britain, France and the Unity of Europe 1945–1951* (Leicester: Leicester University Press, 1984).

—— *Britain and European Unity, 1945–1992* (London: Macmillan, 1993).

—— *France, the Cold War and the Western Alliance. 1944–1949: French Foreign Policy and Post War Europe* (Leicester: Leicester University Press, 1990).

Zeiler, Thomas W., *American Trade and Power in the 1960s* (New York: Columbia University Press, 1992).

Zelikow, Philip, and Rice, Condoleezza, *Germany Unified and Europe Transformed: A Study in Statecraft* (Cambridge, Mass.: Harvard University Press, 1995).

Index

Made in the USA
Lexington, KY
04 February 2013